RIVER COTTAGE
EVERY DAY

HUGH FEARNLEY-WHITTINGSTALL

PHOTOGRAPHY BY SIMON WHEELER

TEN SPEED PRESS

Berkeley

For Marie, for every day

Text copyright © 2009 by Hugh Fearnley-Whittingstall
Photography copyright © 2009 by Simon Wheeler
Additional photography copyright © 2009 by Marie Derôme
(pages 25, 330–31, 354)
Illustrations copyright © 2009 by Mariko Jesse

Originally published in slightly different form in Great Britain by
Bloomsbury Publishing Plc, London, in 2009

Library of Congress Cataloging-in-Publication Data is on file
with the publisher.

ISBN 978-1-60774-098-8

Printed in China

Project editor: Janet Illsley
Copy editor: Jane Middleton
Cover design: Chloe Rawlins
Interior design: Lawrence Morton
Photography: Simon Wheeler
Illustrations: Mariko Jesse (www.marikojesse.com)

The text of this book is set in Avant Garde Gothic and Serifa

10 9 8 7 6 5 4 3 2 1

First U. S. Edition

contents

introduction

Good food prepared from fresh ingredients – ideally seasonal and locally sourced – can and should be at the heart of every happy, healthy family kitchen. Yes, I genuinely believe that cooking from scratch (or with your own leftovers) is a possibility for everybody, pretty much every day. I realize, when so many of us are always in a hurry, and when easy access to fresh, local ingredients is not a universal privilege, that that's a controversial position. But I stand by my conviction, and I've written this book to show you how I think it can be done.

It often seems that there is a divide between people when it comes to food. A crude way of describing the divide is that we fall into two broad categories: those who care about food and those who don't. I have been accused at times of writing only for the first group or, to put it another way, of preaching largely to the converted. I can see why some would say that. I propose a degree of involvement with food – knowing and caring where it comes from, perhaps even growing some of it, or gathering some from wild places – that to many seems patently absurd. To some, I am "that weirdo who eats anything." Of course, to me, eating nettles, rabbits, and such makes perfect sense. It's completely normal. But it has been quite a journey for me to discover and embrace that kind of normality.

As a child, I was one of the fussiest eaters you can imagine. If it didn't come out of a Birds Eye package and get fried up and served with ketchup, then I really wasn't that interested. So I have no qualms imagining that others can make journeys with food – even journeys they haven't yet imagined possible for themselves. In the twenty-odd years since I first became involved in the food business, I have seen entrenched attitudes to food, on the part of both stubborn individuals and monolithic institutions, shift massively. I've witnessed burgeoning excitement, enlightenment even, as more and more people get involved in cooking real food from fresh ingredients. I've seen people's lives and family dynamics transformed by the discovery of good food and by a change of approach to acquiring and preparing food.

If you have watched any of the television programs I've made over the last few years, you'll know I've spent a lot of time trying to persuade various people to change their way of shopping and cooking and to become more engaged with real fresh food. For the most part, I feel I've succeeded, at least to some degree. The individuals and families I've been growing and cooking food with are now, at the very least, a little more skeptical of frozen dinners, factory-farmed produce, and anonymous, pre-packaged fare. Most of them have developed a determination to cook more with fresh ingredients and to make food a bigger part of their interaction with family and friends. But perhaps the most important thing is that all of them, I think it's safe to say, have had a good time. They've discovered how to cook ingredients they'd shied away from and how to get more out of foods they thought "boring," and realized that some truly delicious meals can be thrown together from scratch in very little time at all.

The food media can only do so much to engage public interest in these issues. Luckily there are all kinds of other catalysts that bring about a change for good in people's relationship with food, and many of them can't be marshaled or predicted: a meal at a friend's house; a great dish encountered on holiday; a child coming home with something they've cooked at school; an unexpected gift of a fruit bush or vegetable plant. These can all kick-start a new and exciting future with food – one that turns out to be more accessible than you might have imagined. Buying your food becomes less of a chore, more of a pleasure, an adventure even, as you steer your grocery cart away from the frozen-dinner aisle and over toward fresh produce. Or perhaps start heading for the nearest farmers' market rather than the supermarket. Suddenly it seems that your friends have discovered cooking too – though perhaps it's just that you are hearing the food-related content of their chatter when previously you were filtering it out.

That's why I think the "us and them" view of our food culture is unduly simplistic. I see not two firmly entrenched camps who can never meet but rather a continuum, with those who are already thoroughly involved with the story of their food at one end and those who are

entirely dependent on anonymous, industrially produced food, the origins of which are largely unknown to them, at the other. Everyone, and every household, has a place on this continuum. I see the main challenge of my work as helping people move along it in the direction of more engagement with real fresh food, away from dependence on the industrial food machine. I believe it's a worthwhile enterprise for one simple reason: I'm convinced that a greater engagement with the source of their food makes people happier.

This book is my latest attempt to contribute to that happiness – by writing about the kind of food I eat at home, every day. I describe how bread, meat, fish, fruit, and vegetables are dealt with in our house, how we juggle breakfast for three hungry schoolkids, and how we sort out weekday lunches for two working parents. I reveal why so many of the meals we eat (including some of our absolute favorites) are made from leftovers. I try to show you how to put vegetables and fruit at the forefront of your family cooking, while getting the most from precious foods such as meat and fish. I suggest ways to make entertaining at home less daunting, less expensive, and altogether more fun. And I offer up the recipes I love to cook for my family – and those that, when I'm really lucky, they cook for me.

I make no prior assumptions about where you shop, what you may or may not know about growing vegetables or keeping livestock, whether you can tell the difference between a rutabaga and a turnip, or whether you know what to do with a belly of pork and a breast of lamb. Instead, I show you easy and confidence-inspiring ways with cuts of meat, types of fish, and other ingredients you may not have tried before. And I offer you fresh approaches that I hope will breathe new life into familiar staples, such as rice, potatoes, beans, and your daily bread.

Above all, I intend to tempt you irresistibly toward a better life with food, with a whole raft of recipes that I think you will love. I hope some of them will become your absolute favorites, and the favorites of your dear friends and beloved family. I hope the dishes you like best will infiltrate and influence your cooking, giving you increased confidence and fresh ideas. In short, I hope that before long, cooking simple and delicious food from the best seasonal ingredients becomes second nature and a first priority for you, not just once in a while, but every day.

A few of my favorite things

It's a truism that the quality and nature of your ingredients make all the difference to a finished dish, and I'd expect any cook worth their salt to choose the freshest, finest raw materials they can lay their hands on. However, there are a few staples to which personal preferences (or outright prejudice) also apply. The following basic pantry ingredients appear time and time again in my recipes, so I feel they merit a little extra explanation – and, since I feel pretty strongly about their provenance, a little recommendation, too.

OIL

An entire book could be written about oils – I'm sure there must be several – but let me cut to the chase and tell you what you'll find in my kitchen. My general rule is to opt for organic and unrefined oils (the refining process can involve heating, the addition of solvents, and even bleaching). Cold-pressed oil is also good because, while heating the seed or fruit increases the yield of oil, it affects the flavor and nutritional value, too. On the other hand, for deep- and shallow-frying you do need an oil that can be heated to a high temperature, and that usually (but not always) means a refined oil of some kind.

Canola oil Many British farmers are now producing this wonderful culinary oil, and I use a lot of it. Terrifically versatile, it has an incredible golden-yellow color and a gentle nutty flavor. Canola oil is mild enough to use in mayonnaise but has enough character to contribute to a dressing, or to add flavor when drizzled on bread or soup. In addition, it's stable enough at high temperatures to be used for frying or roasting – though perhaps not prolonged deep-frying. You may well be able to find a good one produced locally.

Olive oil I use quite a bit of olive oil but I don't worship it. I no longer use it much for frying or roasting; canola oil has supplanted it as the first oil I reach for. I'm much more likely to use it for dressings and for general drizzling, and even then only if it's that distinctive olive oil flavor I'm after. That might be in a classic vinaigrette or salsa verde, on sliced tomatoes, or perhaps stirred into pesto. But these days it's always a conscious decision to reach for the olive oil rather than an automatic one.

That means I'm happy to pay a bit more for a good organic extra-virgin olive oil (extra-virgin means the oil has a low acidity level and

is guaranteed unrefined). I don't use the super-expensive "luxury" olive oils – although once in a while, when someone gives me an exquisitely peppery, richly flavored olive oil (usually Tuscan), I am reminded what all the fuss is about.

Sunflower oil This is a very lightly flavored oil with a high burn point, which makes it ideal for general frying, including deep-frying. This is one case where I definitely wouldn't choose an unrefined oil, as the flavor would be too strong and it would most likely be adversely affected by the heat, but I do usually opt for organic and/ or fair trade. After being used for deep-frying, sunflower oil can be recycled by straining it through a coffee filter or cotton cloth (when completely cold) and rebottling it. Don't leave it sitting around in the saucepan or deep-fat fryer, or it will go stale and impart a rancid flavor to the next batch of fried goodies. Peanut oil is a good substitute for sunflower when a neutral frying oil is needed.

Hempseed oil People either love or hate the pungent, grassy, throaty flavor of hempseed oil. I love it. Its intensity means it compares to the very best olive oils and makes a great drizzling and dipping oil. It's full of goodness – loaded with omega fatty acids, which arguably give it the best nutritional profile of any raw culinary oil. I use it on my breakfast toast and in a number of pestos.

VINEGAR

Vinegar (literally *vin aigre*, or "sour wine") is a crucial part of my cooking repertoire, as indispensable as lemon juice when it comes to balancing flavors. I use it almost every day, mostly in dressings and mayonnaise, but also when roasting vegetables, in sauces or marinades, or to deglaze the pan after frying meat. English cider vinegar is the type I turn to most, because it is fruity and robust but not overpowering, but white wine vinegar is a perfectly good alternative, if that's what you happen to have in the pantry.

FLOUR

I like my flour stone ground if possible, as traditional stone grinding involves less heat than modern steel-rolling techniques, thereby preserving more of the grain's goodness. Whole-wheat flour is more likely to be stone ground than white.

Different flours vary enormously, not only in quality but in their color, consistency, and the way they absorb liquid. When you're making bread, pastry, or batters, you should feel confident in adjusting the quantity of flour or liquid to reach the consistency you think is right. Note also that whole-wheat flour tends to absorb more water than white, so you might need to increase the fluid content if you're converting a recipe from white to brown.

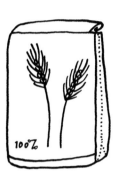

White and whole-wheat flour
If I need all-purpose or pastry flour, then I favor one that's produced from organically grown wheat. However, I'm increasingly turning to whole-wheat flour in order to make our everyday meals more wholesome – I like its toasty, wheaty flavor, too.

I've found there are few traditional "white" recipes that can't be adapted to contain at least some whole-wheat flour – a half-and-half blend of white and whole-wheat flour is often very successful. I'll happily knock out a Victoria sponge using whole-wheat pastry flour, which is fine-ground soft wheat: the result is very nearly as light and fluffy as you get with white flour but with a lovely, nutty flavor that I actually prefer. It also works well with muffins and pancakes.

Bread flour
This is what you should use for most bread recipes. It is milled from a particular type of wheat that is high in gluten, the substance that helps bread form the correct stretchy texture.

Spelt flour
A grain I'm very fond of, spelt is an ancient type of wheat with a distinctive nutty flavor. It differs from conventional wheat flours in that it contains a more delicate kind of gluten, which some people find more digestible. Whole-grain spelt flour makes very good bread and can also be used in cakes and even pastry – or use the refined "white" spelt if you fancy something lighter.

SALT
Top-quality sea salt – sweet, flaky, and fresh tasting – is an essential part of my everyday cooking. It differs from rock salt in that it's harvested from the open sea by traditional evaporation techniques rather than being pumped out of the ground. Fewer of its natural minerals are stripped away and fewer unnatural things, such as anti-caking agents, added. It also tastes much better – do a comparative tasting and I think you'll agree. Maldon sea salt, a flaky, coarse white salt, is a kitchen classic of long standing.

There are times when a fine-grained salt is more appropriate than a coarse one – when seasoning a delicate cake batter, for instance.

In addition, if you need to use salt in large quantities – when mixing up a cure for pork chops, say – using top-notch coarse sea salt would be rather extravagant. In these circumstances, I still opt for sea salt but a fine-grained type – you'll find it at any good natural foods store.

PEPPER AND OTHER SPICES

Spices remain exotic ingredients – precious, fragrant substances that must be imported from regions of the world more lush and tropical than our own. These days it's easy to find excellent examples, grown in a way that's respectful to the environment – and traded in a way that's respectful to the grower, too. Fair-trade and organic spices are available in many supermarkets, but it's online that you'll find the greatest variety.

Black pepper is so ubiquitous that most of us don't give it a second thought, but try a few different varieties and you might be surprised at the way their flavor and heat vary. Wynad peppers, for instance, are fragrant and warm, while Penja berries are incredibly hot.

Wherever your spices come from, certain rules apply: once ground, they lose their flavor and fragrance surprisingly fast. If you can buy whole spices and grind them yourself, you'll get much more bang for your buck. Find the time to dry-roast them gently in a frying pan before pounding them in a mortar, and the results will be even more pleasing.

DRIED FRUIT

Golden and dark raisins, prunes, figs, and dried apricots are pantry essentials in my book (and in my kitchen). Foreign in origin they may be, but they are key to all sorts of traditional sweet and savory dishes. I choose organic where I can and also, as with many imported foods, fair trade if it's available – which, for dried fruit, it often is.

Many dried fruits – golden and dark raisins and currants in particular – have vegetable oil added to keep them from sticking together. I see this as a pretty benign additive, but one I'm less sanguine about is sulfur dioxide, used to preserve a fresh, bright color. You're most likely to find it in dried apricots: if they're bright orange, you'll know sulfur has been used. This chemical also halts the natural oxidation process in the fruit, which is why sulfured apricots taste less rich, complex, and toffeeish than the unsulfured variety. They've got a bit of a sherbety "fizz" to them, which some people like. But I'm afraid it's the sulfur you're tasting there. I prefer the natural, mellow, caramel flavor of organic, nonsulfured fruit.

Dried fruit in general, and apricots, prunes, and figs in particular, are much more luscious, soft, and juicy than they used to be. However, if you find yourself with a dry, tough batch, soaking the fruit in liquid (water, tea, freshly squeezed orange juice, or a hefty slosh of alcohol) – particularly if it's hot – will soon plump it up.

BREAD

You'll see from the Daily Bread chapter just how passionately I feel about the importance of good bread. A robust, well-flavored, crusty loaf brings so much more to a meal than a cotton-woolly, flabby bit of sliced white. I am now a total convert to sourdough, and I use it not only for my daily toast, sandwiches, and general meal-accompanying needs, but also for bread crumbs, croutons, and various other stale bread applications.

I realize that not everyone has access to good sourdough (though you can easily make your own – see page 66), and also that not everyone loves its tangy flavor and hearty texture. But I would nevertheless urge you to seek out a source of good bread – bread that does not dissolve on the tongue and go stale in 12 hours but that has flavor, texture, and longevity – not just for these recipes but for every time you need a slice or two. You can find some good bread in supermarkets but it's the exception rather than the rule, because most supermarket bread is made using modern industrial methods and ingredients. An artisan bakery is a far better bet, or a natural foods store or a farmers' market.

STOCK

A good savory broth, home cooked from meat bones, herbs, and aromatic vegetables, is a precious thing in the kitchen (see the recipes on pages 192 and 196). But I know it's unrealistic to expect everyone to have a pot of stock on the go at all times. I certainly don't. When I need stock instantly, I have various options. The ten-minute vegetable stock (on page 266) is an excellent solution to the no-stock situation (as long as you've got a carrot, an onion, and a bay leaf available, you're in business – a couple of stalks of celery would be ideal, too).

Failing that, or if I'm really in need of a meatier brew, frozen stocks are the best replacement for homemade. But I am no stranger to the stock cube if I'm cooking up a soup super quick. Be aware, though, that cubes, pastes, granules, and other concentrated, ready-made forms of stock are usually quite salty, so you'll need to adjust the seasoning of your dish accordingly.

CHEESE

I'm not about to tell you which cheeses you should eat – though I can give my opinion that you rarely need to look outside your own area of the country for a good cheese, whether you want something hard, soft, semisoft, mild, strong, blue, mold-ripened, etc. However, I would like to let you in on what I personally find to be indispensable when it comes to cheese for cooking, as opposed to just sitting down and eating.

Instead of Parmesan I tend to use a hard, matured goat cheese. It has the same salty, granular texture and exquisite seasoning potential as Parmesan. Soft, fresh goat cheeses are ideal for making cheesecakes (see page 44) or for mixing with herbs and other seasonings. I like to slice and crumble semihard goat cheese over salads (like the one on page 294).

If I cook with Cheddar or a similar hard cheese, then it's really got to be a mature one, otherwise the flavor just doesn't carry. But you don't always need one that's tangy to the point of making your eyes water.

Blue cheese frequently finds its way into my cooking. I tend to forgo the pungency of Stilton in favor of something a little sweeter and creamier, such as Gorgonzola dolce.

OTHER PANTRY ESSENTIALS

It's a sad and sorry day when a scan of my larder doesn't turn up at least some of these tried-and-true standbys:

Organic canned tomatoes and purée Combined with nothing more than garlic, chile, and seasonings, these can turn no supper into Yo, Supper! They can also be an alternative to stock in a soup or curry and are generally indispensable. Canned tomatoes are chunky, of course, whereas purée is sieved.

Dried pasta We all have our own preferences when it comes to pasta shapes, but one of my favorites is orzo. Shaped like fat grains of rice, it has a wonderful texture and is particularly good in soups and for soaking up sauces. I often make an orzo risotto (much quicker than a proper risotto) by simmering orzo in stock and adding sautéed onions and a few leftovers – cold fish or meat, grated cheese, wilted greens, etc.

Dried and canned beans, peas, and lentils We eat
lentils – usually nutty little French lentils – at least once a week. They are quick to cook (no soaking), absorb sauces and dressings deliciously, and are packed with protein. I also keep chickpeas at hand, plus white beans such as cannellini. I prefer to use dried ones, soaking and cooking them from scratch, but I'd be lying if I said I always have time to do this, so I keep some organic canned ones as well.

making breakfast

I've called this chapter "Making Breakfast" to emphasize a point.

Breakfast is in danger of becoming moribund, suffocating under a tower of cereal boxes or being sidelined altogether by commercial breakfast bars.

Now I'm not about to overwhelm you with recipes for a grand, heart-stopping Edwardian breakfast of deviled kidneys and kedgeree followed by a sideboard of cold meats and pickles. And I hesitate to trot out the mantra that breakfast is *the* most important meal of the day, because it's such a tired cliché that it almost seems to provoke the protest of skipping it altogether. I'd rather combine cherished tradition with some sound modern nutritional knowledge and say that breakfast is simply an unmissable opportunity to start the day well.

Of course, not everyone has the same appetite for breakfast, or indeed feels the same way about breakfast from one day to the next. What is required is a modest but effective breakfast repertoire that covers the needs of the whole family on a daily basis, and also allows for special-occasion or weekend breakfasts when everyone has a little more time. And that's what I'm aiming to provide here.

On weekdays at home, we like to factor in just a little more time for breakfast than I suspect may be available in many households. While we're still juggling the usual chaotic rigmarole of unfinished homework, misplaced soccer shoes, and attempts to shirk morning hygiene rituals, we try to make sure there's always time to make hot cereal or pancakes, or a soft-boiled egg with toast, as well as to squeeze some juice from a few oranges (or, in the autumn, from our own apples).

One of the best ways to make this work is to get the children involved from an early age. Easy breakfast dishes are the perfect bunny slopes for young cooks, and a little coaching of junior members of the household so they can do their bit at breakfast soon becomes a great asset to the whole family. Show them how to prepare their own favorite breakfast dish, and before long they can take responsibility, once in a while, for dishing it up for the rest of the gang too.

Oscar, ten, can now knock out pancakes from scratch for the whole family, in about half an hour flat (well, they are pancakes). That's just as well, because we probably have pancakes for breakfast at least once a week. Chloe, twelve, makes wonderful oatmeal and can fix anyone an egg or two just about any way they like it. Freddy's only six, but he's very good at making tomato toast and oily toast (see page 54), sometimes without getting either tomato or oil on his school shirt.

One strategy for taking the heat and rush out of weekday family breakfasts is to do a little basic prep the night before. Nothing too strenuous. But if you mix up a pancake batter and stick it in the fridge, then the job of the designated flipper the next morning is plain sailing. Similarly, presoaked cereal made from steel-cut oats (see page 37) practically cooks itself in the morning. And a ready-made fruit compote (see pages 339–44) chilling overnight in the fridge is at least half a breakfast waiting to happen.

On a Saturday or Sunday morning, I love a pair of eggs on toast or a nice pile of creamy scrambled eggs with mushrooms or smoked salmon, but I'm pretty much a fruit and grains man during the week. Having said that, I certainly won't say no to a pancake or two, and if we've got a good fruit compote/salad on the go – perhaps rhubarb or apple in the colder months or macerated berries in the summer – I'll often have it with some yogurt, and maybe a sprinkling of muesli or wheat flakes on top of that.

Fads for smoothies and the like come and go in our house; currently it's strawberry season, and I'm on an almost daily dose of strawberry and mint smoothie (page 28).

And so you can see that some form of fruit pops up on our breakfast table more days than not, which is clearly a good thing and should satisfy the phantom nutritionist whispering in our ear. But it's also life-affirming in a subtler way. A handful of summer berries for breakfast, or a tangy, crunchy autumn apple, a sweet, juicy winter pear, or a bowl of tart poached or baked spring rhubarb means that you head out of the house not just knowing what day of the week it is, but also what time of the year it is. Call me seasonally sentimental, but I think that counts for a lot.

Talking of heading out of the house, there's no getting away from the rushed-start-to-the-day and resulting missed-breakfast syndromes in some households. But that doesn't make the corner grocery or the gas station counter the right place to sort out the missing calories. A peanut butter and banana sandwich, plus an apple, is a genuinely delicious and actually pretty well-balanced portable breakfast. And the honey and peanut butter booster bars on page 39 will beat any branded so-called breakfast bar every time.

Although first thing in the morning is not the obvious time to be thinking of leftovers, in our house breakfast certainly begs, borrows, and steals from other meals (and other chapters in this book). Our breakfast toast is usually made from our homemade sourdough loaf (page 66), and if it's second- or even third-day bread then it's none the worse (and quite possibly all the better) for that. The same goes for French toast – that lovely, substantial breakfast dish where pancakes and toast collide. And if ever an oversight leaves us breadless at breakfast, I'll soon be raiding the pantry for oatcakes, homemade (see page 87) or otherwise.

Personally, I really like something a little sweet and a little sharp on the morning palate – but not too rich or cloying. So any leftover apple or rhubarb crumble (see page 358) will make an appearance and usually disappear before any other options have even been discussed. Granted, it's more likely to get a dollop of yogurt than custard or cream. Unless, of course, there's some leftover custard or cream . . . By the same token, I wouldn't actually bake a sponge or fruit cake for breakfast, but if a homemade cake happens to be knocking around, I wouldn't hesitate to put it on the table as an option, though I might insist on some fresh fruit as a virtuous counterbalance.

If breakfast at the Fearnleys is starting to sound a bit lawless and outré, then I'm fine with that; because, so often, for so many, it's become the meal most hidebound by convention and tradition. But why is that? Perhaps it's because breakfast was the first of all our mealtimes to fall victim to industrialized food production and the seductive pressures of convenience consumerism. I understand that the box of cereal is a time-saving device that few modern families, including mine, would wish to abandon altogether. But do those multinational corporations who manufacture such products actually have to own our breakfast? Of course not!

So let's reclaim breakfast as an actual meal, and not just a calorie-delivery system. Let's find things to savor and share that don't just fill us up, but make us feel good. And if we must squabble at breakfast time (it's in the DNA of most families, isn't it?), then let's cross spoons over the last strawberry or pancake, and not just scrabble for the plastic toy at the bottom of the cereal box. Then we can tackle the adventure of the day ahead with something good and wholesome and homemade inside us. You can call it breakfast, or you can call it love.

Seasonal smoothies

I'm sure I'm not the only parent who gives thanks for the advent of the smoothie – an irresistible and fun way to funnel fresh fruit into otherwise reluctant children. Smoothies can be great for fruit-shy adults too, packing a satisfyingly high dose of goodness into a single glass.

The following recipes are mere guides; you can, and should, tailor-make your smoothie to suit your taste and mood – and, of course, your fruit bowl. Be led by what is seasonally available, add lemon juice to reduce sweetness, yogurt for more creaminess, or oats to make your smoothie a thickie – whatever floats your boat.

The best way to ensure your smoothies are nice and cool is to chill the ingredients beforehand. Alternatively, add two or three crushed ice cubes, though they will slightly dilute the fruit.

SPRING

Rhubarb and orange smoothie

Serves 2

2 to 3 rhubarb stalks, about 6 ounces, cut into 1-inch lengths

Finely grated zest and juice of 2 oranges

3 to 4 teaspoons honey

3 to 4 tablespoons plain yogurt

Put the rhubarb in a saucepan with the orange zest and juice, honey, and 2 tablespoons of water. Stir over low heat until the honey dissolves. Cover the pan and stew the rhubarb very gently for about 8 minutes, until it softens. Add a little water if it starts to look dry. Turn off the heat and let cool completely. (You can, of course, prepare the rhubarb a day ahead and keep it chilled overnight.)

Put the rhubarb mixture in a blender with the yogurt and blend until smooth. Taste and add a little more honey, if you like. Pour into 2 glasses and drink right away.

SUMMER

Strawberry and mint smoothie

Serves 2

1 cup ripe strawberries, hulled

1/4 cup plain yogurt

2 teaspoons finely chopped fresh mint

1 to 2 teaspoons honey or sugar

Blend everything in a blender and serve right away.

SUMMER

Peach Melba smoothie

Serves 2

2 handfuls raspberries

2 large ripe peaches or nectarines, peeled, pitted, and quartered

A small glass of freshly squeezed orange or apple juice

1 to 2 tablespoons honey

1 teaspoon vanilla extract

Put everything in a blender and blend until smooth. Serve immediately.

VARIATION
Apricot and raspberry smoothie
Use 4 ripe apricots in place of the peaches.

LATE SUMMER/AUTUMN
Dan's breakfast juice

This concoction from River Cottage baker Dan Stevens sounds weird but tastes great. You do need a proper juicer to make it.

Serves 2

1 apple
1 pear
1 banana
1 carrot
2 celery stalks
1/2 beet, peeled
1-inch piece fresh ginger, peeled
2 or 3 sprigs parsley

Ideally, chill all the ingredients in the fridge for an hour or two before you juice them.

Simply turn on your juicer and feed all the ingredients through. For a richer, thicker drink, don't juice the banana but place it in a blender, pour the other juiced ingredients over, then blend.

Serve right away and feel the goodness flow through you.

AUTUMN
Pear and cinnamon smoothie

Serves 2

2 very ripe pears
1 cup plain yogurt
1 1/2 tablespoons maple syrup or honey
1 teaspoon ground cinnamon, plus a little extra for sprinkling
1 teaspoon fresh lemon juice
1 teaspoon grated fresh ginger

Peel, halve, and core the pears and cut into chunks. Put into a blender with all the rest of the ingredients and blend until smooth.

Pour into 2 glasses and sprinkle a little more cinnamon on top, if you like.

WINTER
Banana and oat thickie

Serves 2

2 ripe bananas
1 1/4 cups ice-cold milk (or half milk and half plain yogurt)
2 tablespoons quick oats
2 ice cubes

Put all the ingredients in a blender and blend until smooth.

Honey-baked rhubarb

Rhubarb, I confess, is one of my very favorite fruits (though to be accurate, it's actually a vegetable with an identity crisis). I never tire of finding new ways to enjoy it. This sweet and fragrant breakfast compote is a fairly recent discovery, and I absolutely love it.

Try it on French toast (page 47) or perfect pancakes (page 43), or spooned on to your customized muesli (page 34) or thick yogurt. Alternatively, serve with vanilla ice cream for a pretty dessert.

From January till early April, you can buy elegant, slender stems of indoor-grown "forced" rhubarb. This gradually gives way to the thicker, darker, more robust outdoor-grown crop. Either will work in this recipe.

Serves 6

2 pounds rhubarb, cut into 2- to 4-inch lengths

Juice and finely grated zest of 1 orange

1/4 cup honey

Preheat the oven to 300°F.

Put the rhubarb in an ovenproof dish large enough to hold it in a single layer, then scatter over the orange zest and pour in the juice. Drizzle over the honey and gently mix everything together.

Cover loosely with foil and bake for 45 minutes to 1 hour, until the rhubarb is tender, giving it a gentle stir halfway through. The pieces of rhubarb should keep their shape rather than cook to a mush.

Let cool before serving. This can be covered and kept for a week or so in the fridge.

Two (or more) fruit salad

There's no syrup or juice here, no maceration is required, and sugar is an optional extra. It's really just a plate of fruit. The key thing is that you've taken the trouble to peel and slice or otherwise prepare it (a squeeze of lemon or lime juice is, for instance, a wonderful way to dress up a ripe banana and give it a bit of attitude). Children can eat this with their fingers or a fork.

1 banana per person, peeled and sliced

Plus 1 (or more) of the following per person:

A few strawberries, hulled, large ones halved or quartered

A few raspberries

A couple of plums, pitted and quartered

1 small or 1/2 large apple or pear, cored and sliced

A lemon wedge

1 to 2 teaspoons superfine sugar (optional)

Arrange the prepared fruit on a plate. Squeeze a little lemon juice over the fruit (mainly on the banana). Sprinkle a scant amount of superfine sugar on the tarter fruits, if you like, and serve at once.

Muesli with apple, orange, and yogurt

If you've never eaten muesli the Swiss way – soaked in freshly squeezed orange juice and dished up with grated apple and yogurt – then you've never really given it a chance. It makes a much more exciting breakfast than muesli with just a slosh of milk. The recipe you see here is merely a guide to compiling a dry muesli mix based on your own preferences. Don't like sunflower seeds? Leave them out. No dried apricots in the cupboard? Use raisins or prunes. The idea is to customize it to suit yourself and your family.

The dried mixture will keep well for several weeks in an airtight jar, so you can put together a nourishing breakfast in minutes. Unsulfured apricots are my favorite dried fruit for muesli – they have slightly more sharpness than your average raisin. And my favorite nuts are almonds.

Makes 10 to 12 servings

2 cups old-fashioned rolled oats

1 cup mixed dried fruit of your choice, such as dark or golden raisins, dried apricots, dates, or prunes

3/4 cup nuts of your choice, lightly toasted if you have time

1 cup wheat flakes (optional)

3 to 4 tablespoons seeds, such as pumpkin, sunflower, sesame, or flax (optional)

To serve (for 1):

1 crisp eating apple, such as Fuji or Gala

Juice of 1 or 2 oranges (or a little milk, if you prefer)

Sugar or honey

Plain yogurt

To make the muesli, put the oats in a bowl. Coarsely chop larger dried fruits, such as apricots, dates, and prunes. Leave the nuts whole, or chop them coarsely if you prefer. Add the fruit and nuts to the oats, together with the wheat flakes and seeds if using, and stir to combine. Empty into an airtight container, seal, and store in a cool, dark place until required.

To serve, put about 1/2 cup of the muesli mix into a bowl. Coarsely grate or finely chop the apple (including the skin) and add this to the muesli. Squeeze the orange(s) and add the juice to the bowl (or use milk, if you like). Stir to blend everything evenly and let soak for about 10 minutes.

Finally, sprinkle over just a little sugar or drizzle over some honey, add a good dollop of yogurt, and serve.

Quick oatmeal

It took a while for me to warm to this classic breakfast, after the experience of lumpy, cement-like porridge (i.e., oatmeal) at school. In fact it was the Wallace oatmeal (see below) that converted me. Now I'd say there is no finer start to the day.

You can scale this up to serve as many people as you like. Just stick to the ratio of 1 part oats to $2^1/_2$ parts water and/or milk.

Serves 2 to 3

1 cup quick oats
$2^1/_2$ cups water or milk
(or half of each)
A pinch of sea salt

To serve:
Milk or cream
Honey, sugar, maple syrup, or jam
Bananas, apples, or raisins (optional)
A pinch of ground cinnamon (optional)

Pour the oats into a pan, stir in the water and/or milk and the salt, and bring to a boil over medium heat. Cook briskly for 3 minutes, stirring constantly. If it's getting too thick, add a dash of hot water.

Serve with a little milk or cream and your choice of sweetener: honey, brown or white sugar, maple syrup, or jam. Feel free to crank it up with sliced bananas, apple slices (gently fried in butter, if you like), raisins, and/or a pinch of cinnamon.

VARIATION
Wallace oatmeal

So called because my friend Andrew Wallace showed me how to make it, this traditional Scottish approach to oatmeal uses steel-cut oats rather than rolled oats for a nuttier, grainier finish, which I love. It needs overnight soaking, and takes a bit longer to cook.

For 4 people, add $1^1/_3$ cups steel-cut oatmeal to a saucepan, add $3^1/_2$ cups cold water, and leave overnight. In the morning, add a good pinch of salt and stir gently over medium heat until it begins to bubble and gloop like hot mud. Turn the heat down low and cook, stirring occasionally, for about 8 minutes, until the oatmeal is cooked through and creamy. If it is a little thick, a dash of boiling water from the kettle will loosen it. Serve with your choice of milk, cream, honey, jam, syrup, or sugar.

Honey and peanut butter booster bars

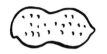

These jam-packed near relatives of the flapjack are my antidote to the devil's work – those big-brand "energy" bars that fester among the chocolate on every gas station counter masquerading as a late breakfast. I wouldn't call these a substitute for breakfast, and I wouldn't make outlandish health claims for them either. But the fruity, oaty, nutty, seedy elements will certainly ensure a hefty dose of natural goodness. Far more importantly, they taste delicious.

Makes 16

¹/₂ cup unsalted butter

²/₃ cup packed brown sugar

¹/₃ cup no-sugar-added crunchy peanut butter

¹/₄ cup honey, plus a little more to finish

Finely grated zest of 1 orange

Finely grated zest of 1 lemon

1¹/₄ cups old-fashioned rolled oats

³/₄ cup dried fruit, such as raisins, chopped apricots, prunes, or dates, either singly or in combination

1 cup mixed seeds, such as pumpkin, sunflower, poppy, flaxseed, and sesame

Preheat the oven to 325°F.

Grease and line an 8-inch square baking pan with parchment paper.

Put the butter, sugar, peanut butter, honey, and grated citrus zests in a deep saucepan over very low heat. Let heat until melted, stirring from time to time.

Stir the oats, dried fruit, and three-quarters of the seeds into the melted butter mixture until thoroughly combined. Spread the mixture out evenly in the prepared pan, smoothing the top as you go.

Scatter the remaining seeds over the surface and drizzle with a little more honey. Bake for about 30 minutes, until golden in the center and golden brown on the edges.

Let cool completely in the pan (be patient – it cuts much better when cold), then turn out and cut into squares with a sharp knife. These bars will keep for 5 to 7 days in an airtight tin.

VARIATION
Banana booster bars
Replace the peanut butter with 1 medium ripe banana (about 6 ounces), mashed. Stir it in after all the other ingredients have been combined.

Whole-wheat pancakes

Once you start eating these, warm and fluffy from the pan, it's hard to stop. They're great for weekend breakfasts, but just as good for afternoon tea. The kids love to help me with them, waiting for the bubbles to appear in the hot batter and judging the perfect moment to flip them over in the pan.

If you can't get hold of self-rising whole-wheat flour, use whole-wheat pastry flour with 2 teaspoons of baking powder added.

Makes 20 to 30

1¹/₂ cups self-rising whole-wheat flour

A pinch of baking powder

A pinch of sea salt

2 tablespoons superfine sugar

2 eggs

About 1 cup milk

3 tablespoons unsalted butter, melted

A little sunflower oil

To serve:

Butter

Superfine sugar

A pinch of ground cinnamon (optional)

Jam, maple syrup, or macerated fruit (see page 336; optional)

Sift the flour, baking powder, and salt into a large bowl and stir in the sugar. Make a well in the center and break in the eggs. Pour in about half the milk. Whisk, gently at first, and then as you start to get a thick paste, add more milk and the melted butter. Beat until you get a creamy batter a little thicker than heavy cream – you might not need all the milk.

Put a large, heavy frying pan or a flat griddle over medium-high heat. Add a few drops of oil and rub with a thick wad of paper towels to oil the pan very lightly. Pour a scant tablespoon of batter into the pan – you should be able to fit 4 or 5 in the pan.

After about a minute, little bubbles will start to appear on the surface of the pancakes. As soon as they cover the surface, flip the pancakes over with a spatula – be warned, the first batch may stick. Cook the other side for 40 to 60 seconds or so, then transfer the pancakes to a warm plate and cover them with a clean tea towel so they stay soft – or hand them over to those people waiting eagerly.

Cook the remaining pancakes in the same way, adjusting the heat level if they start browning too quickly and oiling the pan with paper towels as necessary.

To serve, top with a little butter and sprinkle with some sugar and a fine dusting of cinnamon, if you like. Or serve buttered and spread with jam, maple syrup, or macerated fruit. Eat quickly, while still hot.

VARIATIONS

Raisin and lemon pancakes

Add a little grated lemon zest to the batter and an extra tablespoon of sugar. Sprinkle raisins onto the pancakes as they cook.

Savory pancakes

Omit the sugar. Add about ¹/₃ cup grated Cheddar and a grind of black pepper to the batter, and maybe some crumbled cooked bacon. Very good as a quick supper with baked beans.

Perfect pancakes

Thin, crêpe-style pancakes have a bit of a reputation for being tricky, but I think that's because a lot of us only make them once a year. Confidence is the most important ingredient: the more you make, the better they'll be. They're great, quick breakfast fare, and in our house we have them at least once a week. I like to eat them with a light dusting of sugar and a squeeze of lemon juice, but we also top them with sliced banana and honey, with fridge jam (page 50), or sometimes with a slosh of maple syrup.

The 30-minute rest is important (without it, your pancakes may be a bit wet). If we are thinking ahead, we often make the batter the night before and leave it in the fridge overnight. It won't keep for more than 48 hours though; i.e., two breakfasts in a row, tops.

Makes about 16

2 cups white or whole-wheat pastry flour
A pinch of sea salt
2 eggs, lightly beaten
About 2^1/$_2$ cups whole milk
A little sunflower oil

To serve:
Superfine sugar and a squeeze of lemon juice (or see suggestions above)

Sift the flour and salt into a bowl and make a well in the center. Pour in the eggs, add about ^{1}/$_4$ cup of the milk, and start to whisk, gradually incorporating the flour into the wet ingredients. When you have a thick batter forming in the middle, add a bit more milk and whisk in a bit more flour. Keep going in this way until all the milk has been added, all the flour is incorporated, and you have a smooth batter about the consistency of half-and-half. One of the mistakes people make with these pancakes is to leave the batter too thick. You can also make the batter by blending everything up in a blender or food processor. Either way, let it rest for at least 30 minutes, then check the consistency again. If it's thickened up a bit, add a dash more milk to bring it back to the right consistency.

To cook the pancakes, heat a nonstick frying pan or crêpe pan, about 8 inches in diameter, over medium heat. When it's hot, swirl 1 tablespoon of oil around the pan, then pour out the excess. Add a small ladleful (a scant ^{1}/$_4$ cup) of batter – just enough to coat the bottom of the pan – and swirl it around quickly until it covers the bottom. Cook for a minute or so, until lightly colored underneath, then flip over and cook for a minute more. Depending on the pan, you may need to loosen the edges of the pancake with a palette knife before you flip.

Almost without exception, the first pancake will be a failure. Don't worry, this is normal; the next one will be much better. Dole them out as you make them so they can be eaten hot – sprinkled with sugar and lemon juice.

Baked breakfast cheesecake

I know the idea of cheesecake for breakfast sounds odd, but this simple recipe is a great way to start the day, especially if you serve it with some fresh berries or a fruit compote. It is incredibly easy to throw together since there's no crust, and you can get it on the table in little more than half an hour.

Besides making a luxurious weekend breakfast or brunch, it is also a delicious dessert. Until recently, I thickened the cheese mixture with a little semolina or flour, but I tried using oatmeal instead and the result was so successful that I now usually do it this way.

If using salted goat cheese, don't add salt to the recipe.

Serves 10

21 ounces ricotta cheese or cream cheese, or soft, very mild goat cheese (preferably unsalted)

5 tablespoons unsalted butter, melted and cooled slightly

3 tablespoons quick oats, fine semolina, or whole-wheat pastry flour

A good pinch of sea salt

$1/2$ cup superfine sugar

2 eggs, lightly beaten

Finely grated zest of 2 small oranges, plus 1 tablespoon juice

3 tablespoons raisins (optional)

To serve:

Fresh fruit or fruit compote (see pages 339–44)

Yogurt or sour cream (optional)

Preheat the oven to 325°F.

Generously butter a 9-inch springform cake pan.

Beat the cheese with a wooden spoon until smooth, then add the melted butter, oatmeal, semolina, or flour, salt, sugar, eggs, and orange zest and juice, and mix well (feel free to whiz the ingredients in a food processor). Fold in the raisins, if using.

Spoon the mixture into the prepared pan and bake for about 25 minutes, until just set, with a slight wobble in the center.

Serve hot, warm, or at room temperature with some fresh fruit or fruit compote, and, if you like, yogurt or sour cream.

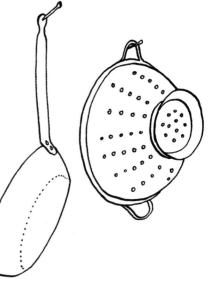

French toast with apples

Known in Britain as "eggy bread," French toast – like pancakes – is a wholesome way for kids to start their day, especially if it is topped with fried apple slices. You could substitute pears for the apples, cooked in exactly the same way, or simply top the French toast with fridge jam (page 50), or macerated fruit (see page 336).

Serves 4

4 eggs
2 tablespoons milk
About 2 tablespoons superfine sugar
4 thick slices slightly stale white bread, crusts removed
Unsalted butter and sunflower oil for frying
1/2 teaspoon ground cinnamon (optional)

For the apples:
1 tablespoon unsalted butter
A drizzle of sunflower oil
2 crisp eating apples, such as Cortland, peeled (or not, as you like), cored, and cut into thin wedges
2 teaspoons superfine or brown sugar (optional)

Beat the eggs together thoroughly with the milk and 1 tablespoon of the sugar, then pour into a shallow dish. Add the bread slices and submerge them in the egg, turning to coat them well. Let them soak, turning occasionally, for at least 10 minutes, or up to half an hour. Ideally, the bread should absorb almost all the egg – but it never quite does!

While the bread is soaking, cook the apples. Heat the butter and oil in a frying pan. Add the apple slices and cook over medium heat, turning them occasionally, for 5 to 10 minutes, until soft and lightly golden. Add a little sugar toward the end, if you like, to create a buttery syrup in the pan. Scoop the apples out and keep them warm.

You can fry the bread in the same pan as the apples – but if you've added sugar you'll have to give it a quick cleaning. Heat the pan over medium heat and add a little more butter and another dash of oil. Lay the bread in the pan (cook it in 2 batches, if necessary) and drizzle any leftover egg on top. Fry for 2 to 3 minutes, until the bottom is golden brown, then flip over and cook for 2 to 3 minutes more. Transfer to warm plates.

Scatter the remaining sugar over the bread (combining it first with the cinnamon, if you like), pile the warm apples and any syrupy juices on top, and serve.

VARIATIONS
- Serve cinnamon-sprinkled French toast with roasted plums (see page 352) or with honey-baked rhubarb (page 30).
- Instead of sprinkling your French toast with sugar, drizzle over some maple syrup and top with blueberries or raspberries.
- Serve plain, unsugared French toast with bacon or fried ham.

Homemade yogurt

We use yogurt all the time at River Cottage – in fruity fools and ice cream, in breads and cakes, and swirled into soups, stews, and curries. We mix it with goat cheese and herbs to make near-instant dips, and with toasted spices to spoon into bowls of soup (see page 274). But it is also, of course, an ideal breakfast food, wonderful with a spoonful of fridge jam (page 50) stirred in, or a drizzle of golden honey on top. Pair it with fresh, dried, or stewed fruit, or muesli (page 34) and it makes an even more satisfying start to the day.

Making your own yogurt can save you money, and it also gives you complete control over what goes into it (organic or even unpasteurized milk, if you choose, and no preservatives). You just need some live yogurt to start you off, a candy thermometer, and a warm bowl in a warm place or, easier still, a Thermos. The powdered milk isn't essential either, though it will help to thicken the yogurt. Make sure you don't eat all your first batch – keep a little back to make your next lot.

Makes about 2¼ cups

2 cups whole milk
⅓ cup powdered milk
3 tablespoons live-culture plain whole-milk yogurt

Pour the milk into a saucepan and whisk in the dried milk powder. Put the pan over medium heat, stand a candy thermometer in it, and stir gently, watching the thermometer carefully, until the temperature reaches 115°F.

Take the saucepan off the heat and pour the milk into a warmed mixing bowl. Check that the temperature hasn't gone beyond 115°F. If it has, stir the milk until the temperature drops back. Whisk in the yogurt. The bacteria within it will start to work on the fresh milk, converting it into yogurt.

Cover the bowl with a lid or some plastic wrap, wrap it in a towel, and put it somewhere warm – above a radiator is good. Alternatively, you can pour the mixture into a warmed wide-mouth Thermos and seal.

Check the yogurt after 6 to 8 hours, or leave it overnight. If it's still runny, leave it wrapped up in the warm place for another 1 or 2 hours. When it has thickened and looks set, pour it into a clean container, seal, and refrigerate. Homemade yogurt isn't as thick as most commercial varieties. If you'd like a thicker finish, you can strain the yogurt through a cheesecloth-lined sieve over a bowl in the fridge for a few hours.

Fridge jam

This "fridge jam" is a sort of halfway house between full-blown preserves and a fresh fruit sauce. With only two-thirds the sugar of a standard jam, it has a softer, looser consistency and a sharper flavor. It's very versatile. You can still serve it on toast, of course, but at home we mostly have it for breakfast with pancakes or on yogurt. It's outstanding with rice pudding, too. Make it with strawberries, raspberries, or gooseberries, or try my favorite cherry jam (see below).

Makes about 6 cups

3 pounds fresh strawberries, raspberries, or gooseberries

Juice of 1 lemon

4 cups sugar

Sterilize some Mason jars or other suitable containers by washing them in hot, soapy water and drying in a very low oven (or put them through a dishwasher cycle).

Divide the fruit in half, putting the smaller berries in one bowl, the larger ones in another (if the small ones are quite big, halve them). Coarsely crush the large ones with a potato masher (or by hand), then add the uncrushed berries, lemon juice, and sugar. Stir to combine, then leave for an hour to draw out the juices.

Transfer the mixture to a preserving pan or a wide, heavy saucepan that is deep enough for the jam to bubble away safely. Bring it quickly to a rolling boil, stirring a few times to make sure all the sugar dissolves, then boil hard for exactly 5 minutes, skimming off any foam from the surface. Take off the heat and let cool for 5 minutes (this helps to keep the whole fruit suspended in the jam).

Pour the hot jam into the warm jars or other vessels and seal tightly. Label jars when cool. Store in the fridge and use within 3 weeks.

VARIATION
Sour cherry fridge jam

Substitute 3 pounds cherries for the berries. I like to leave the pits in, as they lend a special flavor, but you may prefer to remove them using an olive/cherry pitter (tie the pits in a square of cheesecloth and add it to the jam while you boil it up).

Put the cherries in a preserving pan or a wide, heavy saucepan with 6 tablespoons water (no lemon juice) and bring slowly to a boil, stirring often, until the juices run. Simmer gently for about 10 minutes, until the cherries are soft. Add 4 cups sugar, stir until dissolved, then bring to a boil and boil hard for 5 minutes. Seal and serve as above.

Nut butters

Making your own nut butter is so simple and quick, and you can adapt the recipe to your own taste. Try toasting the nuts for a few minutes in a hot oven or leave them raw, or experiment with different nuts, in any combination. Cashew nut butter is my favorite, but almonds, hazelnuts, and, of course, peanuts all work well.

Homemade nut butter is very good spread thickly on freshly baked bread and topped with your favorite jam. You could also spread it on oatcakes (page 87) or digestive biscuits (page 88), or roll it into balls and dip them in melted dark chocolate for a deliciously indulgent treat. It plays a starring role in our favorite "late-for-school" sandwich, too – thick sourdough bread, nut butter, and sliced banana.

Makes ³/₄ cup

1¹/₂ cups nuts (unroasted and unsalted), such as cashews, almonds, hazelnuts, and/or peanuts

3 to 4 tablespoons canola or sunflower oil

1 to 2 teaspoons honey

¹/₂ teaspoon coarse sea salt

Put the nuts in a food processor and pulse until quite fine. Add a tablespoon or two of the oil and process until you have a creamy paste, then add the honey and salt. Add a few more nuts just at the end of processing if you'd like a crunchy nut butter. Store in the fridge in an airtight container, where it will keep for up to 2 weeks.

VARIATION
Nut and seed butters

To any of your favorite nut butters, add ¹/₄ cup sunflower, sesame, or pumpkin seeds, or a combination, at the end of processing to give extra texture and crunch.

Tomato toast

If you have ever had breakfast in Barcelona, there's every chance you were offered *pa amb tomàquet*. That's tomato toast to you and me. I can think of few things more delicious in high summer, when tomatoes are at their fleshy, sunny, flavorsome best. If you grow your own, it's an absolute must.

The messy, pulpy tomato grating is fun for grown-ups and kids – this is one occasion when you're certainly permitted to play with your food.

Serves 2

2 thick slices robust bread (sourdough, page 66, is ideal)

1 garlic clove, halved (optional)

2 ripe, juicy large tomatoes, halved

2 tablespoons fruity extra-virgin olive oil

Sea salt

Toast or grill the bread. If you don't mind a bit of garlic in the morning, rub the cut garlic clove gently over one side. Next, rub on the tomatoes, grating and squishing the cut side messily against the rough surface of the toast and squirting out the pulp as you go. Discard the skins. Drizzle over the olive oil, sprinkle on a pinch of sea salt, and eat immediately.

VARIATION
Oily toast

This is a delicious alternative to hot buttered toast. My kids absolutely love it for breakfast. Rub your hot toast with garlic if you like (we don't in the morning, but do if we're having the toast with soup or salad for supper). Then simply drizzle the toast fairly generously with a good, tasty unrefined oil – we rotate hempseed, canola, and olive oil, and sometimes use a combination. Finish with a sprinkling of sea salt.

Portobello mushrooms on toast

Big, dark-gilled mushrooms, oozing garlicky, buttery juices, make a very easy cooked breakfast or brunch. This is a dish I particularly like to make in autumn, with horse or field mushrooms I've gathered myself. With a salad on the side, this would make a light supper, too – or a simple starter for four.

Serves 2

4 portobello or other large, flat mushrooms, stemmed

About 2 tablespoons unsalted butter

1 fat garlic clove, finely chopped

A large sprig of thyme or lemon thyme

Sea salt and freshly ground black pepper

2 thick slices bread (sourdough, page 66, and soda bread, page 72, are particularly good)

$^1/_2$ lemon

Preheat the oven to 375°F.

Put the mushrooms in a lightly buttered ovenproof dish big enough to hold them in a single layer. Cut the butter into little nuggets and dot them over the top of the mushrooms. Scatter over the chopped garlic, then strip the leaves from the thyme and scatter these over too. Season generously with salt and pepper.

Bake for about 15 minutes, until the mushrooms are tender and overflowing with garlicky, buttery juice. Meanwhile, toast the bread.

Put the toast on 2 warm plates, top with the mushrooms, and drizzle over any juices left in the dish. Finish with a generous squeeze of lemon juice and serve right away.

Smoked salmon and scrambled eggs on toast

Salty, smoky salmon combined with rich, creamy scrambled eggs is one of the great brunch/weekend-breakfast dishes – and a pretty mean supper any day of the week. You may well have your own preferred method for scrambling eggs, but I include mine for those who are not yet set in their ways. As with any simple dish, the quality of the ingredients is everything. Use organically farmed salmon, and the freshest free-range eggs you can find.

Serves 2

About 4 ounces sliced smoked salmon

4 eggs

Fine sea salt and freshly ground black pepper

1 tablespoon unsalted butter, plus a little more for the toast

2 slices good bread

Unwrap the salmon and lay the slices on a plate so they come to room temperature while you cook the eggs.

Break the eggs into a bowl. Add a good pinch of salt and a grind of pepper and whisk with a fork. Place a small nonstick saucepan over low heat and melt half the butter in it. When the butter begins to bubble, pour in the eggs and start stirring with a wooden spoon. Put the bread on to toast now.

As the mixture gets hotter, the eggs will start to thicken into soft lumps. This takes a few minutes – don't rush it by turning up the heat. Keep stirring gently, scraping the bottom and sides of the pan to move any setting egg back into the more yielding middle. As you approach the degree of runniness you like, remove from the heat, stir for another 10 seconds or so, then add the remaining butter, which will, with a final quick stir, help stop the eggs cooking any further.

Quickly butter the toast, lay a couple of slices of smoked salmon on each piece, and pile the eggs on top. Serve right away.

VARIATIONS

Scrambled eggs with ham

Instead of smoked salmon, use ham (sliced from a proper ham) at room temperature. Serve on the toast, under the scrambled eggs, as above.

Scrambled eggs with smoked fish

In place of the salmon, use 8 to 10 ounces smoked pollock or haddock fillet lightly poached in enough milk just to cover, with a bay leaf and a few peppercorns added (bring to a simmer, take off the heat, and let the fish cook in the residual heat for a few minutes, then drain). Break the fish into large flakes, removing the skin and any bones. Gently stir into your scrambled eggs for the last minute or so of cooking.

Many home cooks, some professional chefs, and at least one

semiprofessional home cook (that's me) have culinary blind spots – areas of kitchen endeavor where they rarely attempt to tread. For some it may be pastry, for others fish, and for others perhaps the long, slow cooking of meat, as in braises, stews, and pot roasts. For me, until a few years ago, it was bread making.

Reasons for neglecting a certain set of cookery skills vary with the individual: some fess up to a lack of confidence, or plead restricted opportunity; others may even belittle the speciality in question as simply not worth bothering with. Sometimes it's hard to put your finger on it. It's just a strange, almost imperceptible creeping feeling that the gastronomic pursuit in question is not your thing. This, of course, becomes a self-fulfilling prophecy, as the longer you go without breaking through, the more it seems to be part of the definition of what kind of cook you are, or aren't.

Rarely, if ever, is it because one doesn't enjoy the food in question. I love bread and always have. But I somehow never cast myself as a baker. And the more I didn't bake bread, the more I began to think of myself as a non-bread-baking kind of cook. Then I moved into a house with a fabulous wood-burning bread oven in an ancient inglenook fireplace. I could hardly not try it out. In fact, what better way of reviving it than for our daughter Chloe's tenth birthday party, when we decided to fire up the dormant beast and bash out pizzas, kneaded, shaped, and topped by a gang of frighteningly noisy young girls.

Apart from the sheer joy of the occasion, the pizzas we all put together weren't half bad. In fact, putting aside the fact that they were formed into some rather unconventional shapes (many could perhaps best be described as "protozoan"), they were absolutely delicious. By the end of the day, I had taken the opportunity to knock out a couple of loaves too, pretty much following the instructions on the back of one of the bags of organic flour we had inevitably overinvested in for our pizza-making bonanza. They were also more than respectable. Lovely, in fact. And in one fell swoop, my bread-baking jinx was busted.

Now we've moved house again, and we miss our inglenook-with-ancient-bread-oven like an old friend left behind. But we have a new friend, as we have installed a wood-burning range. It's easy to fire it up to get the top oven to a piping 500°F or more – ideal for bread and pizzas. (Incidentally, as long as you can get your oven to

a temperature of 425°F, you will be able to bake great bread and pizza; if it's any less than that, in all honesty you will struggle.) We now have regular family pizza sessions – they make a fine alternative to a big Sunday roast dinner when you have friends over on the weekend. Personally, I never tire of dabbling with the pizza theme, my current enthusiasm being for tomatoless types of "pizza bianca." The less-is-more concept is taken to its logical conclusion with the "plain pizza" flatbread on page 85 (though I have to say, in my house the younger pizza makers are still deeply committed to the more-is-more approach...).

Lately, it is my wife, Marie, who has really been bitten by the bread-making bug. Rather than starting from scratch every time with commercial yeast, she tends and nurtures a sourdough "starter" (a fermenting batter of flour and water that contains natural airborne yeasts – see page 66) that we acquired from River Cottage baker Dan Stevens. She bakes an outstanding loaf from this just about every other day – often daily on weekends and during the holidays. If she's busy or away, I step in once in a while to start or finish a batch of dough, or bake a risen loaf that's too impatient to await her return. And it is this very soothing, almost daily rhythmic ritual that has finally weaned us, as a family, off commercial bread. I can't tell you how satisfying it is – it's right up there with growing your own vegetables – and I would urge you to give it a go.

I'm not going to pretend that baking bread is easy, however. Traditional yeast-leavened bread is made by a time-honored and time-consuming process, the rudiments of which need to be respected. My point is that they don't need to be feared. Just get started, as I did, and there is every chance you will make delicious bread – and every chance you will greatly enjoy both the bread and the making of it. I hardly need to mention that, for both taste and goodness, the home-baked loaf has factory-made, supermarket-sold bread roundly thrashed every time. And with a little commitment and understanding, your own efforts can easily compete with the best artisan loaves, at a fraction of their (often eyebrow-raising) price.

Can it be done instantly? No. But it can readily be fitted around a busy working day, or week, and become a steady and even relaxing part of your routine. Techniques can be adapted to your timetable – and there's no shame whatever in using a mixer with a dough hook to do the kneading (we do it all the time). Even if you don't go all out for the sourdough starter as a nurtured "family pet" (it needs "feeding" regularly with flour and water), you'll find the overnight "sponge" method, borrowed from the sourdough technique, can be applied to recipes using fresh or dried yeast (see page 70). So . . . mix before bed. Knead in the morning. Put somewhere cool (the fridge) for a long, slow rise. Punch it down at the end of the working day and knead again. Shape your loaf, leave it for a quicker, warmer rise for a couple of hours, then bake. Your freshly baked loaf, started 36 hours previously, is ready for breakfast. Each little intervention takes only a matter of minutes. And you've hardly noticed the effort.

If you want to acquire a bread-baking habit (or perhaps just improve one), this chapter will show you the way. But besides yeast-risen doughs, there is much pleasure (and time) to be gained from more instantly gratifying forms of baking. Making soda bread, for example, is a great shortcut to wholesome and delicious homemade bread. It's really just a giant scone. And once you've got the knack, then adapting the basic recipe by adding seeds, dried fruit, or even cheese and onion is not just acceptable, it's inevitable.

The American take on yeastless breads is dominated by corn bread – in many ways similar to soda bread, except that the principal flour is milled from corn. This beloved staple of American cuisine is falling-off-a-log easy but hugely rewarding.

"Breads" can be even simpler – though less obviously breadlike. Take the oatcake. In Britain, it's thought of as a kind of cracker to be eaten with cheese, but it is really a very basic form of flatbread. Thinking of it this way can only help to emphasize its versatility. I'm just as likely to eat an oatcake for breakfast with marmalade, or for a quick lunch with a chunk of pâté, or alongside my suppertime soup, as I am with a hunk of Cheddar and a dab of chutney. Flatbreads in the more traditional sense don't get much easier, more primitive, or more instant than the recipe on page 78, yet when you produce a batch of these, the chances are you'll feel very pleased with yourself as you serve up a stack with a pile of homemade hummus, or offer them to your guests to tear up and dunk into a soup or stew. This kind of unleavened bread has been around for millennia, but it's just as relevant to the way we cook today as it ever was.

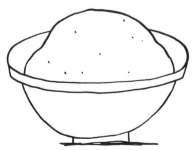

Sourdough loaf

Bread is, of course, a staple, something most of us eat every day, so it's a crying shame that much of it is so poor – tasteless and limp, laced with additives, and completely lacking in character. Baking your own gives you the opportunity to eat really great bread every day – and to have access to wonderful toast and bread crumbs too. Even stale homemade bread is a benefit, with myriad satisfying uses. In short, I urge you to become the baker of your own daily bread. It does require a certain amount of time and commitment, but I promise you, the rewards are phenomenal.

I could offer you a standard simple white bread recipe – the kind you'll find on the back of your bag of bread flour – but I want to go one better. Since I've been baking bread at home, I've discovered that you get a vastly superior flavor and texture in a handmade loaf if it's leavened with wild yeasts, and if those yeasts have been allowed time to develop their personalities. I don't want to get too technical, but, in a nutshell, the more time yeast spends feeding on flour, the more its secretions of alcohol and various acids build up and develop flavor. The truth is, slow-risen bread tastes better.

The bread we make at home now is almost invariably sourdough. It all began, as sourdoughs do, with what is aptly known as a "starter"– a gently fermenting batter of flour and water in which natural airborne yeasts have settled and got to work. We acquired ours from Dan Stevens, my River Cottage baking chef, and you may be able to get hold of one too (from a friendly baker, or a friend who bakes). We're eternally grateful to Dan, who showed us the way with sourdough and helped make it, literally, our daily bread.

But you can also "grow your own" starter from scratch. It may take several days – even a week or two – to get going, but once established, all it needs is regular feeds of flour to keep it frothing happily away. When we want to bake a loaf (which we do, on average, every other day), we take a portion of the starter and combine it with fresh flour and water to make a "sponge." This we leave overnight to ferment and develop flavor. The next morning we combine the sponge with more flour and some salt to make our actual dough, which we knead, rise, shape, prove, and bake.

That may sound like a long-winded process, but I promise you that, while it does take time, it does not take a great deal of effort. Your interventions are relatively brief; the yeasts do their work over several hours, but the baker doesn't do any more hands-on work than the baker of a conventional loaf. If you're still skeptical, all I can do is ask you to take a leap of faith. Try this method and you will produce bread with more flavor and texture than any loaf you've baked at home before. We love it!

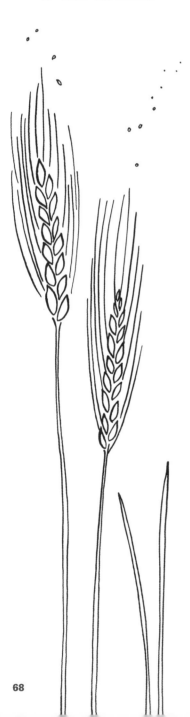

For the starter:
About ³/₄ cup bread flour (at least 50 percent whole-grain flour, such as whole wheat, spelt, or whole-grain rye), plus up to 3 cups bread flour to "feed" the starter

Making the starter

In a large bowl, mix the flour for the starter with enough warm water to make a batter roughly the consistency of thick paint. Beat it well to incorporate some air, then cover with a lid or plastic wrap and leave somewhere fairly warm. A warm kitchen is fine. Check it every few hours until you can see that fermentation has begun – signaled by the appearance of bubbles on the surface and a smell of . . . well, of fermentation (it can actually smell quite unpleasant and acrid at this stage, but don't worry; it will mellow as it matures). The time it takes for your starter to begin fermenting can vary hugely – it could be a few hours or a few days. But make your starter with whole-grain flour (which offers more for the yeast to get its teeth into), keep it warm and draft free, and you should be rewarded with the first signs of life within 24 hours.

Your starter now needs regular feeding. Begin by whisking in another ³/₄ cup or so of fresh flour and enough water to retain that thick batter consistency. You can switch to using cool water and to keeping the starter at normal room temperature – though nowhere too cold or drafty. Leave it again, then, 24 hours or so later, scoop out and discard half the starter, and stir in another ³/₄ cup flour and some more water. Repeat this discard-and-feed routine every day, maintaining the sloppy consistency and keeping your starter at room temperature, and after 7 to 10 days you should have something that smells good – sweet, fruity, yeasty, almost boozy – having lost any harsh, acrid edge. By this stage, it should be actively enticing you into baking with it. But don't be tempted to bake a loaf until it's been on the go for at least a week.

If you're going to bake bread every day or two, maintain your starter in this way, keeping it at room temperature, feeding it daily, and taking some of it out whenever you want to create a sponge (see right). However, if you want to keep it for longer between bakings, you can simply add enough flour (but no water) to turn it from a batter into a stiff dough, then it won't need another feeding for 4 days or so. You'll just need to add more water when you come to make the sponge. Alternatively, you can lull your starter into dormancy by cooling it down – it will keep for a week in the fridge without needing to be fed. You'll then need to bring it back to room temperature and probably give it a fresh feeding to get it bubbling and active again. Combine these two approaches – keep your starter as a stiff dough in the fridge – and you can leave it for 2 weeks before it will need your attention again. If you know you won't be baking for a while, you can even freeze the starter; it will reactivate on thawing.

Makes 1 medium loaf

For the sponge:
About ¹/₂ cup active starter
1¹/₂ cups bread flour (white, whole wheat, or a mixture)

For each loaf:
2 cups bread flour (white, whole wheat, or a mixture)
1 tablespoon canola or olive oil (optional)
2 teaspoons fine sea salt

Making the loaf

The night before you want to bake your loaf, create the sponge: Take about ¹/₂ cup of the active starter and combine it with 1¹/₂ cups flour and 1 cup warm water in a large bowl. Mix well with your hands, then cover with plastic wrap and leave overnight. In the morning it should be clearly fermenting – thick, sticky, and bubbly.

To make the dough, add the 2 cups flour to the sponge, along with the oil, if you're using it (it will make the bread a touch softer and silkier but is not essential), and the salt (which is essential). Squish it all together with your hands. You should have a fairly sticky dough. If it seems tight and firm, add a dash more warm water. If it's unmanageably loose, add more flour, but do leave it fairly wet – you'll get better bread that way.

Turn the dough out onto a lightly floured work surface and knead until smooth and silky. This takes about 10 minutes, but it can vary according to your own style and level of confidence. To knead, place the fingertips of one hand in the middle of the ball of dough, then use the heel of your other hand to push the dough away from you in a long stretch. Fold the dough back on itself, then repeat the maneuver. Keep going, stretching and folding, giving the dough a quarter turn every few stretches, until it is silky and smooth. Alternatively, use the dough hook on your mixer!

Put the dough in a lightly oiled bowl and turn it to coat with the oil. Cover with lightly oiled plastic wrap, or put the bowl into a large plastic bag, and let rise. Don't expect it to whoosh up to twice its original size in an hour, as a conventional loaf does. Sourdough rises slowly and sedately. The best thing is to knead it in the morning, then simply leave it all day – perhaps while you're out at work – in a fairly cool, draft-free place until it has more or less doubled in size and feels springy if you push your finger gently into it; alternatively, you could knead it in the evening and then leave it to rise overnight.

Knock back (deflate) the risen dough by punching it down with your knuckles on a lightly floured surface. You now need to "prove" the dough (i.e., give it a second rising). You are also going to be forming it into the shape it will be for baking. If you have a proper baker's proving basket, use this, first dusting it generously with flour. Alternatively, rig up your own proving basket by lining a medium-sized, fairly shallow bowl with a clean tea towel, then dusting it with flour. Place your round of dough inside, cover again with oiled plastic wrap or a clean plastic bag, and let rise, in a warm place this time, for 1¹/₂ to 3 hours, or until roughly doubled in size. Then the dough is ready to bake.

Preheat the oven to 500°F (or at least to 450°F, if that's your top limit). If possible, have ready a clean spray bottle full of water – you'll be using this to create a steamy atmosphere in the oven, which helps the bread to rise and develop a good crust. (You can achieve the same effect with a roasting pan of boiling water placed on the bottom of the oven just before you put the loaf in, but the spray bottle is easier – and much more fun.)

About 5 minutes before you want to put the loaf in the oven, place a baking sheet in it to heat up. Then take the hot baking sheet from the oven, dust it with flour, and carefully tip the risen dough out of the proving basket/bowl, upside down, onto the baking sheet; it will now be the right way up. If you like, you can slash the top of the loaf a few times with a very sharp serrated knife, or snip it with a pair of scissors, to give a pattern to the crust.

Put the loaf into the hot oven and give it a few squirts from the spray bottle over and around it. After 15 minutes, reduce the heat to 400°F, give the oven another spray, and bake for a further 25 to 30 minutes, until the well-browned loaf vibrates and sounds hollow when you tap its bottom. Let cool for at least 20 minutes before you plunge in with the bread knife – it's okay to slice it warm, but not piping hot.

An alternative and very satisfying way to bake your sourdough loaf is by placing the dough directly on the floor of the oven – but you can only do this in a cast-iron range. Tip the proved dough carefully onto a well-floured baking sheet or, better still, a baker's paddle, and slide it onto the floor of the oven. We do this every time, and it gives a lovely toasty, chewy, nearly-but-not-quite-burned bottom crust to the loaf.

VARIATION

Cheaty yeasty sponge loaf

If you don't have a starter on the go, you can still take advantage of the overnight sponge method to produce bread with better-than-average flavor and texture. Combine $1^1/_2$ cups bread flour with $1^1/_2$ teaspoons instant yeast, then beat in $1^1/_3$ cups warm water to form a thick batter (alternatively, dissolve 3 teaspoons fresh yeast or $1^1/_2$ teaspoons active dry yeast in the water, then beat it into the flour). Cover with plastic wrap and leave overnight to ferment. The next morning, add another $1^1/_2$ cups flour and 2 teaspoons fine sea salt, then knead as above. Let rise for an hour or two in a warm place, until doubled in size, then punch down, shape, rise again, and bake as above.

Classic soda bread

I frequently turn to soda bread when the bread box is bare. If there's nothing for lunch or to serve with soup for supper, it's a quick and simple answer – and sustaining, too. This classic recipe lends itself to endless tweaking and variation. Add it to your repertoire and you'll never regret it.

Cultured buttermilk, which reacts with the baking soda to make the bread rise, is pretty widely available these days. However, if you can't find it, live-culture whole-milk yogurt makes a great alternative.

Makes 1 medium loaf

4 cups white pastry flour
2 teaspoons baking soda
1 teaspoon fine sea salt
About 1²/₃ cups buttermilk or live-culture yogurt
A little milk, if necessary

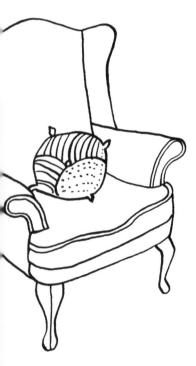

Preheat the oven to 400°F.

Sift the flour and baking soda into a large mixing bowl and stir in the salt. Make a well in the center and pour in the buttermilk, stirring as you go. If necessary, add a tablespoon or two of milk to bring the mixture together; it should form a soft dough, just this side of sticky. Empty it out onto a lightly floured work surface and knead lightly for about a minute, just long enough to pull it together into a loose ball but no longer – you need to get it into the oven while the baking soda is still doing its stuff. You're not looking for the kind of smooth, elastic dough you'd get with a yeast-based bread.

Put the round of dough on a lightly floured baking sheet and dust generously with flour. Mark a deep cross in it with a sharp serrated knife, cutting about two-thirds of the way through the loaf. Bake for 40 to 45 minutes, until the loaf sounds hollow when tapped underneath.

Cool on a wire rack if you like a crunchy crust, or wrap in a clean tea towel if you prefer a soft crust. Soda bread is best eaten while still warm, spread with salty butter and/or a dollop of your favorite jam. But if you have some left over the next day, it makes great toast.

VARIATION
Six-seed soda bread

Mix together 2 tablespoons each of sunflower, pumpkin, sesame, poppy, and flaxseeds, plus 1 teaspoon fennel seeds; set aside. Follow the main recipe but use half white flour and half whole-wheat pastry flour. Add all but 1 tablespoon of the seeds to the dry ingredients before proceeding as above. After cutting a cross in the top of the loaf, brush it with a little buttermilk or ordinary milk and sprinkle with the remaining seeds. Bake at 400°F for 40 to 45 minutes.

Parsnip and thyme bread

Dan Stevens, our baker at River Cottage, created this, inspired by Delia Smith's oatmeal-and-potato bread. It's a really lovely type of soda bread and, like all soda loaves, is great if you want to whip up some bread quickly to go with soup. It has a light sconelike texture, and when it's warm from the oven, it's difficult not to devour the whole thing in minutes, spread thickly with butter.

Makes 1 small loaf

1 tablespoon canola or sunflower oil

1 large onion, sliced

1 cup plus 2 tablespoons self-rising flour

$1/2$ teaspoon sea salt

1 teaspoon fresh thyme leaves

$1/4$ cup grated Parmesan, hard goat cheese, or sharp Cheddar

1 cup grated parsnip

Freshly ground black pepper

1 egg, lightly beaten

2 to 3 tablespoons whole milk

Preheat the oven to 350°F.

Heat the oil in a frying pan, add the onion, and cook gently for about 10 minutes, stirring occasionally, until soft and lightly colored. Remove from the heat and cool slightly.

In a large bowl, mix together the flour, salt, thyme, cheese, grated parsnip, and some pepper. Add the onion, followed by the egg and 2 tablespoons of milk, then mix to form a soft dough, adding the extra milk if needed. Don't overwork the dough; just bring it together with a little light kneading. Shape into a round and place on an oiled baking sheet.

Bake for 40 to 45 minutes, until the loaf is golden and makes a hollow sound when tapped on the bottom.

Let cool for a few minutes on a wire rack, then slice and serve while still warm.

Corn bread

This American favorite is another of those simple, quick, yeast-free breads that can be put together in next to no time. It's not bread at all really, more a sort of savory cake.

The plain version is delicious with bacon for breakfast, or as an accompaniment to hearty, beany stews or soups. However, if you add a few extra tasty ingredients (see suggestions below), it becomes almost a meal in itself, and you don't need much with it except maybe some scrambled eggs or salad.

Makes 12 pieces

$^3/_4$ cup cornmeal or fine polenta (or use half fine and half coarse polenta for a crunchier texture)

$^3/_4$ cup white pastry flour

2 teaspoons baking powder

1 teaspoon fine sea salt

$^1/_2$ teaspoon baking soda

2 eggs

1 tablespoon honey or brown sugar

$^2/_3$ cup buttermilk (or plain whole-milk yogurt)

$^2/_3$ cup whole milk

2 tablespoons unsalted butter, melted

Preheat the oven to 425°F.

Grease a 9-inch square baking pan about $1^1/_2$ inches deep.

In a large bowl, mix together the cornmeal, flour, baking powder, salt, and baking soda. Make a well in the middle.

Whisk together the eggs, honey or sugar, buttermilk or yogurt, milk, and melted butter. Pour into the well in the dry ingredients and stir until everything is just combined. Don't overmix; a few lumps in the batter are fine. You need to get it into the oven as quickly as possible once the baking soda and buttermilk start reacting.

Pour the batter into the pan and bake for about 20 minutes, until the cornbread is golden and has shrunk slightly from the sides of the pan. Place the pan on a wire rack to cool for a few minutes before cutting the bread into squares. Serve warm.

VARIATIONS

Corn bread lends itself to customization. You might want to try adding fried bacon bits, fried diced chorizo, chopped olives, mushrooms (fried with a little garlic and well seasoned), and chopped fresh herbs, such as cilantro and chives.

Cheddar, chile, corn, and green onion corn bread

Gently cook 6 sliced green onions and $^1/_4$ to 1 seeded and finely chopped green or red chile in a tablespoon of canola or olive oil until soft but not colored. Combine with $1^1/_4$ cups cooked corn kernels. Make the corn bread as above, stirring $^1/_3$ cup grated sharp Cheddar cheese into the dry ingredients and adding the corn mixture with the wet ingredients.

Flatbreads

I love these wonderful, soft but slightly charred yeast-free breads (also known as flour tortillas). I could eat a whole pile of them, hot from the pan, just drizzled with oil and sprinkled with salt. However, they are incredibly versatile and the ideal partner to everything from hummus (pages 124–29) to a bulgur wheat salad such as tabula kisir (page 117). They are also ideal for wrapping burgers, sausages, kebabs, and other grilled meats or vegetables, and for mopping up a good wet curry or stew.

Makes 8

1³/₄ cups all-purpose flour
1 teaspoon fine sea salt
1 tablespoon canola, olive, or sunflower oil

Sift the flour into a large bowl and add the salt. Add the oil to ²/₃ cup warm water, then pour this liquid into the flour in a thin stream, stirring well with a wooden spoon or your hands to form a slightly sticky dough. Turn the dough out onto a lightly floured work surface and knead for about 5 minutes, until it feels smooth and plump, sprinkling on a little more flour only if the dough feels very sticky. Cover the ball of dough with the upturned mixing bowl and let it rest for at least 15 minutes.

When you're ready to cook and eat the flatbreads, roll the dough into a sausage shape and divide it into 8 pieces. Roll each piece into a ball. Flour the work surface and rolling pin, then roll out each ball of dough into a round about ¹/₈ inch thick, using plenty of flour as the dough is liable to stick.

Place a heavy nonstick frying pan – or a cast-iron griddle – over high heat and, when it's good and hot, turn the heat down a bit. Have ready a plate lined with a clean tea towel so you can put your cooked flatbreads on it to keep them warm and soft.

Shake off any excess flour and carefully lay a flatbread in the hot pan. Let it sit for a minute or two, until the dough looks "set" on top and is starting to lift away from the pan. Look at the underside and, if you can see dark brown patches forming, flip it over with a spatula or tongs. Cook the second side for 30 to 45 seconds. Wrap the cooked flatbread in the tea towel while you cook the others. If the flatbreads are coloring too quickly, lower the heat a bit.

Serve the flatbreads while still soft and warm. Once cold, they won't be quite the same. But they can be recycled by tearing them into pieces, brushing with a little oil, then crisping them up in an oven preheated to 425°F to make dipping chips, or flat croutons for soups and salads.

Focaccia

This soft, tasty bread, with its light oily, salty crust, is eminently tearable and dippable. Add some dukka (page 134) and a few sliced ripe tomatoes – perhaps a bottle of chilled rosé – and the scene is set for a very good evening.

Makes 12 pieces (to serve 4 to 6)

3¼ cups bread flour

2 teaspoons fine sea salt

1½ teaspoons active dry or instant yeast

2 tablespoons canola or olive oil

To finish:

Canola or olive oil

Coarse sea salt

Leaves from 2 sprigs rosemary, finely chopped

Put the flour and salt in a large bowl and mix together. If you're using ordinary dry yeast, dissolve it in 1⅓ cups warm water. If using instant yeast, add it straight to the flour. Add the yeast liquid or 1⅓ cups warm water to the flour and mix to a very rough, soft dough. Add the oil and squish it all in.

Scrape the dough out onto a lightly floured work surface. With lightly floured hands, knead until it is smooth and silky – anywhere between 5 and 15 minutes. As it's a very sticky dough, you'll need to keep dusting your hands with flour; it will become less sticky as you knead.

Shape the dough into a round, put it in a lightly oiled bowl, turn to coat with oil, then cover with lightly oiled plastic wrap or a clean tea towel and let rise in a warm place until it has doubled in size; this will take about an hour. Punch down the dough and, if you have time, let it rise again in the same way. Meanwhile, lightly oil a shallow baking pan, about 10 by 14 inches.

Press the dough out into a rough rectangle on a floured surface, then put it in the baking pan and press it right into the corners. Cover with oiled plastic wrap or a tea towel and let rise for about half an hour.

Once the dough is risen, preheat the oven to its highest setting (at least 450°F). Use your fingertips to poke rows of deep dimples across the surface of the dough. Drizzle the top generously with oil, then sprinkle with salt and rosemary. Bake for 15 to 20 minutes, turning the oven down after 10 minutes if the focaccia is browning too fast. Serve just warm, or let it cool completely.

VARIATIONS

Focaccia is a bit of a blank slate: you can make it your own by adding all manner of different flavorings. Here are a few ideas:

• Add some finely chopped rosemary and/or thyme, or red pepper flakes to the flour at the start.

• Knead some chopped black or green olives and/or sun-dried tomatoes into the dough after the first rising.

• Push some thyme sprigs, sage leaves, or strips of roasted pepper into the dough when you poke the dimples before baking.

Pizza

There's pizza and then there's pizza. There are thick-based, soggy, drooping excuses-for-pizza, covered with a mélange of oversalted, barely identifiable odds and ends. And then there's thin-crust, crisp, slightly charred, and smoky pizza, topped with choice tidbits – salty ham, garlicky scraps of mushrooms, crumblings of good cheese – ingredients that function almost as mere seasonings for the glorious bread base, which is, quietly, the real star. No prizes for guessing what I'm presenting you with here. Once you've kneaded this easy dough, cranked up your oven to its highest setting, and baked your first proper pizza, you'll never look back.

The tomato sauce suggested on page 84 is just one possibility – you could use instead a few spoonfuls of the sieved roasted tomatoes that go into the sauce on page 142. Then again, you could cook a sauce with peeled, diced fresh tomatoes when they're in season. However you do it, the important thing is not to use too much – you're after a thin covering, not a swamping, so that you can still see patches of pizza crust showing through. Don't be afraid to forgo the tomato sauce altogether, as I have for the pizza illustrated here – just drizzle the dough generously with good olive oil flavored with grated garlic before you apply the toppings.

Makes 4 to 5 pizzas (each serves 1 generously)

For the pizza dough:

1²/₃ cups all-purpose flour

1²/₃ cups bread flour

2 teaspoons fine sea salt

1¹/₂ teaspoons active dry or instant yeast

2 tablespoons canola or olive oil

Cornmeal, fine polenta, or semolina, for dusting (optional)

For the quick tomato sauce (optional):

2 tablespoons canola or olive oil

1 garlic clove, finely sliced

2 (14-ounce) cans chopped tomatoes (or 1 can plus 1 can tomato pureé)

Sea salt and freshly ground black pepper

A pinch of sugar

Optional toppings:

Scraps of ham, or crisp nuggets of cooked bacon or chorizo

An egg, broken onto the pizza just before baking

A handful of sliced mushrooms, sautéed in oil with garlic until dry

Cheese – strips of buffalo mozzarella, coarsely grated hard cheese, or crumbled blue or goat cheese

Coarsely chopped olives

Anchovies, rinsed and drained

Sardines in oil, drained and coarsely flaked

Capers

Coarsely chopped fresh rosemary or thyme

For adding after baking:

Shredded fresh basil or arugula, or torn fresh flat-leaf parsley, or fresh thyme leaves

To make the dough, combine the flours and salt in a large bowl. If you're using ordinary dry yeast, dissolve it in 1¹/₃ cups warm water and let stand for 10 minutes or so. If you're using instant yeast, mix it into the flour. Add the yeast liquid or 1¹/₃ cups warm water and the oil to the flour, mix to form a rough dough, then turn out onto a lightly floured surface and knead for about 10 minutes, until silky and elastic (follow the kneading technique on page 69). Don't be tempted to add too much extra flour, even if the dough seems sticky – it will become less so as you knead.

Put the dough in a lightly oiled bowl, turning it so it gets a coating of oil, cover with plastic wrap, and let rise in a warm place until doubled in size; this will probably take at least an hour.

Meanwhile, make the tomato sauce, if using: heat the oil in a frying pan over a gentle heat. Add the garlic and let it sizzle very gently for a minute or so. As soon as it starts to turn golden, add the tomatoes. Let them bubble gently, stirring often, for 10 to 15 minutes, until you have a thick sauce. Transfer to a pitcher and purée with an immersion blender (if you do it in the pan, the sauce will go everywhere), or just crush the chunks of tomato in the pan with a fork until you have a reasonably smooth sauce. Season to taste with salt, pepper, and the sugar.

Preheat the oven to 475°F, or as high as it will go, and put 2 baking sheets in it to heat up.

Punch the risen dough down on a floured surface and cut it into 4 or 5 pieces. Use a rolling pin or your hands (or both) to roll and stretch each piece into a thin circle or square, or a strange, amoeba-type shape, whichever you prefer; it should be no more than ¹/₄ inch thick – thinner if you can get away with it.

Carefully take one of your hot baking sheets from the oven, scatter it with a little flour or, even better, some cornmeal, polenta, or semolina, and lay the dough on it. Thinly spread a little tomato sauce – a couple of tablespoons should be enough – over the dough (or drizzle with garlicky olive oil; see page 82). Now add the toppings of your choice and grind over some pepper. Bake for 10 to 12 minutes, until the crust is crisp and golden brown at the edges.

While it is cooking, roll out the next piece of dough and prepare the next pizza in the same way. Serve hot, in big slices, drizzled with a little more oil.

VARIATIONS
Pizza bianca

This is pizza without tomato sauce. A tangle of soft, sweet onions tops the dough, seasoned with thyme or oregano and enriched with a little mozzarella or crème fraîche – a lovely, simple meal.

Make the dough (see left). While it is rising, heat $1/4$ cup olive or canola oil in a large frying pan, add 2 pounds very finely sliced onions and a good pinch of salt, and cook gently for 20 to 25 minutes, stirring occasionally, until the onions are soft and translucent. Spread them over the rolled-out dough, scatter over some thyme or chopped oregano, then add a few dollops of crème fraîche or some mozzarella, broken into small pieces. Grind over some pepper, drizzle with a little oil, and bake (see left).

Plain pizza

This is an excellent type of flatbread. Simply roll out the pizza dough (see left) and bake it, absolutely unadorned, for about 8 minutes, until crisp and golden. Remove from the oven and drizzle generously with your very best extra-virgin oil. Scatter with coarse sea salt, grind over some pepper, then serve. It's delicious with dips as a starter and also makes a good partner to soups or salads.

Grissini

The pizza dough can also be used to make grissini (bread sticks) for nibbling and dipping. Just shape small sausages of the punched-down dough into long, thin sticks. Leave them plain or brush lightly with oil and sprinkle with coarse sea salt, or seeds, spices, or herbs of your choice. Transfer to an oiled baking sheet, let rise for half an hour, then bake in a preheated 425°F oven for 15 to 20 minutes.

Bill's Rona oatcakes

At the end of a long day's fishing and filming on the Isle of Rona in the Inner Hebrides, Bill Cowie, the island manager, made us a batch of these for tea. We devoured the lot, some with marmalade, some with honey, and some with cheese and homemade chutney. This is now my standard oatcake recipe.

Makes about 20

1¹/₃ cups quick oats

1¹/₃ cups old-fashioned rolled oats

¹/₂ teaspoon fine sea salt

A few grinds of black pepper (optional)

A small handful of sunflower or other seeds (optional)

¹/₃ cup extra-virgin olive, canola, or hempseed oil

Preheat the oven to 350°F.

Mix all the dry ingredients together in a bowl and make a well in the center. Pour the oil into the well, stir, and then pour in just enough boiling water (about ³/₄ cup) to bind it into a firm dough. Work quickly and don't worry if you overwater a bit – you can remedy the situation by adding more oatmeal, if necessary.

Shape the dough into a ball and let it rest for a few minutes. Roll it out on a lightly floured surface, or between 2 sheets of parchment paper, until about ¹/₄ inch thick. Cut out rounds with a 2¹/₂-inch cookie cutter. You can reroll the pieces to make more oatcakes, but the dough will become increasingly crumbly the more you work it.

Place the oatcakes on 2 lightly floured baking sheets and bake for 20 minutes. Turn the oatcakes, over and bake for a further 10 minutes. Let cool on a wire rack.

The oatcakes will keep for up to a week in an airtight container.

Digestive biscuits

These whole-grain cookies (called "biscuits" in the UK) are also known as sweet-meal biscuits. I give two options for the sugar quantity in the recipe below: the less-sweet biscuits are better suited to pâtés and charcuterie, while the sweeter ones are good with cheese, or naked and unadorned with a cup of tea. If you like, make them with half whole-wheat and half spelt flour, or entirely with spelt flour, to give a slightly nuttier taste.

Makes 35 to 40

1³/₄ cups whole-wheat flour, or whole-grain spelt flour

1 cup (2 sticks) unsalted butter, cut into small cubes and slightly softened

3 cups quick oats

¹/₃ to ¹/₂ cup packed brown sugar, depending on how sweet you want your biscuits

2 teaspoons fine sea salt

2 teaspoons baking powder

About 1 tablespoon milk

Pulse the flour and butter together in a food processor until the mixture resembles fine bread crumbs, or you can do this in a large bowl by rubbing the butter and flour together with your fingertips. Add the oatmeal, sugar, salt, and baking powder and mix together with your hands, adding a little milk a few drops at a time until everything comes together into a slightly sticky dough.

Dust with more flour, then press into a disk about 10 inches in diameter. Wrap in plastic wrap and chill for at least 30 minutes, to rest and firm up a bit. The dough will keep well in the fridge for a few days. Remove it from the fridge about an hour before you want to roll it out, as it will become very hard.

Preheat the oven to 375°F.

Dust the dough with flour and roll it out carefully, dusting regularly with more flour to keep it from sticking, until it is about ¹/₈ inch thick. As it is quite sticky and brittle, you may find it easier to roll between 2 sheets of waxed paper or plastic wrap, also dusted with flour.

Cut the biscuits out with a 2¹/₂-inch cookie cutter and use a spatula to transfer them to nonstick baking sheets (or ordinary baking sheets lined with parchment paper). Bake for up to 10 minutes, checking regularly after the first 5 minutes. They should be golden brown around the edges and lightly colored on top.

Remove from the oven and leave the biscuits to cool and firm up on the baking sheet for a few minutes before transferring them to a wire rack to cool completely.

As Tina Turner might have sung, "What's lunch got to do with it?"

The fact is that for most of us these days, during the week at least, lunch is an irrelevance. Not so much because we don't eat it – we still generally manage to shovel some kind of calorific concoction into our mouths between the hours of noon and 2 p.m. No, the problem is that we scarcely notice we're eating it. We devour our food on autopilot, barely savoring the taste and texture, as our brains continue to go over the day's workload.

To me, this is clearly so wrong. That's why the message of this chapter is simple. If you want to improve the quality of your working day, then improve the quality of your daily lunch. For anyone who is any kind of a home cook, the best way to do that, without a doubt, is to pack a lunch box.

The homemade packed lunch works on so many levels. It ensures that you always eat something you like for lunch, because you (or someone who loves you) have prepared it specially. It slots neatly into a thrifty approach to feeding the family, because more often than not it will largely be made up of (top-quality) leftovers. And it gives you more time to enjoy the break in the middle of your working day, as you don't have to line up for the same old sandwich. (I've got nothing against the sandwich, by the way. Many of the recipes in this chapter can be happily adapted to go between two slices of bread – and the resulting lunch will knock the product of your average sandwich counter into a cocked hat.)

Freed from the need to fight your coworkers for access to second-rate fast food, you can concentrate on finding somewhere nice – the park, the roof – to enjoy your own homemade lunch (or someone nice to enjoy it with). And it certainly saves you money. Even a relatively gourmet lunch box (spiced chicken couscous; mackerel fillet with French lentils and pesto; beet hummus and goat cheese sandwich . . .) will cost you just a few dollars if it's put together at home. And for less than $25 a week, I reckon you can lunch like a king. So, the notion of the portable working lunch is central to the recipes that follow. All but a very few are suited to making the journey with you to your place of work.

I feel passionately about lunch boxes because I make one several times a week for my wife, who goes out to work (and, of course, I feel passionately about her). Most of these recipes, or close variations thereof, have featured on her lunchtime menu at one

time or another, and so, of course, have many other wholesome combinations that I've never written down and probably never will.

However, there is a set of guiding principles that produces well-balanced combinations – always delicious, if rarely ever quite the same twice. It initially involves scouring the fridge for significant leftovers. In our house, this search is most fruitful in the early part of the week, since weekend menus usually have leftovers for weekday lunches factored in.

The first tier of the scavenge is the search for protein: generally meat or fish, so there might be some shreds of cold roast chicken, lamb, or pork. A little more exotically, there could be some leftovers from a more elaborate recipe – for example, sticky glazed spareribs (page 210). Gosh, they're good cold.

Next comes a scan for leftover starch and/or grains or beans. Some cold new potatoes? Cooked rice or pasta? Lentils, perhaps? If this draws a blank, there's still the option of cooking something quick from scratch while we have our breakfast. French lentils are ready after boiling for just 20 minutes or so and cool very quickly if spread out on a plate. Couscous is practically instant. If time is tight and other options limited, you can always open a can of chickpeas.

In summer, there may be time to pick a few handfuls of green beans from the garden and fling them into a pan of simmering water for 5 minutes, or wash and pack a little bunch of baby carrots or crisp radishes, or simply throw in a handful of cheery cherry tomatoes.

Having two or three primary ingredients in hand, it's time for a little creative thought. Nothing too taxing, you understand; you're just asking yourself the question, "What can I add now to make this really nice?" A scattering of capers or cornichons, a little crumbled goat cheese, or good old grated Cheddar? Some seeds/nuts/dried fruit, perhaps? And it's always worth keeping some dukka (page 134) handy – it's a lunch-box winner.

The final touch is usually some kind of dressing. It might just be a glug of good oil and a squeeze of lemon, or a thoroughly shaken and emulsified mustardy vinaigrette (see page 97). It could be a blob of mayonnaise from a jar – and you might want to add some lemon juice, a smidgeon of crushed garlic, and a good blob of mustard. Or you might want to go to another level of premeditation with one of the fresh pestos on page 132. These will keep for several days, and

will instantly transform an otherwise bland combo of leftover meat/
fish and grains/beans into a really excellent lunch.

If you have the facilities to heat food at work, a whole separate raft
of options opens up. Marie has a microwave at work and, unlike me,
she's not afraid to use it. So if there's some leftover stew and some
leftover mashed potatoes, or the remains of a big, hearty soup (you'll
find several of these in the Thrifty Meat chapter), then the job of
sorting the lunch box is done before it's begun. Sometimes a little
customizing is in order. If there's stew but no potatoes, or a soup
that's full of lively vegetables but light on substance, some quickly
cooked couscous, rice, or pasta, or canned beans, can be
incorporated. If you can organize some plain hot pasta at work,
by way of microwave, kettle, or stove top, then your lovingly
homemade pesto can reassert itself in a more conventional role,
simply tossed with a mound of hot buttered spaghetti (or noodles).

Even if there are no leftovers at all, a lovely lunch box can still be
composed from scratch if you have some reasonable resources
to draw on. In the summer, the combination of pantry plus the
vegetable garden (or farm box), with perhaps some good cheese
standing by, should provide the makings of any number of substantial
and really quite sophisticated salads. That's where the seasonal
slaws (pages 120–23) are coming from. If you have the foresight/
organizational skills to do something about your lunch the evening
before, a whole load of lovely salads that use cooked vegetables
as a main ingredient can then enter the fray. The two most frequently
occurring examples in our kitchen are beets and squash. If ever
we're cooking (usually roasting) either vegetable as a side dish,
we'll try to cook enough for a lunch box outing in the days ahead.

You'll have grasped by now that cooking more of something in order
to enjoy the leftovers as lunch pickings is second nature in my kitchen,
and pretty fundamental to my family's approach to eating. So much
so that sometimes we actually cook something solely in order to be
able to use it as leftovers. That sounds a bit batty, I know, but having
a bowl of cooked French lentils or couscous standing by in the fridge
means you always have a quick lunch (or indeed a quick supper,
come to that) in waiting. Even if all you mix it with is a few scraps of
leftover roast lamb and a dab of that oh-so-useful pesto.

Clearly these guiding principles of lunch box assembly need not
always lead, literally, to a lunch in a box. My own weekday working
lunch is similar to, but different from, Marie's. If I'm working at home,

I usually raid the fridge/pantry/garden in much the same way as I do for her lunch box – only I don't have to be quite so disciplined (by which I mean tidy), as there's no need to pack it all away in a neat, portable packet. I'm more likely to spread out the bounty of my raiding party on the kitchen table and pick and mix to my heart's content.

In fact, it's an extension of this process that very often gives us our most enjoyable family lunches on weekends. I'm talking about a generous smorgasbord of leftovers (cold cuts of meat or fish, often tossed with dressed beans), just-pickeds (salad and/or crudités from the garden or grocery store), ready-to-eats (good homemade or locally made ham, pâté, or salami), and one or two quick and easy things that have been cooked specially. The latter might be one of my favorite hummus recipes (on pages 124–29), a big bowl of one of the slaws (on pages 120–23), or, when we've got plenty of eggs, a large frittata (on pages 106–9).

I am more than happy to extend this lovely way of eating to accommodate even quite large numbers of guests – especially in summer, when most lunches will effectively be picnics at the table, either inside or out. Besides the recipes in this chapter, many of the ones in the Vegetables Galore chapter fit perfectly into this scheme.

Sitting down for a more traditional Sunday lunch of big roast, big stew, or big baked fish, plus trimmings and more or less traditional accompanying vegetables, isn't something we do every weekend. But when we do, then no sooner is my plate clean than I'm eyeing what's left of the meal, imagining the myriad ways in which they might enhance the lunches (and suppers) of the coming week.

Tomato, chipolata, and new potato lunch (box) with mustardy vinaigrette

This is comfort food for work days: herby chipolatas (small spicy sausages), tangy tomatoes, and potatoes, all lightly coated in a mustardy dressing. If this doesn't cheer you up at lunchtime, nothing will. And if you think your lunch box might leak, take the dressing in the screw-top jar you mixed it in and add it before eating.

Serves 1

For the dressing:

1 teaspoon English (or other strong) mustard

1¹/₂ teaspoons cider vinegar or white wine vinegar

2 tablespoons canola or extra-virgin olive oil

A small pinch of sugar

Sea salt and freshly ground black pepper

About 4 cold boiled new potatoes, cut into chunks if large

A handful of sweet, ripe cherry tomatoes, halved

2 to 3 cold cooked herby chipolata or other small sausages, or sliced cooked large sausages

To make the dressing, whisk all the ingredients together in a bowl, or shake them in a small screw-top jar to combine.

Put the potatoes and tomatoes in a bowl, drizzle over most of the dressing, and toss together. Transfer to your lunch box. Place the chipolatas on top and drizzle on the remaining dressing. Seal your lunch box and don't forget to take a fork and napkin with you.

Sardine niçoise lunch (box)

I am a great fan of canned sardines and never tire of thinking up new ways to use them. With some cold potatoes and crunchy green beans along for the ride, it makes a healthy and delicious summer lunch (box). Feel free to embellish with other classic salade niçoise components: hard-boiled eggs, olives, anchovies, capers, etc. But even without them, this is a very decent lunch.

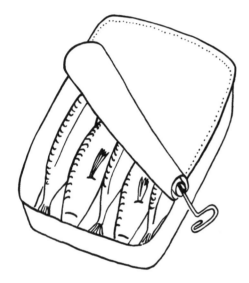

Serves 1

2 to 3 cold cooked potatoes

About ½ cup cold cooked green beans

Sea salt and freshly ground black pepper

2 to 3 canned sardines, drained

1 to 2 tablespoons canola or extra-virgin olive oil

A lemon wedge

Slice the potatoes thickly and arrange in a layer in your lunch box (or on a plate). Scatter the beans over the top, followed by some salt and pepper. Add the sardines, broken into rough chunks if you like. Drizzle on the oil, tuck in the wedge of lemon for last-minute squeezing, and seal your lunch box (or serve up).

Beef with mustardy lentils and mint

This works as a portable lunch box, picnic dish, or part of a cold-cuts lunch or buffet spread. Lentils are best served slightly warm or at room temperature, so you can prepare them ahead.

You can also make this with leftover roast pork or chicken, cooked sausages, or cold tongue or corned beef, leaving the salt out of the dressing if you are using cured meat.

Serves 4

1 cup French lentils

1 bay leaf

2 tablespoons canola or olive oil

1 onion, finely chopped

1 celery stalk, finely chopped

About 6 ounces cold roast beef, cut into strips or torn into rough shreds

2 tablespoons coarsely chopped fresh mint

For the dressing:

2 good teaspoons English mustard

2 teaspoons cider vinegar

3 tablespoons canola or extra-virgin olive oil

Sea salt and freshly ground black pepper

Put the lentils in a saucepan, cover with plenty of cold water, and add the bay leaf. Bring to a boil, turn down to a simmer, and cook for about 20 minutes, until the lentils are al dente. Keep an eye on them, and taste after about 15 minutes, as they can go from al dente to soft very quickly. Top up with more water if necessary during cooking.

Meanwhile, heat the oil in another pan, add the onion and celery, and cook gently for about 5 minutes, stirring occasionally, until softened but still with a bit of crunch. Remove from the heat and set aside.

When the lentils are done, drain them, remove the bay leaf, and return the lentils to the warm pan. Whisk together all the dressing ingredients and pour into the warm lentils, along with the sautéed onion and celery. Stir well and let cool.

Toss the beef and mint into the lentils, taste, and add some more seasoning if you like.

VARIATIONS

Beef with horseradishy lentils

If you have horseradish sauce left over along with your beef, use a couple of teaspoons of this in the dressing instead of the mustard.

Leftover mackerel lunch box

For a fantastic lunch for two, use about half the quantity of lentils listed above and toss with $1/2$ cup or so of flaked cold cooked mackerel (or other cold cooked fish), loads of coarsely chopped fresh parsley, and a tablespoon of small capers, rinsed.

101

Chicken, green bean, and almond salad

Another simple three-way-combo salad that makes an easy summer lunch box, not to mention light supper. If you can get hold of plump, sweet Marcona almonds, it will be particularly special. You can, of course, substitute other nuts and seeds – cashew, pumpkin, etc., and combinations thereof. There's a touch of honey in the dressing to bring out the sweetness of the nuts and beans – replace with a pinch of sugar, if you prefer.

Serves 2

About 6 ounces green beans, trimmed

A good handful of blanched almonds

About 1 cup shredded cold cooked chicken

For the dressing:

$1/4$ to $1/2$ garlic clove, crushed

$1/2$ teaspoon Dijon mustard

1 teaspoon cider vinegar or white wine vinegar

About $1/2$ teaspoon honey

2 tablespoons canola or extra-virgin olive oil

Sea salt and freshly ground black pepper

Cook the green beans in a large pan of boiling salted water for 3 to 5 minutes, until just tender but still with a bit of bite. Drain, refresh immediately under cold running water, and pat dry.

Scatter the almonds in a dry frying pan and toast over medium heat for a few minutes, shaking the pan occasionally, until golden brown. Let cool.

Whisk all the ingredients for the dressing together in a bowl or shake in a screw-top jar to combine.

Put the beans, shredded chicken, and almonds in a large bowl and toss together with your hands. Drizzle over the dressing, toss well, and serve. Or, if you want to make a lunch box of this, transfer the undressed salad to a plastic box or other suitable lidded container and seal. Take the dressing with you separately in a small screw-top jar and add just before you dig in.

Chicken with couscous, honey, and cinnamon

While I've got nothing against a good chicken sandwich, there are many more exciting things you can do with a few shreds of cold roast chicken. Couscous is a very useful medium for leftover meat, and this is one of my favorite ways to eat cold chicken. Take a tub of this with you to work, or serve up with crisp lettuce leaves as a quick supper.

Serves 2

$^2/_3$ cup blanched almonds

2 tablespoons canola or olive oil

1 onion, finely chopped

1 garlic clove, chopped

Sea salt and freshly ground black pepper

1 teaspoon ground cinnamon

$^2/_3$ cup couscous

1 tablespoon honey

About 1 cup boiling water, or chicken or vegetable stock

About 1 cup chopped cold cooked chicken

1 small preserved lemon, pulp discarded and skin finely chopped (or the grated zest of $^1/_2$ fresh lemon)

A good squeeze of lemon juice

1 tablespoon chopped fresh parsley or mint

Put the almonds in a dry frying pan and toast over medium heat for a few minutes, tossing occasionally, until golden brown. Let cool, then chop them very coarsely.

Heat the oil in a small saucepan, add the onion, garlic, and some salt and pepper and cook gently for about 10 minutes, until softened. Add the cinnamon, then take off the heat and stir in the couscous.

Stir the honey into the boiling water or stock until dissolved, then pour over the couscous (it should just cover it) and put a tight-fitting lid on the pan. Let stand for 10 minutes, until the couscous has swollen up and absorbed all the liquid. Fluff it up with a fork, transfer to a bowl, and let cool.

Toss the chicken pieces, almonds, preserved lemon or zest, and the lemon juice into the couscous and season to taste.

Pack into a lunch box, or pile into a serving dish for serving at the table. Either way, finish with a sprinkling of parsley or mint and a good grinding of black pepper.

VARIATION

Leftover lamb with couscous, lemon, and mint

Prepare the couscous as above, leaving out the cinnamon and honey. Toss about 1 cup shredded cold roast lamb into the couscous, along with the grated zest and juice of 1 lemon and 2 tablespoons of chopped mint. You can keep the almonds or not, as you prefer, and/or add a couple of handfuls of chopped dried apricots, if you like.

Three frittatas

A frittata is simply a thick, chunky omelette made with some vegetables and usually a little cheese. Served warm, in wedges, it makes an excellent supper. Cooled, then sliced into chunks, it's robust enough to pack into a lunch box or picnic basket. In fact, it's ideal prepare-ahead food.

Quite apart from this, frittata appeals to me because you can add almost anything you like to it: bacon or cooked sausage, flaked fish, any kind of cheese, peas or fava beans, asparagus, kale, spinach or broccoli, mushrooms, and so on. My only caveat is to avoid "wet" ingredients such as tomatoes, which will keep the eggs from setting properly.

Spinach, bacon, and goat cheese frittata

Serves 4

1 tablespoon canola or sunflower oil

3 ounces pancetta or bacon, cut into small cubes

4 shallots, thinly sliced

3 cups young leaf spinach

8 eggs

$1/4$ cup grated Parmesan, Cheddar, or other hard cheese

A grating or two of nutmeg

Sea salt and freshly ground black pepper

$1/2$ cup crumbled soft goat cheese

Preheat the oven to 350°F or preheat the broiler to medium-high.

Heat the oil in a 9-inch nonstick ovenproof frying pan over medium heat. Add the pancetta or bacon and sauté until golden, then remove with a slotted spoon; set aside. Add the shallots to the pan, lower the heat, and cook gently for about 10 minutes, until soft but not colored. Add the spinach and stir until just wilted, then remove from the heat.

Lightly beat the eggs in a bowl, then stir in the pancetta or bacon, spinach and shallots, grated cheese, nutmeg, salt, and pepper. Put the frying pan back over low heat, pour in the egg mixture, and cook gently, without stirring, letting the eggs set slowly from the bottom up. After about 5 minutes, give the pan a little shake: the bottom half of the frittata should be set, with a layer of wet egg still on top.

Dot the goat cheese over the top. If you're baking the frittata, place it in the oven for 5 to 10 minutes, until just set. Or put the frittata under the broiler, ideally not too close to the heat, for about 5 minutes. Let cool slightly (or completely) before slicing and serving.

Frittata niçoise

A French salad reinterpreted through the medium of an Italian omelette? Why not? The proof is in the eating. Please use only sustainably sourced, pole-and-line-caught tuna. Alternatively, you can make this with canned sardines, using the oil from the can to fry the onions.

Serves 4

2 tablespoons canola or sunflower oil

About 6 green onions, sliced on the diagonal

1 garlic clove, finely chopped

8 eggs

About 1 cup thickly sliced cold cooked new potatoes

About $1/2$ cup cold cooked green beans, cut into 1-inch lengths

About 3 ounces canned tuna, drained and coarsely flaked

About 20 pitted black or kalamata olives in oil, drained

Sea salt and freshly ground black pepper

Preheat the oven to 350°F or preheat the broiler to medium-high.

Heat the oil in a 9-inch nonstick ovenproof frying pan over medium heat. Add the green onions and garlic and cook gently for 3 to 4 minutes, until soft but not colored, then remove from the heat.

Lightly beat the eggs in a large bowl, then stir in the potatoes, beans, tuna, and olives. Add the green onions, season, and mix well.

Return the frying pan to low heat and add the egg mixture, making sure the olives are evenly distributed. Cook gently, without stirring, just letting the eggs set slowly from the bottom up. After about 5 minutes, give the pan a little shake: the bottom half of the frittata should be set, with a layer of wet egg still on top.

If you're baking the frittata, place it in the oven for 5 to 10 minutes, until just set. Or put the frittata under the broiler, ideally not too close to the heat, for about 5 minutes. Allow to cool slightly (or completely) before slicing and serving.

Onion frittata

The classic Spanish potato tortilla is similar to an Italian frittata. You can turn this recipe into a tortilla by simply adding about 1^1/$_2$ cups thickly sliced cold cooked waxy potatoes to the beaten egg with the softened onions.

Serves 4

3 tablespoons canola or sunflower oil

2 large onions, chopped

Sea salt and freshly ground black pepper

8 eggs

1 to 2 tablespoons finely chopped fresh flat-leaf parsley

^{1}/$_4$ cup finely grated Parmesan, Cheddar, or other hard cheese

Preheat the oven to 350°F or preheat the broiler to medium-high.

Heat the oil in a 10-inch nonstick ovenproof frying pan over medium heat. Stir in the onions and a sprinkling of salt, then lower the heat and cook for about 15 minutes, until the onions are very soft and translucent but not colored.

Lightly beat the eggs in a bowl and then mix in the parsley and two-thirds of the cheese. Season with salt and pepper (remember, the cheese is quite salty), then stir in the onions.

Put the frying pan back over low heat, pour in the egg mixture, and cook gently, without stirring, just letting the eggs set slowly from the bottom up. After about 5 minutes, give the pan a little shake: the bottom half of the frittata should be set, with a good layer of wet egg still on top.

Sprinkle over the remaining cheese. If you're baking the frittata, place it in the oven for 5 to 10 minutes, until just set. Or put the frittata under the broiler, ideally not too close to the heat, for about 5 minutes. Allow to cool slightly (or completely) before slicing and serving.

Three savory pasties

Inspired by the great original, the Cornish pasty, these are all filling, portable meals, neatly wrapped in their own edible packaging. If you don't have time to make the rough puff pastry, you could make short crust (page 328), or use a good, ready-made all-butter puff or flaky pastry. Eat the pasties hot from the oven, cold at your desk or in the park, or even – dare I say? – reheated (thoroughly) in the office microwave.

Chicken and leek pasties

Serves 4

For the rough puff pastry:
2 cups all-purpose flour
A pinch of sea salt
$^2/_3$ cup chilled unsalted butter, cut into small cubes

For the filling:
2 tablespoons unsalted butter
2 to 3 leeks (about 1 pound), trimmed and finely sliced
1 teaspoon coarsely chopped fresh thyme leaves
$^2/_3$ cup heavy cream
1 teaspoon English mustard
Sea salt and freshly ground black pepper
About 12 ounces boned chicken thigh and breast meat (or leftover cooked chicken), cut into thick slices
1 tablespoon canola or olive oil (if using fresh chicken)

To finish:
1 egg, lightly beaten with 1 teaspoon milk, for glazing

To make the pastry, mix the flour with the salt, then add the cubed butter and toss until the pieces are coated with flour. Stir in just enough ice water (8 to 10 tablespoons) to bring the mixture together into a fairly firm dough.

Shape the dough into a rectangle with your hands and, on a well-floured surface, roll it out in one direction, away from you, so you end up with a rectangle about $^3/_8$ inch thick. Fold the far third towards you, then fold the nearest third over that (rather like folding a business letter), so that you now have a rectangle made up of 3 equal layers. Give the pastry a quarter-turn, then repeat the rolling, folding, and turning process 5 more times. Wrap the pastry in plastic wrap and rest it in the fridge for about 30 minutes, or up to an hour.

To make the filling, melt the butter in a frying pan, add the leeks and thyme, and cook gently for 5 to 10 minutes, until the leeks are very tender. Stir in the cream and cook gently for 4 to 5 minutes to reduce and thicken. Stir in the mustard, season well, and let cool.

If using fresh chicken, season well and fry in the oil in a frying pan over medium-high heat until evenly browned. Set aside.

Preheat the oven to 375°F.

Roll out the pastry on a lightly floured work surface to about $^1/_8$ inch thick. Using a plate or a cake pan as a template, cut out four 8-inch circles; you may have to gather up the trimmings and reroll them to get your fourth circle.

Spoon the leek mixture on to one half of each circle and pile the chicken on top. Brush the pastry edges with a little water, fold the other half of the pastry over the filling to form a half-moon shape, and crimp well to seal.

Place on a lightly oiled baking sheet and brush the tops of the pasties with the egg wash. Bake for about 25 minutes, until golden brown. Eat hot or cold.

Leftover-stew pasties

Practically any stew will do for this, but particularly good are the oxtail stew with cinnamon and star anise (page 228), rabbit ragù (page 219), and the pot-roast pheasant with chorizo, butter beans, and parsley (page 234). If you don't have enough stew left for the filling, you could also add some leftover cooked vegetables, such as diced potatoes or carrots or shredded greens, or a handful of cooked beans or lentils.

Serves 4

Rough puff pastry
(page 110)

For the filling:
About 2^1/$_2$ cups cold
leftover stew

To finish:
1 egg, lightly beaten
with 1 teaspoon milk,
for glazing

For the filling, drain off any excess juices from the stew so that the meat and vegetables are just lightly coated in gravy. Take any large chunks of meat or vegetables and chop them up coarsely before stirring back together. Taste the stew and make sure it's seasoned to your liking. Let cool completely.

Preheat the oven to 375°F.

Roll out the pastry on a lightly floured work surface to about ^{1}/$_8$ inch thick. Using a plate or a cake pan as a template, cut out four 8-inch circles; you may have to gather up the trimmings and reroll them to get your fourth circle.

Spoon the stew onto one half of each circle. Brush the pastry edges with a little water, fold the other half of the pastry over the filling to form a half-moon shape, and crimp well to seal.

Place on a lightly oiled baking sheet and brush the tops of the pastries with the egg wash. Bake for about 25 minutes, until golden brown. Eat hot or cold.

Lentil and squash pasties

If you don't fancy making pastry, double the quantities to make a delicious filling for a vegetarian shepherd's pie.

Serves 4

Rough puff pastry
(page 110)

For the filling:
1 tablespoon canola
or olive oil

1 small onion, finely
chopped

1 small celery stalk,
finely chopped

1 small carrot, finely
chopped

1 garlic clove, finely
chopped

Sea salt and freshly
ground black pepper

$1/3$ cup white wine
(optional)

$1/2$ cup green or brown
lentils

$1^1/4$ cups stock (such as
ten-minute vegetable
stock, page 266)

1 bay leaf

A sprig of thyme
(optional)

$1^1/2$ cups finely diced
butternut or other
squash

2 teaspoons balsamic
vinegar

2 teaspoons hot English
mustard

To finish:
1 egg, lightly beaten
with 1 teaspoon milk,
for glazing

For the filling, heat the oil in a saucepan, add the onion, celery, carrot, garlic, and some salt and pepper and cook gently for 10 to 15 minutes, until soft. Add the wine, if you're using it, and let it bubble away to nothing. Add the lentils and stock, season well, then add the bay leaf and thyme, if using. Stir well, cover, and simmer gently for about 10 minutes.

Add the squash and simmer for another 20 minutes, or until both lentils and squash are tender. If the filling looks a bit wet, you can either drain off some of the liquid and/or take out a couple of spoonfuls of the lentils, mash them, then stir them back in to thicken the sauce. Stir in the balsamic vinegar and the mustard and check the seasoning. Let cool.

Preheat the oven to 375°F.

Roll out the pastry on a lightly floured work surface to about $1/8$ inch thick. Using a plate or a cake tin as a template, cut out four 8-inch circles; you may have to gather up the trimmings and reroll them to get your fourth circle.

Spoon the filling onto one half of each circle. Brush the pastry edges with a little water, fold the other half of the pastry over the filling to form a half-moon shape, and crimp well to seal.

Place on a lightly oiled baking sheet and brush the tops of the pastries with the egg wash. Bake for about 25 minutes, until golden brown. Eat hot or cold.

Tartiflette toastie

Lunch doesn't get more comforting – or indulgent, frankly – than this sumptuous version of cheese on toast, which is also a great way to use up leftovers. It's not something you can take to the office, granted, but it is just the sort of thing I like to rustle up for lunch when I'm at home. It's inspired by the Savoyarde dish *tartiflette*, a rich baked combination of potatoes, cheese, and bacon. *Tartiflette* is usually made with Reblochon, but any semisoft washed-rind cheese, such as Brie (not too ripe), works well, or try a semihard cheese, such as Cheddar.

Serves 1

1 tablespoon canola or olive oil

2 bacon slices, or a slice of cold ham, cut into small strips

1 cold cooked potato (baked, boiled, or even roasted), thickly sliced

1 to 2 tablespoons heavy cream or crème fraîche

Sea salt and freshly ground black pepper

1 large, thick slice bread

3 to 4 thick slices (about 1 ounce) semisoft or semihard cheese

A few crisp, bitter salad greens, such as chicory, radicchio, or frisée, to serve

Heat the oil in a small frying pan over medium heat. If you are using bacon, add it to the pan and fry for a few minutes, until cooked. Add the potato and fry until it is heated through and starting to color a little. If you're using ham, add it now and stir until well heated through.

Stir in the cream or crème fraîche and allow it to bubble and reduce for a couple of minutes. Remove from the heat and season to taste.

Toast the bread, pile the mixture on top, then cover with the sliced cheese and put under a hot broiler. As soon as the cheese is melted and bubbling, whip out from under the broiler and transfer to a plate. Serve at once, with a few crisp, bitter salad greens on the side.

Tabula kisir

This is a lovely herby, spicy bulgur wheat dish from Turkey, similar to tabouli. It's the piquant dressing that makes it special. Despite the lengthy list of ingredients, it is quick and easy to make. When my greenhouse tomatoes are in full swing, I often double the quantity of tomatoes, leaving out the peppers. And you can make a very respectable version using couscous instead of bulgur wheat.

Serves 4 to 6

1 cup bulgur wheat

$^1/_3$ cup walnuts

12 ounces ripe tomatoes

3 to 4 green onions, top green part discarded

1 red bell pepper, cored and seeded

1 green bell pepper, cored and seeded

5 tablespoons finely chopped fresh flat-leaf parsley

$^1/_4$ cup finely chopped fresh mint

3 tablespoons finely chopped fresh dill

For the dressing:

$^1/_4$ cup fresh lemon juice

1 tablespoon tomato paste

Pinch of red pepper flakes

1 teaspoon ground cumin

1 teaspoon paprika

1 teaspoon sea salt

1 teaspoon freshly ground black pepper

5 tablespoons canola or extra-virgin olive oil

To serve:

Pita bread and/or Little Gem or romaine lettuce

Place the bulgur wheat in a large bowl, pour over $^3/_4$ cup boiling water, stir, then cover and leave for 20 minutes. The bulgur should retain some bite at this stage.

Meanwhile, make the dressing. Mix together the lemon juice, tomato paste, pepper flakes, cumin, paprika, salt, and pepper, then whisk in the oil. Pour the dressing over the warm bulgur and stir well. Let cool completely.

Preheat the oven to 350°F. Put the walnuts in a pie pan and toast in the oven for 5 to 7 minutes, until fragrant. Let cool and then chop coarsely.

Meanwhile, core, seed, and dice the tomatoes. Slice the green onions finely, and cut the peppers into dice.

Once the bulgur is cool, combine it with the tomatoes, peppers, green onions, walnuts, and herbs. Let stand for at least 20 minutes so the flavors can mingle, then taste and adjust the seasoning, adding more salt, pepper, and/or pepper flakes if you like. Serve with pita bread and/or lettuce leaves.

VARIATION

Zucchini kisir

Omit the green and red peppers. Slice, season, and quickly fry about 1 pound small zucchini (follow the recipe for lemony zucchini on toast on page 263, if you like), then add them to the salad with the tomatoes. Very firm, fresh young zucchini can be added raw – chop into small dice rather than slice.

Egg tartare

This feisty little mixture is so named because it combines all the elements of a classic tartare sauce. However, I've jiggled the quantities so the eggs become the main event, deliciously bound together with all the other ingredients. It makes the best egg sandwich you could ever tuck into your lunch box. Alternatively, served on a single slice of bread, it makes a lovely and surprisingly elegant starter.

Makes enough for 4 substantial sandwiches, or serves 4 to 6 as a starter

6 eggs, at room temperature

4 green onions or 2 small shallots, finely chopped

3 to 4 gherkins, finely diced

1 tablespoon capers, rinsed

2 tablespoons finely chopped parsley

1 tablespoon finely chopped dill (optional)

2 to 3 tablespoons mayonnaise (page 282)

A dab of Dijon mustard

2 to 3 dashes of Tabasco sauce (optional)

Sea salt and freshly ground black pepper

Slices of sourdough, rye, whole-wheat, or your favorite bread, to serve

First, boil the eggs. They should be what I call soft-hard-boiled – that is, the whites completely set but the yolks just a bit runny in the middle. I achieve this pretty reliably by putting them in a pan of hand-hot water, covering it, and bringing it quickly to the boil, then boiling for exactly 4 minutes – 5 if they are extra-large. Then I run the eggs under cold water and peel them as soon as they are cool enough to handle.

Coarsely chop the eggs and mix with the green onions or shallots, gherkins, capers, parsley, and dill, if using.

In a small bowl, whisk together the mayonnaise, mustard, and Tabasco, if using. Gently combine this mixture with the eggs and season with salt and pepper. Serve on whole-wheat, sourdough, or rye bread, as closed or open sandwiches.

Three seasonal slaws

I make crunchy slaws of grated roots and shredded cabbage throughout the year, using whatever vegetables are in season. You need to take your time slicing and grating everything finely, but once you've got a big bowlful in the fridge, you need only transfer a portion to a lunch box (or plate), add a little cold meat, cooked egg, cheese, or other protein-rich finishing touch, and you have a filling, wholesome lunch.

To make a complete meal of these slaws, accompany them with one of the following:

- A couple of oatcakes and some shredded cold chicken, ham, pork, or lamb.
- A slice of pork pie.
- A chunk of blue cheese, crumbled over the top, plus some lightly toasted walnuts.
- A wedge of cold frittata (see pages 106–9).
- A whole-wheat roll filled with soft, mild goat cheese sprinkled with salt and pepper.

Summer slaw

Serves 4

8 fat radishes, trimmed

A few small summer carrots, scrubbed

1 large or 2 small fennel bulbs

1/2 small red onion

1 tablespoon finely snipped fresh chives

4 small lettuce hearts, such as Little Gem (optional)

For the vinaigrette:

1 teaspoon English mustard

1 tablespoon cider vinegar or white wine vinegar

3 tablespoons canola or olive oil

Sea salt, freshly ground black pepper, and a pinch of sugar

Very finely slice the radishes and carrots, using a mandoline if you have one, and place in a large bowl. Trim the bottoms and tops off the fennel bulbs and remove the tough outer layers. Quarter the bulbs, remove the cores, then slice very finely and add to the radishes. Chop the red onion very finely and add to the bowl, along with the chives if you're using them.

Make the dressing by whisking everything together, then adjust the seasoning to taste. Toss the vegetables with the dressing. Taste the slaw and adjust the seasoning, if necessary.

If you're serving this at home, make sure you let it sit for at least half an hour before eating. Cut the lettuce hearts into quarters, if using, and arrange them around the edge of a large bowl. Spoon the slaw into the middle and serve – try it with crumbled blue cheese on top or some cold meats on the side. For a lunch box, pile the slaw into a suitable container with the lettuce and other savory items.

VARIATION

For a creamier slaw, dress with mayonnaise rather than vinaigrette.

Two-root slaw

In this lovely winter salad, I've simply added carrot to what is essentially a fairly classic *céleri rémoulade*. You could include a little shredded green cabbage, which would take you further from rémoulade and closer to a traditional coleslaw.

Serves 6

2 to 3 large carrots

1/2 celery root (about 12 ounces)

For the dressing:

1/4 cup good mayonnaise (page 282)

2 teaspoons English mustard

Juice of 1/2 lemon, or a dash of cider vinegar

1 tablespoon caraway seeds, lightly toasted in a dry frying pan (optional)

Sea salt and freshly ground black pepper

Peel the carrots and celery root and coarsely grate them into a bowl (or use a mandoline on the matchstick setting, if you have one).

Beat together all the ingredients for the dressing, pour them over the grated vegetables, and stir to coat thoroughly.

Pack in your lunch box or serve at home, allowing the flavors to develop for an hour or so beforehand. It's good with cold meats, especially ham and tongue, or after a stew or shepherd's pie.

VARIATION

For a lighter dressing, make a mustardy vinaigrette, such as the one on page 120.

Purple slaw

This is a favorite autumn lunch for me, and a great way to use red cabbage. It always looks vibrant and stunning.

Serves 6

12 ounces red cabbage

6 ounces lightly cooked beets (see page 294)

1/2 cup walnuts, toasted and coarsely chopped

1/3 cup raisins

For the dressing:

2 tablespoons canola or extra-virgin olive oil

2 tablespoons walnut oil

1 tablespoon cider vinegar

1 teaspoon honey

Sea salt and freshly ground black pepper

Finely shred the red cabbage and place in a bowl. Coarsely grate the beets (or cut it into matchsticks on a mandoline) and add to the cabbage along with the walnuts and raisins.

Whisk together all the ingredients for the dressing, adding salt and pepper to taste. Stir the dressing into the salad.

Either transfer a portion to a lunch box or serve the salad at the table, after letting it rest for at least half an hour. This slaw is particularly good with ham or cold beef.

Three hummuses

Or should that be hummi? Authentic hummus is, of course, made with chickpeas and tahini, but I love the idea of making thick, dippable purées with fresh vegetables too. These are a few of my favorites. For lunch boxes, they make delicious sandwich fillings, but don't discount the idea of a portable hummus dip. Pack in a tub and take along some simple crudités – celery, cucumber, broccoli, cauliflower, peppers, etc. – and pita bread. Or have as part of a meze lunch box, with a few olives, some flatbreads (page 78) or pita, and some ready-made falafel or cubes of halloumi cheese.

Very lemony hummus

You might like to try this hummus in a sandwich with sliced tomatoes and a smear of harissa paste, or with grated carrot and a few torn mint leaves. If you are short of time, instead of cooking dried chickpeas, you can use canned, well drained and rinsed; add a little water to them for the initial puréeing.

Serves 4 to 6

²/₃ cup dried chickpeas
1 bay leaf
Sea salt and freshly ground black pepper
Juice of 2 lemons
¹/₂ to 1 small garlic clove, crushed with a little salt
2 to 3 tablespoons tahini (sesame seed paste)
2 to 3 tablespoons canola or extra-virgin olive oil
A pinch of ground cumin (optional)

Rinse the chickpeas thoroughly, then place them in a large bowl with enough water to cover them well. Let soak for at least 12 hours, or overnight.

Drain the chickpeas and put them in a saucepan with the bay leaf and enough cold water to cover generously. Bring to a boil, then turn the heat right down and partially cover with a lid. Simmer gently for about 3 hours, until the chickpeas are really soft, skimming the surface and topping up with boiling water as necessary to keep the chickpeas covered. Add ¹/₂ teaspoon of salt near the end of cooking. Drain the chickpeas, reserving the liquid, and discard the bay leaf.

Put 3 to 4 tablespoons of the hot cooking liquid into a food processor or blender with half the chickpeas, ¹/₄ cup of the lemon juice, and the garlic. Whiz for a few seconds. Add the remaining chickpeas, 2 tablespoons of tahini, and 2 tablespoons of oil, then whiz again until you have the consistency you like. Scrape into a bowl.

Season with salt and plenty of pepper. If you think it needs more oil, lemon juice, or tahini, add a little at a time, beating well, until you're happy with the flavor. Top with a sprinkling of cumin, if you like.

VARIATION

Add 3 or 4 tablespoons of finely chopped flat-leaf parsley, chervil, or chives – or all three – to create a lovely, green-flecked purée.

Beet and walnut hummus

This glorious purple concoction – a revelation for people who claim not to like beets, or walnuts come to that – is wonderful with crisp crudités, in a sandwich with goat cheese, or scooped up with flatbreads (page 78).

Serves 4

¹/₃ cup walnuts

1 tablespoon cumin seeds

1 slice stale bread, crusts removed

2 cooked beets (not pickled), cut into cubes

1 tablespoon tahini (sesame seed paste)

1 large garlic clove, crushed

Juice of 1 lemon

Sea salt and freshly ground black pepper

A little olive or canola oil (optional)

Preheat the oven to 350°F. Put the walnuts in a pie pan and toast in the oven for 5 to 7 minutes, until fragrant. Let cool.

Warm a small frying pan over medium heat. Add the cumin seeds and dry-fry them, shaking the pan almost constantly, until they start to darken and release their aroma – this should take less than a minute, so be careful not to burn them. Crush the seeds with a mortar and pestle or a spice grinder.

Break the bread into small chunks, put in a food processor or blender with the walnuts, and blitz until fine. Add the beets, tahini, most of the garlic, a good pinch of the cumin, half the lemon juice, a little salt, and a good grind of pepper, then blend to a thick paste.

Taste the mixture and adjust it by adding a little more cumin, garlic, lemon, salt, and/or pepper, blending again until you are happy with it. Loosen with a dash of oil if you think it needs it. Refrigerate until you want to eat it, but bring back to room temperature to serve.

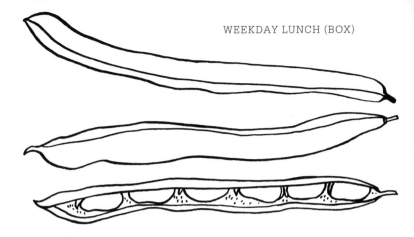

Fava bean hummus

Toward the end of the summer, when fava beans get fat and floury and a little bitter, I like to whiz them up into this hummus. As well as making a fine dip, it is a great lunch box addition – pack with some Little Gem lettuce leaves, crumbled ricotta, and flatbreads (page 78); or use to fill a bun or pita bread, along with a slice of ham.

Serves 4

2 cups shelled fava beans (late-season larger beans are fine to use)

$1/2$ to 1 garlic clove, crushed with a little salt

About 3 tablespoons canola or extra-virgin olive oil

A generous squeeze of lemon juice

Sea salt and freshly ground black pepper

Put the fava beans in a pan, cover with water, and bring to a boil. Lower the heat and simmer for 5 to 10 minutes (depending on the beans' age and size) until tender, then drain. Set aside to cool, then slip the beans out of their skins.

Put the peeled fava beans in a food processor or blender with the garlic, 3 tablespoons of oil, a good squeeze of lemon juice, and some salt and pepper. Process to a thick, slightly coarse purée, adding more oil if it seems too thick and dry.

When you're happy with the texture, transfer the purée to a bowl. Taste and adjust the seasoning with more salt, pepper, and lemon juice as needed.

Pestos

Traditionally, pesto is tossed with hot pasta or spooned into classic Italian minestrone, but I'm much more likely to use it as part of my lunchtime repertoire. I love to add it to sandwiches made with cold roast meat, tomatoes, and crisp lettuce leaves. In fact, if I've got some really good, fresh white bread, I'm happy to anoint it with a generous slick of pesto and nothing else. It's also very good as a dressing for lunch box salads. You could even take some to work to augment hot soup or a plain baked potato from the office canteen.

Classic pesto is, of course, made with basil, pine nuts, garlic, Parmesan, and olive oil – and lovely it is too, especially if you've grown the basil yourself and harvested it minutes before blitzing. But the basic notion of pesto – a nutty seed (or seedy nut) pulverized with herbs, hard cheese, and richly flavored oil, is ripe for experimentation and customization. At River Cottage we've had a lot of fun, and a lot of success, inventing pesto variations. Parsley is my favorite pesto herb, since it is so abundant and easy to grow. Here are a few favorite pestos. They will keep in the fridge for several days, or longer if the surface of the pesto is covered with a thin layer of oil.

Parsley and pumpkin seed pesto

Makes 6 to 8 tablespoons

$^1/_2$ cup pumpkin seeds

1 garlic clove, coarsely chopped

A large bunch of flat-leaf parsley, leaves only

$^2/_3$ to $^3/_4$ cup canola or extra-virgin olive oil

$^1/_3$ cup grated Parmesan or matured hard goat cheese

Sea salt and freshly ground black pepper

Juice of $^1/_2$ lemon

Put the pumpkin seeds and garlic in a food processor or blender and pulse until the seeds are in coarse grains. Add the parsley leaves and pulse briefly until finely chopped and blended with the seeds. Then, with the machine running, pour in the oil in a slow, steady stream until you have a fairly thick, nicely grainy paste.

Scrape the mixture into a bowl. Stir in the cheese, thin with a little more oil if you want, then taste and adjust the seasoning with salt, pepper, and lemon juice.

VARIATIONS

Parsley and walnut pesto

Make as above, but with $^1/_2$ cup lightly toasted walnuts instead of the pumpkin seeds.

Basil and pumpkin seed pesto

Simply replace the parsley with basil (or include both herbs).

Parsley, walnut, and blue cheese pesto

Make as above, but use $^1/_2$ cup lightly toasted walnuts instead of pumpkin seeds, and replace the suggested cheese with Gorgonzola or another crumbly blue.

Brown bread, hempseed oil, and parsley pesto

Makes 6 to 8 tablespoons

1 cup coarse whole-wheat bread crumbs

A large bunch of flat-leaf parsley, leaves only

1 small garlic clove, coarsely chopped

$^2/_3$ to $^3/_4$ cup hempseed oil

$^1/_3$ cup grated Parmesan or matured hard goat cheese

Sea salt and freshly ground black pepper

Juice of $^1/_2$ lemon

Toast the bread crumbs in a small frying pan for a few minutes, until crisp and nutty, then leave to cool.

Put the parsley leaves and garlic in a food processor and pulse until finely chopped (or chop them by hand, if you prefer). Transfer to a bowl and stir in enough oil to create a thinnish paste. Stir in the cheese and bread crumbs, thin with a little more oil if you want, then adjust the seasoning with salt, pepper, and lemon juice.

The bread crumbs give this pesto a coarse, chunky texture. It's absolutely delicious with baked potatoes.

Use these pestos in the following ways:

- Spread thickly between slices of white bread, along with shreds of cold cooked chicken, pork, or beef and a few lettuce leaves.

- Combine in a sandwich with some of the fava bean hummus on page 129.

- Spread thinly over a flatbread (page 78) or tortilla and top with crumbled goat cheese or thickly spread soft cheese. Add a little leftover ham or cooked bacon, if you have some, then finish with a few peppery lettuce leaves and roll up into a neat parcel.

- Toss with cooked white beans, such as cannellini (canned or cooked at home from scratch), plus diced tomatoes and some cold cooked potatoes to make a substantial lunch-box salad.

- Mix with leftover peas and/or leeks, then combine with some torn buffalo mozzarella and pack into a pita bread.

- Cook 4 cups pasta shapes, drain, and toss with one batch of pesto while still hot. Let cool. Use this as the base for various portable salads by adding cheese, cubes of ham or chicken, flakes of sardine, mackerel or cold leftover fish, coarsely chopped hard-boiled eggs, cooked beans, or chopped cold roasted vegetables.

- Use a heaping tablespoon of pesto to replace the parsley and Parmesan in the onion frittata on page 109.

- Pesto thinned down with a little extra oil and lemon juice makes a good dressing for any of the slaws on pages 120–23, or the tabula kisir on page 117.

- To make pesto bread, slice a ciabatta or baguette diagonally at $1^1/_2$-inch intervals, without cutting right through to the base. Spread any pesto thickly between the slices and drizzle with a little oil. Place on a baking sheet, cover with foil, and bake in an oven preheated to 375°F for 10 minutes, removing the foil for the last 3 to 4 minutes. Especially good for summer barbecues, and to serve with soups.

Dukka

This Egyptian blend of coarsely ground seeds, spices, and nuts is traditionally used with olive oil as a dip for bread. Its fragrant flavors and pleasing crunch make it a great addition to salads (sprinkled on top) or dips (blend with a little oil and drizzle over), too. You could also include it in a flatbread (page 78) wrap with hummus, toss it into a beany salad, or add it to a lunch-box tub of leftover roast vegetables and chunks of halloumi cheese. Dukka can be kept in an airtight container in the fridge for a few weeks.

A handful of hazelnuts

$^1/_2$ tablespoon cumin seeds

1 tablespoon coriander seeds

2 tablespoons sesame seeds

$^1/_2$ teaspoon red pepper flakes

$^1/_2$ teaspoon sea salt

A small handful of fresh mint leaves, finely shredded

First, toast the hazelnuts. Preheat the oven to 350°F. Spread the hazelnuts out in a pie pan in a single layer and toast in the oven for about 5 minutes, until they are lightly colored and the skins are blistered and cracked. Wrap them in a clean tea towel for a minute and then rub them vigorously with the towel until the skins fall off.

Toast the cumin and coriander seeds in a small frying pan over medium heat until they just begin to release their fragrance – barely a minute. Bash them with a mortar and pestle until broken up but not too fine. Put the sesame seeds into the pan and heat gently until just golden. Add the hazelnuts, sesame seeds, pepper flakes, and salt to the spice mix and bash again until the nuts are broken up into small pieces. Stir in the mint, and the dukka is ready to use.

The simplest and most fun way to eat it is with some delicious fresh white bread (ideally sourdough) and a little bowl of your best culinary oil: olive, canola, pumpkin seed, or walnut, for example. Tear off a small hunk of bread, dip it in the oil, then dip lightly in the dukka so it picks up a dusting of the nutty, spicy seeds. This is delicious with a glass of chilled rosé.

fish
forever

Fish is an exceptionally good food, but increasingly a worrying one.

The main purpose of this chapter is to make sure that the fish you eat always tastes delicious. But before we get to that, I think it's vital to consider briefly the worrying aspects of choosing to make fish a regular part of our diet.

The demand for fish is unprecedented, as are the technologies and resources being applied to extract it from our oceans. At least a quarter of humanity – coastal dwellers around the globe – relies on it as its primary source of protein. Meanwhile, another quarter – the wealthy West – rates it so highly that it is prepared to spend almost without limit to see it brought to the table. The result of this pressure on fish stocks is as predictable as it is depressing: all over the globe, the most sought-after species are on the brink of collapse.

As it happens, the last book I wrote before this one was *The River Cottage Fish Book*, coauthored with my friend, Nick Fisher. In it we considered in some depth the complex issues of how our fisheries are run and the implications for various species both in the UK and across the world. Of course, I'd love you to get a copy, if you haven't already, and to bone up on the rather alarming story of what's happening to our fish and what you can do about it. But I realize that not everyone can become a fully informed fish conservationist in their spare time. Nevertheless, with a bit of guidance on how to shop for fish responsibly, everyone who wants to enjoy fish can do so in the knowledge that their net contribution is to the solution rather than the problem.

Fish to avoid

1 Cod (Atlantic, imported Pacific)
2 Chilean sea bass
3 Flounders, soles (Atlantic)
4 Groupers
5 Sharks
6 Mahimahi (imported)
7 Bluefin, tongol, longline-caught albacore, bigeye, yellowfin, canned tuna (except troll/pole)
8 Salmon (CA, OR wild)
9 Orange roughy
10 Monkfish
11 Red Snapper
12 Swordfish (imported)
13 Tilapia (Asia farmed)
14 Catfish

So let us cut to the chase: the overarching question for the conscientious fish buyer is surely, "What fish should I avoid at all costs?" My answer to that would be, first, don't buy any species that are known to be in ecological crisis, and second, try to avoid fish of any species caught using methods that harm the marine environment. There is a big overlap between these two considerations, but they are not quite the same thing. There is sustainably fished line-caught sea bass, for example, and unsustainably fished trawled sea bass. For this reason, lists of "fish to avoid" will inevitably contain the odd qualification. But I think such lists are worthwhile, and I'm happy to offer my current "black list" (see left).

Now when it comes to lists, clearly it's a boon to fish lovers to have a few ticks as well as a bunch of black crosses. So I've also given a list

Fish to eat more of

1 Mackerel (Atlantic, particularly line caught)
2 Pollock (Alaska wild)
3 Arctic char (farmed)
4 Pacific cod (Alaska longline)
5 Pacific halibut
6 Black cod/sablefish
7 Tilapia (US farmed)
8 Rainbow trout (US farmed)
9 Salmon (Alaska, WA wild)
10 Flounders, sole (Pacific)

Sustainable shellfish

1 Clams (farmed)
2 Crab (Dungeness, stone)
3 Mussels (farmed)
4 Scallops (but only hand dived, not dredged)
5 Oysters (farmed)
6 Squid
7 Shrimp (US, Canada)

of fish that it's generally reckoned we could eat more of, in order to help alleviate some of the pressure on threatened species.

And if you're on the lookout for guilt-free seafood, shellfish is often a better bet than finfish, provided the method of catching/gathering is not damaging to the marine or shore environment – or, if the shellfish is farmed, it's being done in a sustainable way. Below is a list of some to feel good about. Since we have different fish in the UK than you do in the US, these lists have been rewritten to reflect that.

The good news is that you should be able to find most of the "eat-more-of" and sustainable species without too much trouble. The only caveat is that the assessment of what is and isn't sustainable is under constant review – so that if you're reading this a year or more after the time of writing, the list of "fish to eat more of" is likely to look rather different. The best way to keep up with the latest scientific and environmental thinking on fish stocks in the States is to log on to montereybayaquarium.org and print out their Seafood Watch lists for your area, or the national version. It lists Best Choices, Good Alternatives, and Fish to Avoid.

Besides favoring sustainable species over blacklisted fish, it's also helpful to know the method by which a fish has been caught. The most destructive fishing techniques are generally the least selective, and the ones that do permanent damage to the sea floor. Worst of the lot are beam trawling and dredging: both drag heavy gear along the bottom of the sea, which disturbs and destroys the soft corals and invertebrates that are the foundation of life on the seabed. "Static bottom nets" are better because they are lowered and raised to and from the bottom without having much physical impact on the sea floor itself.

Line fishing is generally regarded as the most sustainable means of commercial fishing for two key reasons: first, the fish are usually alive when they reach the boat, meaning that untargeted species and undersized fish can be returned unharmed to the sea. Second, the hooks, lines, and weights are generally fished clear of the bottom. Although there is some snagging, it is the hooks and lines that are inclined to break, rather than the marine features to which they have become attached.

So where should you go in search of top-quality sustainable fish? A well-stocked and busy fishmonger's shop is certainly a good place to find the best quality, but as far as sustainability goes you are likely

to encounter a mixed bag. Very few fishmongers, if any, restrict themselves to the sale of sustainable species. However, some are more committed than others, and the best will always be prepared to tell you where a fish comes from and how it was caught. (If he or she can answer neither of these questions, then I would suggest you go elsewhere.)

If you are a regular customer, you can undoubtedly cultivate a somewhat privileged relationship with your fishmonger – and you shouldn't be in the least bit shy about doing so. Assuming you are in every week and he or she knows what you like, then you'll be looked after. When you're on the hunt for something really special, a phone call a couple of days in advance will stand you in good stead when the fishmonger places his or her order or goes to market.

Things tend to be very different in supermarkets, where those serving at the fish counter are rarely experts on the fish they are selling. On the other hand, some supermarkets are taking the issue of sustainability very seriously and have even banned certain species or rejected certain fishing methods. I would urge you to look hard for signs of genuine commitment in the way fish is presented and labeled in supermarkets, and reward meaningful initiatives with a purchase – provided, of course, the fish in question is in tiptop condition.

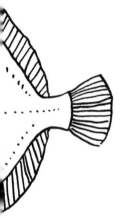

And that brings me to the most important factor in choosing fish, at least from the point of view of your own pleasure: it should be spanking fresh. A really fresh fish has an aura about it that simply shouts, "Buy me!" It is shiny and plump, in head as well as body. It looks as if, were you to drop it accidentally into the sea, it might just perk up and swim away. Its eye is bright and seems to be looking at you; its scales are glistening and sparkle with the light.

Ideally, two further operations will confirm your suspicions that a fish either is or isn't in perfect shape. Ask to have a look at the gills: the pinker they are, the better. A little sticky red blood is not a bad sign, but a slimy, gummy, gray-brown mucus suggests time has marched on since the fish met its end – and you should march on too. Finally, if you are allowed to handle the fish on the slab, prod the thickest part of the flesh gently. It should be firm – if super-fresh, almost rock hard. If it gives to your finger and you leave a little dent behind, then walk on by . . .

Remember that your mission is to find the best possible fish available for the money you are prepared to spend. In fact, many of the fish on the fish-to-eat list are very good value, and definitely at the cheaper end of the fish spectrum. So don't get hung up on species. In the recipes that follow, there's plenty of flexibility. Even where a specific fish is named in the recipe title, alternatives are always given, and further alternatives could be found too.

Now, I know that cooking fish makes some otherwise highly competent home cooks just a little bit jumpy, particularly as they are nervous of committing the perceived arch-crime of fish cuisine – overcooking it. So the best general tip I have for you is this: a piece of fish is cooked as soon as it is hot – technically about 131°F. If the heat has reached the middle of the fish, or fillet, so that the outside is just too hot to touch, it's done, and you should cook it no longer. Furthermore, if the fish is hot, it will have changed color – usually from some more or less translucent shade of white, buff, or red/brown to an opaque version of the same. And it will "flake," so that it comes away from both the next flake and the bone.

The various tests for doneness are based on these straightforward, dependable, observable events. You can take the temperature in the middle of your fish by inserting the tip of a knife, then touching it to your fingertip or lip: if it's hot, the fish is cooked. Similarly, slip a thin blade into the thickest part of the fillet/fish and check whether it is opaque/flaky in the middle/next to the bone.

Finally, here is one surefire therapy for anyone who is, for whatever reason, just not quite getting along with fish in their kitchen. Go fishing. Cook what you catch. Eat it with friends. You'll never look back, I promise.

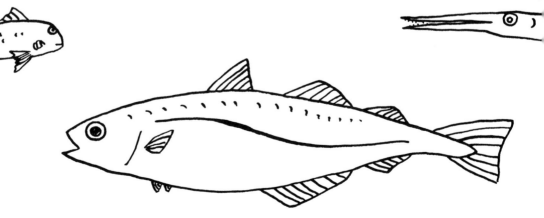

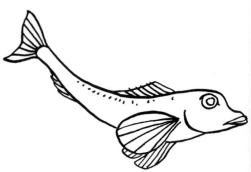

Five ways with fish fillets

Each of the following simple treatments works well with fillets of sustainable white fish, such as Pacific halibut, black cod, US farmed tilapia, and Pacific cod (Alaska longline).

Fried fish fillets with roasted tomato sauce

An ideal dish for late summer and early autumn, when I've usually got more home-grown tomatoes than I know what to do with. In fact, I often make up a really big batch of the sauce, without the sugar and vinegar, and freeze it for use in soups, stews, and curries later in the year.

Serves 4

For the roasted tomato sauce:

3 pounds ripe, flavorful tomatoes, such as plum tomatoes, halved

3 garlic cloves, finely chopped

A few sprigs of thyme (optional)

2 tablespoons canola or olive oil

Sea salt and freshly ground black pepper

1 bay leaf

A little brown sugar

A little white wine vinegar or cider vinegar

Ground mace

1 to 2 tablespoons sunflower oil

3 to 4 tablespoons all-purpose flour

4 fish fillets (see above), ideally with the skin on

First, make the tomato sauce. Preheat the oven to 350°F. Lay the tomato halves, cut side up, in a single layer in a large baking pan. Scatter over the garlic and the thyme, if using, drizzle over the oil, and season generously. Place in the oven and roast for an hour, or until the tomatoes are soft and starting to brown. Tip them into a large sieve and rub through with a wooden spoon; discard the peel and seeds.

Measure the sieved tomato purée, then put it into a wide saucepan with the bay leaf. For every 2 cups purée, add 1 heaping teaspoon of brown sugar, 1 tablespoon of vinegar, and a pinch of mace. Bring to a simmer and cook gently, stirring often, until reduced by one-third to one-half to form a thick, glossy sauce – not quite a ketchup, but quite saucy nonetheless. Season to taste and adjust the sugar/vinegar content too, if you like. Set aside while you cook the fish.

Pour the oil into a large frying pan and place over medium heat. Put the flour on a plate and season it well. Lightly dust the fish fillets in the seasoned flour, shaking off the excess, then transfer to the pan, skin side down. Sizzle gently for 4 to 5 minutes, until the skin is crisp, the edges lightly browned, and the flesh about two-thirds cooked through. Turn over and cook for 1 to 2 minutes longer.

Spoon the sauce onto warm serving plates, add the fried fish, and serve with pasta, noodles, or sautéed potatoes.

Breaded fish fillets with tomato salsa

Here's another variation on the fried-fish-with-tomatoes theme – the tomatoes are fresh and zesty this time, the fillets in a crisp crumb coating. However, you could easily swap the sauces around – for this and the previous recipe. As an alternative to tomatoes, you could serve the fillets with caper mayonnaise (see page 152).

Serves 4

For the tomato salsa:

1 pound ripe, tasty tomatoes, diced

1 shallot or $^1/_2$ small red onion, very finely diced

1 to 2 tablespoons tiny capers, rinsed (optional)

A small squeeze of lemon juice

2 to 3 tablespoons canola or extra-virgin olive oil

Sea salt and freshly ground black pepper

A tiny pinch of sugar

A few fresh mint or flat-leaf parsley leaves, finely chopped

4 fish fillets (see page 142)

3 to 4 tablespoons all-purpose flour

1 egg, lightly beaten

About $^1/_2$ cup fine fresh bread crumbs (or half fresh, half dried)

Sea salt

A pinch of cayenne pepper or hot smoked paprika (optional)

1 teaspoon very finely chopped fresh thyme (optional)

Sunflower or peanut oil for frying

For the tomato salsa, combine the tomatoes, shallot or onion, and capers, if using, in a bowl. Whisk the lemon juice and oil together in a small pitcher, season well with salt and pepper, and add the sugar. Add to the salsa with the chopped mint or parsley and toss lightly; set aside.

If you prefer your fish skin-free, use a sharp knife – ideally a filleting knife – to slice the fillets neatly off their skin (you could ask the fishmonger to do this when you buy them).

Put the flour on a plate and season it well. Pour the beaten egg into a shallow dish. Put the bread crumbs on another plate and season them with a little salt and a pinch of cayenne or paprika, and the thyme leaves, if you like.

Dip each fillet first in the seasoned flour, shaking off the excess, then in the egg until lightly coated, and finally in the seasoned bread crumbs, patting them on so they form an even layer all over.

Heat a layer of oil, $^1/_2$ inch to $^3/_4$ inch deep, in a large frying pan over medium-high heat. To test whether it is hot enough, throw in a few bread crumbs; they should immediately bubble vigorously in the oil.

Put the crumbed fillets into the pan (you might need to cook them in 2 batches). Fry for about 3 minutes (more like 2 minutes if you're using a flat fish), resisting the urge to move the fish until the bread crumbs are crisp and crunchy underneath. Carefully turn the fillets over and cook for 2 to 3 minutes on the other side. Transfer to a plate lined with paper towels to drain.

Serve the fish immediately, with the tomato salsa. Some good bread and a leafy salad on the side wouldn't go amiss.

Fried fish fillets with herbs and lemon

This simple dish relies on a sort of deconstructed salsa verde – a mixture of fresh herbs, lemon, and capers – which is thrown in with the frying fish to flavor it and create an instant, aromatic sauce. It is one of my favorite ways to cook white fish fillets, but it also works with fillets of trout and salmon, and oily fish like mackerel and sardines.

Serves 2

For the herb mix:
1 small garlic clove
A small bunch of flat-leaf parsley, leaves only
10 to 12 fresh basil or mint leaves
2 teaspoons capers, rinsed and dried
Juice and finely grated zest of 1 small lemon
Sea salt and freshly ground black pepper
A little canola or olive oil

A dash of sunflower or peanut oil
2 fish fillets (see page 142)
Sea salt and freshly ground black pepper
1½ tablespoons unsalted butter, at room temperature

Start with the herb mix: Chop the garlic finely, then add the parsley, basil or mint, capers, and lemon zest to the board and chop the whole lot together fairly finely. Scrape the mixture into a bowl, add the lemon juice, some salt and pepper, and just enough oil to make a thick purée; set aside.

To cook the fish, heat a little sunflower or peanut oil in a large frying pan over medium heat. Season the fish fillets with salt and pepper. When the pan is hot, put the fish in, skin side down, and fry for about 3 minutes, until crisp and well colored underneath. Turn it over carefully and cook for another 1 to 2 minutes.

When the fish is just about done, add the butter and the herb mix. As the butter melts, stir it together with the herbs and spoon them over the fish in the pan – this last stage of cooking, with the herbs and butter going over the fish, should last only 30 seconds or so.

Transfer the fish to warm plates, spoon all the buttery, herby juices over, and serve right away – with a generous spoonful of creamy mashed potatoes and perhaps a green salad to follow.

Roast fish fillets with roast potatoes

Though unconventional, this dish makes a lot of sense. Roasting potatoes to perfection takes a little effort – heating the oil in the roasting pan, parboiling the spuds, roughing them up a little – but when you get it right, you have something worth celebrating. And if you've got a tray of sizzling hot oil on the go in the oven, you also have an ideal medium for cooking a nice fat fillet of well-seasoned fish. Surely it makes sense to take advantage . . .

Serves 2

1 pound russet potatoes, peeled and cut into small chunks

Sea salt and freshly ground black pepper

3 to 4 tablespoons sunflower, peanut, or canola oil, or goose fat

About 1 pound fish fillets

A few bay leaves

Preheat the oven to 400°F.

Put the potatoes in a pan, cover with cold water, and add a good pinch of salt. Bring to a boil, simmer for 8 minutes, then drain well and return to the empty pan to steam for a few minutes.

Put the oil or fat in a large roasting pan and place in the oven until smoking hot. Meanwhile, generously season the potatoes in their pan, then rough them up: either hold the lid on and give the pan a little shake or use a sharp fork to scratch their surfaces.

When the oil is smoking hot, add the potatoes. Baste them well with the oil, then return the pan to the oven for 45 minutes, giving them a stir after about 30 minutes. By this stage, the potatoes should be almost done – i.e., have a golden crust all over but look as if they could still take a bit more crisping up. Create a space in the middle of the pan for the fish.

Add the fish to the pan, sprinkle it with salt and pepper, then tuck in the bay leaves. Return to the oven for 10 to 15 minutes, until the fish is just cooked. Serve at once, with pea purée (page 156) or mushy squash (page 311) and, by all means, ketchup – or roasted tomato sauce (page 142).

Foil-baked fish fillets with fennel, ginger, and chile

Baking fish scrunched up in a foil parcel with a handful of aromatics
is an easy and delicious option. And it's not just fillets that benefit
from the foil parcel approach. In fact, this is one of my favorite ways
to cook small-to-medium whole fish (see variation).

Serves 2

2 tablespoons sunflower
or peanut oil

2 fennel bulbs, trimmed,
quartered, and thinly
sliced

2 garlic cloves, finely
sliced

1 teaspoon grated or
finely chopped fresh
ginger

1 small red chile, seeded
and finely sliced

2 large (5 to 6 ounces
each) or 4 small (3 to
4 ounces each) fish
fillets

Sea salt and freshly
ground black pepper

Soy sauce

Preheat the oven to 375°F.

Heat half the oil in a pan, add the fennel, and cook gently for a few
minutes, until it starts to soften. Add the garlic, ginger, and chile
and cook for a few minutes more, so everything starts to soften and
release its flavor. Remove from the heat and set aside.

Take 2 pieces of aluminum foil, roughly 10 inches square, and oil them
well with the remaining oil. Pile half of the fennel mixture in a little
mound in the middle of each one. Season the fish fillets generously
and curl them around the fennel mixture – either 2 small fillets or one
large per packet. Sprinkle a little soy sauce and a good grinding of
black pepper over each pile, then bring up the sides of the foil and
scrunch them together tightly to form well-sealed but baggy packets.

Place the packets on a baking sheet, transfer to the oven, and bake
for 15 minutes. Open up the steaming, fragrant packets and pile the
contents, including all the lovely juices, onto 2 warm plates. Serve
with noodles, mashed potatoes, or rice and some wilted greens, such
as spinach, bok choy, or choy sum.

VARIATION

Whole fish baked in foil

Almost any small-to-medium fish will do, including trout, bass, large
mackerel, or flatfish such as sole. You need a one- or two-person-sized
fish, between 1 and 2 pounds. Get your fishmonger to gut and clean it
for you.

Lay the fish on the well-oiled foil. Put a few bay leaves and lemon
slices in the cavity and some more under the fish. Add extra
herbs – parsley, fennel, and/or thyme – if you like. Dot the fish
with butter. Bring up the sides of the foil a little and pour in about
half a glass of white wine and a squeeze of lemon juice. Season
the fish generously. Scrunch the foil together to form a tightly
sealed but baggy packet. Bake at 375°F. Allow 15 to 20 minutes
for small flatfish; 20 to 25 minutes for a 1- to 1$1/2$-pound fish; 30 to
35 minutes for 1$1/2$- to 2-pound fish.

Flatfish in a bun

This is a very quick lunch, and a great way to use flatfish, such as sole.

The caper mayonnaise is a kind of pared-down tartare sauce – miles better than anything you can buy in a jar. I serve it with all sorts of fried fish dishes.

Serves 1

For the caper mayonnaise:

2 tablespoons good mayonnaise (page 282)

2 teaspoons capers, drained and finely chopped

1 tablespoon chopped fresh flat-leaf parsley

Lemon juice (optional)

1 tablespoon unsalted butter, plus extra for the bun

1 tablespoon sunflower or peanut oil

2 tablespoons all-purpose flour

Sea salt and freshly ground black pepper

2 flatfish fillets, about 3 ounces each, skinned if you prefer

1 large, white floury bun

Lettuce leaves

A squeeze of lemon, a dash of Tabasco sauce, and a squirt of ketchup (all optional), to serve

First, combine the mayonnaise, capers, and parsley, adding a squeeze of lemon juice too, if you have any. Set aside while you cook the fish.

Heat the butter and oil in a nonstick frying pan over medium heat. Put the flour on a plate and season it well. Dust the fish with the seasoned flour, shaking off the excess, and fry for about 2 minutes on each side (if you are leaving the skin on, fry it skin side down first for about 3 minutes, then give it a minute on the other side to cook through).

Slice the bun in half and butter it generously. Lay a few lettuce leaves on the bottom half and put the fish on top, seasoning it further, if you like, with lemon juice, Tabasco, and/or ketchup. Dollop on the mayonnaise, then close the bun and eat right away, while the fish is still warm.

Roasted slashed fish with aromatic paste

This simple way of cooking a whole fish involves slashing the flesh to let the pungent flavorings penetrate. For bigger fish, to feed more people, increase the quantities for the paste and extend the cooking time.

Serves 2 to 3

For the aromatic paste:
$3/4$- to 1-inch piece of fresh ginger, finely grated

2 fat garlic cloves, finely grated

$1/2$ to 1 small, hot red chile, seeded and finely chopped (optional)

1 small shallot, grated

1 star anise pod, pounded with a mortar and pestle

Sea salt and freshly ground black pepper

About 1 tablespoon soy sauce

1 whole fish, about 2 pounds, gutted and scaled

A few bay leaves

1 tablespoon sunflower or canola oil

Preheat the oven to 375°F.

First, make the paste: Combine the ginger, garlic, chile, shallot, and star anise. Season with salt and pepper, then add just enough soy sauce to make a thick paste.

Lay the fish on a well-oiled baking sheet. Using a sharp knife, make 3 or 4 slashes, $3/8$ to $3/4$ inch deep, in the thickest part of the fish, being careful not to go through to the bone. Turn and repeat on the other side. Using your fingers, rub the aromatic paste into the slashes, smearing the rest inside the cavity and over the top of the fish.

Tuck bay leaves into the slashes and cavity. Drizzle a little oil over the fish, place in the oven, and roast for 20 to 25 minutes, until the fish is just cooked through. Check by pushing a fine-bladed knife into the thickest part, between 2 slashes: the flesh should be opaque and just coming away from the backbone.

Bring the fish to the table in its roasting dish and ease large chunks of the flesh away from the bones with a knife and fork. Turn the fish over and remove the remaining flesh, then spoon any aromatic pan juices onto each portion. Serve with plain rice or noodles, and stir-fried greens flavored with a little ginger, garlic, and soy.

VARIATIONS

Herby paste

Mix 2 tablespoons of finely chopped parsley, 1 teaspoon each finely chopped thyme and rosemary, 1 finely chopped garlic clove, and the grated zest of $1/2$ lemon with 1 to 2 tablespoons of canola or olive oil to make a thick paste. Season with salt and pepper. Proceed as above.

Spicy paste

Heat 2 tablespoons of sunflower oil in a frying pan and fry 1 teaspoon of brown mustard seeds briefly until they start to pop. Add a finely chopped large shallot and cook until soft. Add a finely chopped garlic clove and a grated $3/4$-inch piece of fresh ginger, then take off the heat. Grind $1/2$ teaspoon each of coriander and cumin seeds with a pinch of fennel seeds and a pinch of red pepper flakes and stir into the shallot mix with $1/2$ teaspoon of ground turmeric and some salt and pepper, adding more oil, if necessary, to make a thick paste. Proceed as above.

Scallops with pea purée and ham

I adore scallops, especially when partnered with some salty pork. I often cook them with little nuggets of Mexican chorizo (page 206), frying them in the spicy red fat released by the meat. But they're also great with slivers of air-dried ham – lightly fried until crisp – or you could use thin slices of bacon.

I always buy diver-caught scallops. Dredging, the most common method of retrieving them, can have a disastrous effect on the seabed. In any case, diver-caught shellfish are invariably fresher too, and less gritty.

The combination of scallops with a warm pea and mint purée was devised by chef Rowley Leigh and has since become a classic. In the autumn you can achieve an equally delightful effect with a purée of squash – just substitute mushy squash (see page 311) for the pea purée.

Serves 4 as a starter

For the pea purée:

2 1/2 cups fresh or frozen baby peas

1 tablespoon canola or olive oil

1 small garlic clove, finely chopped

3 tablespoons unsalted butter

Leaves from 1 large bunch of mint, chopped

Sea salt and freshly ground black pepper

1 tablespoon sunflower or peanut oil

4 large, paper-thin slices serrano ham or prosciutto (or 8 thin cooked bacon slices)

12 diver scallops, cleaned

A little extra-virgin olive or canola oil, to serve

First, make the pea purée: Cook the peas in boiling salted water until tender, then drain, reserving the cooking water, and empty the peas into a blender or food processor. Put the oil and garlic in a small pan and allow to sizzle gently for barely a minute until the garlic just begins to color. Quickly pour it into the blender with the peas. Add the butter, mint, and a pinch each of salt and pepper. Blend to a purée, adding a little of the cooking liquid if necessary to give a consistency similar to that of coarse hummus. Taste and adjust the seasoning; keep warm.

To cook the scallops, put a large, nonstick frying pan over medium-high heat and add the oil. Tear the ham into large shreds and add to the pan, turning the pieces over in the oil as soon as they start to crisp – this should take less than a minute. Transfer to a warm plate. Season the scallops, add them to the pan, and cook for about a minute, until golden brown underneath. Turn them over and cook for a minute on the other side.

Immediately transfer the scallops to 4 warm plates, adding a few scraps of ham to each one. Put a good dollop of pea purée next to the scallops, drizzle with a little extra-virgin oil plus the juices from the scallop pan, and grind over some pepper. Serve right away.

Salt and pepper squid with quick sweet chile dipping sauce

Just a little more elaborate – and piquant – than basic squid rings, this salty, spicy combination is a real winner.

Serves 4 as a starter

2 teaspoons Szechuan peppercorns

1 teaspoon black peppercorns

$^1/_2$ teaspoon red pepper flakes (optional)

2 tablespoons sea salt

1 cup cornstarch

About 4 cups sunflower or peanut oil for deep-frying

1 pound squid, cleaned and cut into rings about $^3/_8$ inch thick, plus the tentacles, washed and dried but left intact

1 egg white, lightly beaten (optional)

For the sweet chile dipping sauce:

3 tablespoons red currant or crab apple jelly

1 tablespoon cider vinegar

1 teaspoon soy sauce

1 red chile, seeded and very finely chopped

1 small garlic clove, very finely chopped

A few grinds of black pepper

Toast all the peppercorns in a small, nonstick frying pan for a couple of minutes until they become fragrant (this is not essential, but it does enhance the taste). Remove from the heat and grind with the red pepper flakes, if using, and the salt, using a mortar and pestle or a spice grinder, until well combined. Mix with the cornstarch until evenly combined. This seasoning for the squid can be made in advance and kept in a jar.

To make the dipping sauce, simply combine all the ingredients in a small saucepan and stir over low heat until the jelly has dissolved and you have a silky syrup. Bring to a simmer and allow to bubble gently for a few minutes. This will mellow the harshness of the garlic. Allow to cool and serve at room temperature. If the sauce resets to a jelly when cool, whisk in a splash of warm water.

To cook the squid, heat the oil to 350°F in a deep-fat fryer or a heavy, high-sided saucepan. If you don't have a cooking thermometer, test that it's hot enough by dropping a small piece of bread into the oil – it should bubble and fizz, turning golden brown in about a minute.

The squid rings should be slightly damp and sticky, but not dripping wet, for the seasoning mixture to coat them well. If they are too dry, you can massage them with a little beaten egg white. The easiest way to coat them is to place a few pieces of squid in a sieve with a few tablespoons of the mixture, then shake the sieve until the squid is evenly coated and any excess seasoning has dropped through.

Fry the seasoned squid in the hot oil, a few pieces at a time, for about a minute, until just golden. Transfer to a baking sheet lined with paper towels and continue to cook the rest. Serve straight away, with the sweet chile dipping sauce.

Leek, celery root, and smoked pollock soup

This soup combines all the classic elements of a chowder: a milky base, potatoes, and chunks of fish. Celery root, which is a very fish-friendly root, adds another dimension. Smoked pollock, which we call "smollock" at River Cottage, is a favorite ingredient of mine. You can substitute smoked haddock. Kippers (smoked herrings) will also work well, though they have a stronger, oilier flavor.

Serves 6

1 pound smoked pollock or kipper fillets

4 cups whole milk

1 bay leaf

A bunch of flat-leaf parsley, leaves chopped, stems reserved

1 tablespoon butter

2 large leeks, white part only, finely diced

2 boiling potatoes, peeled and finely diced

2 cups finely diced celery root

1 tablespoon finely snipped fresh chives

Sea salt and freshly ground black pepper

Put the smoked fish in a pan and add the milk, bay leaf, and parsley stems. Place over low heat. As soon as the milk comes to a simmer, turn off the heat and cover the pan. The fish will keep on cooking in the hot milk. After about 5 minutes, it should be just cooked through; if not, leave it in the hot milk for a little longer, then drain in a sieve placed over a bowl, reserving the milk. Discard the bay leaf and parsley stems.

Heat the butter in a large, heavy saucepan, add the leeks, cover, and cook over low heat for about 5 minutes. Stir in the potatoes and celery root, then add the warm, fishy milk. Bring to a simmer and cook gently for about 10 minutes, until the vegetables are tender.

Meanwhile, flake the fish into smallish pieces, removing the skin and any bones.

Stir the fish back into the soup and season to taste, being generous with the pepper. Ladle into deep bowls, scatter over the chopped parsley and chives, then serve.

Thrifty fish soup with cheaty rouille

This is a pleasingly frugal recipe. You buy an inexpensive fresh fish, get the fishmonger to fillet it for you, then use the head, skin, and bones to make a flavorful stock. The broth is enhanced with a few herbs and vegetables, the fish flesh goes in at the end, and you can splash out on a bit of squid or a few scallops, if you like. The finishing touch is a swirl of garlicky, chile-hot rouille, though I have to say, the soup is delicious even without it. And croutons, made from leftover bread, add crunch.

Serves 4

1 firm-fleshed fish,
1¹/₂ to 2 pounds, filleted
and skinned, skin, head,
and bones saved

For the stock:
2 celery stalks, chopped
1 garlic clove, peeled
1 onion, coarsely chopped
1 large carrot, sliced
A sprig of thyme
1 bay leaf
Stems from 1 bunch
flat-leaf parsley, leaves
reserved
A few black peppercorns
A splash of white wine

For the soup:
2 garlic cloves
1 large onion
2 celery stalks
2 leeks
1 pound russet potatoes
2 tablespoons canola or
olive oil
¹/₂ teaspoon fennel
seeds, coarsely crushed
4 to 6 ounces cleaned
squid, or 4 to 8 scallops
(optional)
Leaves from the parsley
bunch, finely chopped
Sea salt and freshly
ground black pepper
Whole-wheat croutons,
to serve

For the rouille (optional):
1 hot red chile
Mayonnaise (page 282),
made with 1 garlic clove

First, make a simple fish stock: Put the fish head, skin, and bones in a saucepan with all the other ingredients for the stock. Add 4 cups cold water and bring to a gentle simmer. Cook very gently for half an hour; do not allow it to boil hard, as this spoils the flavor. Strain the stock, discarding the fishy bits and vegetables.

For the soup, finely chop the garlic, onion, celery, and leeks. Peel the potatoes and cut into ¹/₂-inch cubes. Heat the oil over low heat in a large saucepan, add the fennel seeds, garlic, onion, celery, and leeks, then cover and cook for about 10 minutes, until soft. Add the potatoes and the stock and return to a gentle simmer. Cook for 15 minutes, or until the potatoes are tender.

Meanwhile, make the rouille, if you are serving it, by chopping the chile very finely and mixing it with the garlic mayonnaise; set aside.

Now, slice the fish fillets into bite-sized pieces. If using squid, slice the pouches into rings; if using scallops, clean and slice horizontally in half. Add all the fish and any shellfish to the simmering broth. Cook for 2 minutes, until the fish is just done, then remove from the heat. Add the parsley and season to taste.

Serve the soup in warm bowls, topped with a few crisp croutons and a good blob of rouille, if you like.

VARIATION

When fennel is in season, in summer and autumn, try using it instead of the leeks.

Mussels with cider, leeks, and pancetta

Mussels are the ultimate fast seafood, and their sweetness goes brilliantly with salty bacon. You could try this with white wine instead of cider, if you prefer.

Serves 2 as a main course, 4 as a starter

2 pounds mussels

1 tablespoon unsalted butter

1 to 2 tablespoons canola, olive, or sunflower oil

3 ounces pancetta, chopped

1 large or 2 medium leeks, white part only, finely sliced

1 teaspoon thyme leaves

1 bay leaf

1 cup medium-sweet cider

1 teaspoon whole-grain mustard

2 to 3 tablespoons heavy cream

Sea salt and freshly ground black pepper

Lots of chopped fresh flat-leaf parsley, to serve

Scrub the mussels and remove any wiry little "beards" that are attached to the shells. Discard any open mussels that don't close when given a sharp tap.

Place a large saucepan over medium heat and add the butter and oil. When the butter is foaming, add the pancetta and cook for 4 to 5 minutes. Stir in the leek, thyme, and bay leaf and cook for 2 to 3 minutes, until the leek softens a little.

Turn the heat up high, pour in the cider, and bring to a boil. Stir in the mustard, then add the mussels and place a lid on the pan. Steam the mussels for 2 to 3 minutes, giving the pan a good shake once or twice. When the mussels have nearly all opened (discard any that remain firmly shut), stir in the cream.

Season with salt and pepper and serve in deep bowls, scattered with parsley and accompanied by plenty of bread – or, even better, home-cooked *frites* – to soak up the sauce.

Thai fish curry

This looks like a complicated recipe, but it isn't really. I like to make the paste in double or triple quantities and freeze some, so I can whip up a curry quickly. You can vary the fish and shellfish, adding strips of squid or thickly sliced scallops if you like, or increasing the proportion of white fish in relation to shellfish for a more economical dish.

Serves 4

For the curry paste:

2 to 6 small green chiles, according to heat, seeded if you like

3 to 4 small shallots or 1 small onion, chopped

1-inch piece fresh ginger, peeled and chopped

4 garlic cloves, peeled

2 tablespoons galangal paste (optional)

3 lemongrass stalks, white part only, tough outer layers removed, finely sliced

2 teaspoons ground coriander

2 tablespoons ground cumin

Juice and grated zest of 1 lime

4 kaffir lime leaves, chopped (optional)

1 teaspoon Thai shrimp paste

1 teaspoon sea salt

2 tablespoons sunflower or peanut oil

$1^3/_4$ cups coconut milk

$^3/_4$ cup fish stock or water

2 tablespoons Thai fish sauce (nam pla)

2 teaspoons sugar

4 ounces green beans

4 green onions

1 pound firm fish fillets, such as Pacific halibut or tilapia, skinned

10 ounces fresh crabmeat

A handful of cilantro and Thai basil or ordinary basil leaves, coarsely torn

Put all the curry paste ingredients into a food processor or blender and blend to a fairly smooth paste, adding a tablespoon of water to help it along if necessary.

Heat the oil in a heavy saucepan, then scrape in the curry paste. Fry over medium-low heat for 3 to 4 minutes, stirring often, without letting it color. Add the coconut milk, stock or water, fish sauce, and sugar. Bring to a gentle simmer and cook, uncovered, for 20 to 25 minutes.

Meanwhile, cut the green beans into $^3/_4$- to $1^1/_4$-inch lengths and slice the green onions on the diagonal. Add these to the curry sauce and cook for 5 minutes.

Cut the fish fillets into large bite-sized pieces. Add these to the pan, cover with a lid, and simmer gently for 2 to 3 minutes, until the fish is just cooked. Stir in the crabmeat and heat through gently for another minute.

Serve in deep bowls, scattered with the cilantro and basil and accompanied by steamed rice.

Hot-smoked trout pâté

I like to serve this with rye bread as a starter, or on toast as a canapé with drinks. It keeps quite well for a week or so in the fridge: just spoon it into a jar, pressing down carefully to ensure there are no pockets of air, then seal the top with a layer of clarified butter. The recipe works well with hot-smoked mackerel, too.

Serves 4 as a starter

10 ounces hot-smoked trout (or mackerel or salmon) fillet, skinned

2 to 2$^{1}/_{2}$ teaspoons English mustard

1 heaping tablespoon crème fraîche

$^{1}/_{2}$ teaspoon superfine sugar

1 tablespoon fresh lemon juice, or to taste

1 teaspoon coarsely ground black pepper

2 to 3 tablespoons chopped fresh dill or chives

$^{1}/_{2}$ teaspoon paprika (optional)

Put half the smoked fish into a food processor or blender with the mustard, crème fraîche, sugar, and lemon juice and blend until smooth. Transfer to a bowl.

Break the remaining fish into flakes and stir it into the blended mixture with the pepper and dill or chives. Taste and add more lemon juice, if necessary. Ideally, let rest in a cool place for an hour or two before serving.

Serve the pâté with a dusting of paprika, if you like, and with buttered bread or toast. A scaled-down version of this, on small pieces of toast, makes a lovely canapé.

Crab cakes

Very simple and very,
very crabby, these make
a great starter served
with a delicate side
salad – but you can also
eat them as a snack or
canapé, dipping them
into the garlicky mayo
with your fingers.

Serves 4

1 pound fresh crabmeat
Grated zest of 1 lemon
1 tablespoon finely
chopped fresh flat-leaf
parsley and/or chives
Sea salt and freshly
ground black pepper
1 to 2 tablespoons crème
fraîche (optional)
$^1/_4$ cup all-purpose flour
1 egg, lightly beaten
1 cup slightly stale white
bread crumbs
1 tablespoon unsalted
butter
$^1/_4$ cup sunflower or
peanut oil

To serve:
Mayonnaise (page 282),
made with 2 crushed
garlic cloves (or more)
Lemon wedges
A few lettuce leaves and
chives (optional)

Put the crabmeat into a bowl with the lemon zest, parsley and/or chives, and plenty of salt and pepper. Mix together, adding a little crème fraîche if necessary to bind the mixture. Divide into 8 and shape each portion into a fat cake about $^3/_4$ inch thick. Chill for about an hour.

Put the flour on a plate and season it well. Pour the egg into a shallow dish, then scatter the bread crumbs on another plate. Take a crab cake and dip it into the flour, turning it over so that it is lightly coated on both sides, then dip it into the beaten egg and finally into the bread crumbs. Set aside on a plate. Repeat with the rest of the crab cakes.

Heat the butter and oil in a large frying pan. When the butter starts to sizzle gently, add the crab cakes to the pan and fry over medium heat for 3 to 4 minutes, until crisp and golden brown underneath. Turn them over and cook for another 2 to 3 minutes, checking from time to time that they're not coloring too quickly and adjusting the heat as necessary.

Serve immediately with the mayonnaise and lemon wedges, along with a few lettuce leaves and chives if you like.

Kippers with smashed new potatoes

Kippers are an honorable part of the proud fish-smoking tradition we have in the UK. If you choose properly smoked ones without dyes or artificial flavorings, I think you'll find this a wonderfully satisfying dish. Of course, you can substitute any other smoked fish.

Serves 4

2 pounds new potatoes, scrubbed

Sea salt and freshly ground black pepper

4 double kipper fillets

1 tablespoon unsalted butter

1 to 2 tablespoons canola or olive oil

2 tablespoons finely chopped fresh flat-leaf parsley and/or chives

Lemon juice

Boil the new potatoes in a pan of lightly salted water until tender.

Meanwhile, skin the kipper fillets, removing any pin bones, and cut or tear the flesh into large bite-sized pieces. Heat the butter and oil in a frying pan and fry the kipper pieces gently for a couple of minutes, until cooked through. Take off the heat and stir in the herb(s).

When the potatoes are cooked, drain well and return them to the pan. Using a potato masher or wooden spoon, smash them lightly to form a coarse, very chunky mash.

Combine the fish and any juices in the pan with the smashed potatoes. Season well with black pepper and lemon juice and serve, just warm, with a crisp lettuce salad to follow or on the side.

Smoked fish and spinach omelette

Loosely based on the famous Omelette Arnold Bennett, this is a fantastic way to use up leftover cooked fish. Smoked fish work best (smoked pollock is my favorite, though salmon, mackerel, trout, or almost any other fish would do). You could also make it with fresh fish if you poach the fish in the milk and strain off the milk before mixing it with the egg yolks. In all cases, the rich omelette allows you to make a little bit of fish go quite a long way. It makes a very decent lunch for two, or a nifty starter for four.

Serves 2 as a main course, 4 as a starter

³/₄ cup whole milk, or a mixture of heavy cream and whole milk

2 egg yolks

About 6 ounces cold cooked smoked fish, such as mackerel, salmon, trout, pollock, or kippers, broken into large flakes

3 tablespoons unsalted butter

1 small onion, finely chopped

Sea salt and freshly ground black pepper

1 bunch fresh spinach, tough stalks removed

4 eggs

¹/₂ cup grated mature Cheddar or Gruyère cheese

Preheat the broiler.

Put the milk, or milk and cream, in a saucepan, bring to just below a boil, then remove from the heat. Lightly beat the egg yolks together in a bowl. Slowly pour in the hot milk, whisking constantly, to form a smooth custard. Stir in the flaked fish.

Heat half the butter in a frying pan, add the onion and a pinch of salt, and fry gently for about 10 minutes, until soft. Meanwhile, cook the spinach in a large pan of boiling salted water for just a minute, until wilted. Drain, let cool enough to handle, then squeeze out the water with your hands. Chop coarsely. Stir the spinach and onion into the fish mixture and season with a few grinds of black pepper.

Lightly beat the 4 whole eggs together with a pinch each of salt and pepper. Heat the remaining butter in a 9- to 10-inch nonstick frying pan over medium heat. When it's foaming, pour in the beaten eggs. As they cook, gently move the set egg around a bit with a fork to allow the uncooked egg to run over the base of the pan. When the omelette is half-cooked – set on the bottom but still quite wet on top – take the pan off the heat.

Spoon the fish and spinach mixture over the omelette, scatter the grated cheese on top, and put the whole thing under the broiler for a few minutes, until golden, bubbling, and slightly puffed. Let the omelette cool for a couple of minutes, then slice it in the pan. Serve with some peppery salad greens to cut its richness.

Curried fish pie

Few meals, indeed few things in life, are as comforting and reassuring as a fish pie, piping hot from the oven – and I've recently discovered that adding some gently cooked onion and a good whack of curry powder to my usual recipe produces a startlingly good result. You could, of course, leave out the curry-flavored onion to make a classic fish pie, but I would urge you to give this one a go. If you don't fancy pastry, top the pie with mashed potato instead.

Serves 4 to 6

For the fish:

2 fillets (about 1¼ pounds) of firm white fish

6 ounces smoked pollock or kippers

3 cups whole milk

1 onion, coarsely chopped

1 large carrot, coarsely chopped

1 celery stalk, coarsely chopped

1 bay leaf

A few peppercorns

For the pie:

5 tablespoons unsalted butter

½ cup all-purpose flour

Sea salt and freshly ground black pepper

1 tablespoon sunflower or peanut oil

1 large onion, finely chopped

1 tablespoon fairly hot curry powder or curry paste (or try the spicy paste on page 154)

1 to 2 handfuls of cooked peeled shrimp (optional)

1 tablespoon chopped fresh cilantro

8 ounces puff pastry (either the rough puff pastry on page 110, or ready-made all-butter puff)

A little beaten egg for glazing

Preheat the oven to 400°F.

Put the fish fillets and pollock in a pan and add the milk, vegetables, bay leaf, and peppercorns. Place over low heat. As soon as the milk comes to a simmer, turn off the heat and cover the pan. The fish will keep on cooking in the hot milk. After about 5 minutes, it should be just cooked through; if not, leave it in the hot milk for a little longer, then drain in a sieve placed over a bowl, reserving the milk. Discard the vegetables, bay leaf, and peppercorns.

Now make a béchamel sauce: Melt the butter in a saucepan, add the flour, and stir well to make a roux. Cook gently for a couple of minutes, stirring every few seconds, then gently whisk in a third of the fishy milk. Add another third of the milk, whisking all the time, and then the final third, so that you end up with a smooth, creamy sauce. Season with salt and pepper, turn the heat down low, and cook very gently for 2 minutes.

Peel the skin off the fish, check for any bones, and gently break the flesh into chunks.

Heat the oil in a saucepan, add the onion, and cook gently for about 5 minutes, until translucent and soft. Stir in the curry powder or paste and cook for another 5 minutes or so. Add the curry-flavored onion to the béchamel, then stir in the flaked fish, the shrimp, if using, and the cilantro. Taste the sauce and add more salt, pepper, or curry powder/paste if you think it needs it.

Roll out the pastry on a lightly floured work surface and cut it to fit the top of the dish. Put the filling into the dish. Dampen the rim of the dish, lift the pastry over the filling, and press down the pastry edges to seal. Brush with a little beaten egg and place in the oven. Bake for about 30 minutes, until the pastry is golden and puffed and the fishy sauce is bubbling underneath. Serve with buttered peas or greens.

thrifty meat

Meat is the most precious of foods, I've said it before and I'll say it

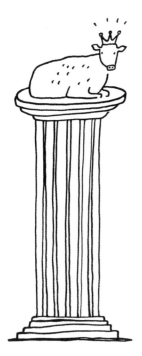

again. It has its special status by virtue of being the flesh of animals, which must be killed in order to provide it. I won't reprise the several hundred pages I spent exploring this theme in *The River Cottage Meat Book*, but I will summarize thus: To my mind, in order to feel good about meat, we have to feel good, or at the very least okay, about how the animals who provided it have lived and died. My preferred way to do that is to raise the animals myself. But it can also be done simply by buying meat from trustworthy sources that you know place a vital emphasis on the importance of good animal husbandry.

More on sourcing meat shortly, but first let's consider some of the practicalities of cooking this great food. Strange as it may seem, cooking meat has an ethical dimension too. And the exciting thing is that it dovetails very nicely with the economic considerations – at least it does to my way of thinking. That's because if we want to do the right thing by the animals we've raised for food, then instead of wasting their meat we should put all of it to the best possible use. That means learning to make delicious meals from the less obvious types of meat – or "secondary cuts" (as opposed to primary cuts).

These pieces of meat tend to be tougher, comprising harder-working muscles with more sinew and sometimes more fat and bone too. This is one of the reasons they are cheaper. The other, related, reason is the assumption many people make that getting the best from this kind of meat is going to be hard work. But don't panic. Because it isn't. You don't have to be a butcher, or an anatomist, or a Michelin-starred chef. You just have to know what to ask for and what to do with it. Dishes made from these cuts are usually both straightforward and forgiving. It's your stove, not you, that does most of the work.

What makes it worthwhile is that the very features that render this meat more affordable – a tougher grain and a bit more skin and bone – mean that, given the right treatment, it is absolutely packed with flavor. That treatment is usually the long, slow application of gentle heat, either from the oven or beneath the slowly simmering stewpot. But sometimes the grill, broiler, or frying pan will also come into play.

As it happens, making the best of these cuts of meat is one of my great passions – and the principal focus of this chapter. I'm not planning to overwhelm you with a comprehensive list of obscure body parts. I'm just going to concentrate on a few that are easy to acquire, straightforward to prepare, and completely delicious to eat. Here is a rough summary of the cuts I think it pays to be familiar with, and which will be the main ingredients for the recipes that follow:

Beef: brisket, oxtail, shank, top round, ground
Pork: shoulder, belly, spareribs, ham hocks, ground
Lamb: shoulder, breast, neck (or neck chops), ground
Chicken: whole ones, sometimes jointed
Game: pheasants, wild rabbits, whole or jointed
Venison: shoulder, ground
Offal: pig's liver, chicken livers, and lamb's hearts

If you are not accustomed to cooking these cuts of meat, you could use the list above as a way of opening up new avenues in your meat cookery. Choose a cut from the list that you haven't cooked before and ask for it next time you're at the butcher's (or try to find it at the supermarket). Have a go at one of the recipes and, if you like the results, peruse other cookbooks to find more dishes using that ingredient. It may soon become a trusted friend. Then move on to another unfamiliar cut of meat. Before you know it, your repertoire will be expanding rapidly.

So where should you go to buy your meat? Call me old-fashioned, but how about your local butcher's? A good butcher really can provide all the meat you'll ever want. If you're lucky enough to have one near you, then you really should support him (or her) with your trade. It's having enough regulars like you that will keep them in business, and keep the quality of their offerings high.

The best butchers source their meat locally and actually visit the farms they source from. They can usually tell you which farm any given piece of meat has come from and what breed of sheep, cow, or pig is being raised there. They offer free-range pork and chicken, stock game in season, and make not only their own sausages but a few specialties – meat pies, perhaps, or meatballs. They may even cure their own bacon, and cure and bake their own hams. They may or may not sell naturally raised meat as a matter of course, but they should be able to get hold of it if you ask nicely. Most of all, though, they should be talkers: always ready to tell you about the meat on offer, happy to cut it this way or that, as it suits you, perhaps even ready to suggest a recipe or two.

Unfortunately, just because the word *butcher* appears above the shop door, you cannot take it for granted that these ideal standards will be upheld. The brutal truth is that a second-rate butcher's is really

no better a place to buy your meat than the supermarket, and quite possibly worse. If little or no information is offered about the origin of the meat, and moreover the staff show a marked reluctance to engage in conversation on that matter, then I would say you are entitled to assume the worst. Such shops are not really butchers' at all. They are clearinghouses for cheap meat. It's not hard to identify such an emporium and, having done so, you should avoid it.

If you are not blessed with a good local butcher, then perhaps you have access to a good farmers' market. This can be an excellent place to find meat of the highest quality. Usually the meat will be pre-packed in some way, as the hoops you need to jump through to be allowed to cut and wrap meat in a market stall are considerable and prohibitive. My preference is for meat that has been tray-wrapped rather than vacuum-packed, as the latter method tends to draw blood from the meat, then bind it back to the surface in a kind of "blood marinade." It's not terminal, but if you do buy meat like this it's worth freeing it from its pack as soon as you get it home. Wipe it dry and let it breathe a bit, keeping it on a plate or tray in the fridge either wrapped in waxed paper or covered with a cotton cloth.

At a farmers' market, anyone selling meat should be able to answer *all* your questions about their product. That's because, if they are playing by the rules, they should be a family member or employee of the farm on which the meat was raised. To me that's the ultimate transparency, and the best possible reason to support your local farmers' market – not just for meat but for all truly local produce.

Having said that, I understand that many people find it irresistibly convenient to buy meat at the supermarket. Now it's no secret that I have a few opinions on the way our major retailers deal with our farmers, and on the consequences of that for the welfare of our farm animals. You've perhaps noticed that I've been particularly exercised about chickens. They may provide our favorite meat, but, on the evidence of how the vast majority are treated, you'd be forced to conclude that they are one of the least cared-for creatures on the planet. The same is true of pork, and pigs.

In fairness to the supermarkets, I should point out that many of them are now selling good-quality meat reared to high welfare standards, including excellent free-range and organic chickens and pork from outdoor-reared pigs. The problem is that such meat is usually marketed as a premium brand, and therefore perceived by many as a luxury item. If I were to buy meat from the supermarket, I would choose only products that gave me sufficient assurance about both the welfare of the animals and the quality of the meat – organic or free-range poultry, organic pork and grass-fed, well-aged beef. If that means favoring only the premium brands, then so be it. If enough supermarket shoppers express their concerns about meat quality and animal welfare by shopping in this way, supermarkets will improve the extent of their "ethical meat" offerings, and will eventually raise their standards across the board. I know this is the case because it is already happening in a genuine and encouraging way in the world of chickens.

Finally, don't overlook the Internet as a means of buying meat. Some of the best meat reared in the States is now sold online. Farms that do business in this way tend to have a "unique selling point," which they will emphasize in the marketing of their product. It might be that their meat is organic, or from specialized or rare breeds, or both. Although this kind of meat tends to be expensive, by cutting out the middleman and selling direct, farmers can manage to keep online prices reasonable, especially if you buy in bulk. Many farms that sell meat online do a whole- or half-lamb box, and similar "mixed cut" packages for pork and beef.

I wholeheartedly approve of this way of selling meat, as it encourages a holistic approach to the carcass. You'll need a freezer, of course, to help manage the meat. By "managing," I mean making sure you don't accumulate a pile of "difficult cuts" – breasts of lamb, fresh hocks of pork – lurking in the darker corners. And that's where I'm delighted to offer my help. I promised they wouldn't be difficult, and here are the recipes to prove I'm as good as my word.

Lamb chops with garlic, thyme, and capers

This is such a good way to serve up lamb chops. They are packed with fantastic flavors, and the pan juices make a delicious gravy.

Serves 4

1 large or 2 medium heads of garlic

A little canola or sunflower oil

4 lamb loin chops, or 8 neck cutlets

Sea salt and freshly ground black pepper

2 tablespoons capers, rinsed

A good handful of thyme sprigs

A few sprigs of rosemary

A small glass of white wine or strong cider

Preheat the oven to 400°F with an ovenproof dish in it. Release all the cloves from the head of garlic, but do not peel them. Just squash them a little with the flat of a knife to help release their flavor.

Heat a little oil in a large frying pan, add the garlic cloves, and fry for a few minutes over medium heat. Add the chops and brown them lightly on both sides, seasoning as you go. Transfer to the preheated dish. Remove the garlic cloves from the frying pan too, and scatter them over the chops with the capers and the sprigs of thyme and rosemary, tucking some underneath as well.

Return the pan to the heat and pour in the wine or cider. Let the liquid bubble away, stirring to deglaze the pan, until it has reduced by half. Tip the contents of the pan over the chops, along with a small glass of water. Season well and return the dish to the oven.

Roast for 15 to 20 minutes, until the meat is cooked through, the fattier edges of the chops are crisping nicely, and the garlic cloves are sweet and tender. Serve with mashed root vegetables (pages 308–11) and steamed cabbage or greens.

Overnight home-cured bacon chops

Curing meat is not the sole preserve of the experts. There are simple, small-scale curing methods that any cook can use to excellent effect. This is one of them: a fail-safe technique for curing pork overnight that will introduce you to the simple principles of the process – i.e., using salt not merely to preserve but also to intensify the flavor of the meat.

Once you've familiarized yourself with the cure recipe and the method, you're only a step away from creating your own home-cured bacon (see variation), which can be used wherever bacon is called for in sauces, soups, and stews.

Serves 4

For the cure:
3 tablespoons fine sea salt

2 tablespoons superfine sugar or soft brown sugar

3 bay leaves, finely shredded

12 to 16 juniper berries, crushed

1 teaspoon freshly ground black pepper

4 large pork chops
2 tablespoons sunflower or peanut oil

Combine all the ingredients for the cure and put them into a plastic container or ceramic dish (a metal one is liable to react with the cure). Add the pork chops and rub the cure lightly all over the meat with your fingers.

Cover the container and leave in a cool place (a cool larder or fridge) overnight or for at least 12 hours, or 24 hours for extra-large or thick-cut pork chops, but no longer. Turn the chops once or twice, if you remember. Then rinse them well and pat dry. That's it: your pork is now cured. They can be used immediately but will keep in a sealed container in the fridge for 5 to 6 days, and the flavor will improve all the time. They also freeze well.

To cook the chops, heat the oil in a large frying pan over medium heat and fry them fairly gently for about 6 minutes per side, until cooked through. Or you can grill them, brushed lightly with oil. Season with pepper and serve with mashed potatoes or a mixed root mash (page 308), and leeks with greens (page 300) or just greens.

VARIATION

Home-cured bacon

Instead of chops, use 2 pounds pork belly, off the bone but skin on. Cut into strips $1\frac{1}{4}$ to $1\frac{1}{2}$ inches thick and cure in the same way, but this time for 48 hours, turning the meat over a few times. After rinsing, the bacon belly strips can be kept in the fridge for 5 to 6 days or frozen.

You'll struggle to turn this bacon into slices without a meat slicer, but – like pancetta – it's perfect for cutting into chunks or small dice and browning gently in a frying pan to add to sauces or stews. Or try scattering fried matchsticks over salads or scrambled eggs.

Pig's liver with sage and onions

It's essential that you use the freshest pig's liver you can get your hands on. Otherwise, this lovely dish asks little of the cook – it's very straightforward, and also works brilliantly with venison or lamb's liver.

Fried pig's liver, cut into little chunks and served on toast, makes a very tasty and quick canapé, too.

Serves 4

2 to 3 tablespoons sunflower oil, lard, or goose fat

20 to 25 baby onions, halved

About 1 pound fresh pig's liver

1/4 cup all-purpose flour

1 teaspoon sea salt

1 teaspoon freshly ground black pepper

6 to 8 sage leaves

6 tablespoons aged cider vinegar or balsamic vinegar

Heat 2 tablespoons of the oil or fat in a large, heavy frying pan, add the onions, and cook gently for about 20 minutes, stirring regularly, until they are caramelized on the outside and tender all the way through. Transfer to a warm dish while you prepare the liver. (Alternatively, you could roast the onions in the oven at 375°F for 30 to 40 minutes, turning them over every 10 minutes or so.)

Meanwhile, peel any membrane from the liver and trim out any tough ventricles. Using a sharp knife, cut the liver into slices about 3/8 inch thick, or even thinner if you prefer.

Mix the flour with the salt and pepper. Dip the liver slices into the seasoned flour until well coated, then shake off the excess.

Pour the rest of the oil or fat into the frying pan, place over high heat, and, when very hot, add the liver slices along with the sage leaves. Cook for 45 seconds to 1 1/2 minutes on each side, depending on the thickness and how you like your liver. Transfer to a warm plate while you quickly finish the dish.

Deglaze the pan by pouring in the vinegar and letting it bubble while you scrape up any tasty brown bits from the base of the pan. Simmer the liquid until it has reduced to a tablespoon or two. Return the caramelized onions and liver to the pan and spoon the juices over the liver. Serve with some creamy mashed root vegetables.

Deviled lamb's hearts

It's not just the traditional kidney that responds well to simple deviling. Livers and hearts are also delicious in this piquant but creamy sauce. If you want to make more of a meal of this, you could serve it with French lentils, cooked as for the recipe on page 101 and tossed with oil, salt, pepper, and lemon juice.

Serves 2 to 3 as a lunch

4 lamb's hearts

1 small onion, coarsely chopped

1 carrot, sliced

1 celery stalk, chopped

1 bay leaf

A sprig of thyme

A few black peppercorns

2 to 3 thick slices of good bread

A little unsalted butter

A little sunflower or peanut oil

Sea salt and freshly ground black pepper

A small glass of dry sherry

1 tablespoon white wine vinegar or cider vinegar

1 teaspoon red currant jelly

A few good shakes of Worcestershire sauce

A good pinch of cayenne pepper

1 tablespoon English mustard

1 tablespoon heavy cream

2 tablespoons chopped fresh flat-leaf parsley (optional)

Cut the lamb's hearts into quarters. Rinse them well under cold running water to remove any blood, then trim away the tough tubes from the top (don't worry about any little bits of white fat). Put them in a pan with the onion, carrot, celery, bay, thyme, and peppercorns and pour on enough cold water just to cover. Bring to a simmer and cook very gently for 1½ to 2 hours, until completely tender. Take out the hearts and let cool. Trim them again, if necessary, then slice thickly.

Put your bread in the toaster, or fry it in butter with a dash of oil until crisp. Keep it warm while you quickly devil the hearts.

Heat a dash of oil in a small frying pan over high heat. Add the heart pieces, season with a pinch of salt, and sizzle for just a minute to brown them, tossing them occasionally. Then add the sherry and let it bubble for a moment. Add the vinegar and red currant jelly and stir until the jelly dissolves. Add the Worcestershire sauce, cayenne pepper, mustard, and plenty of black pepper. Let it all bubble down and reduce until thick and glossy – about 2 to 3 minutes if the heat is high enough.

Finally, add the cream and let it bubble for another minute or two, shaking the pan occasionally, until the sauce is reduced and nicely glossy again. Taste and add more salt or cayenne and black pepper, if you like.

If you've toasted the bread, butter it now. Pile the hearts on to the toast or fried bread, sprinkle with the parsley, if you're using it, and serve right away – as it is, or accompanied by a green salad.

Spring chicken broth

If I buy a chicken for roasting, I always make stock from the carcass. One of my favorite ways to use it is in a simple soup, like this one. I cook three or four seasonal garden vegetables in the simmering stock, sometimes adding a handful of barley, rice, or small pasta, and if there's any chicken meat left over from the roast, that will go in too. No two chicken broths are ever quite the same: the ingredients change with the seasons and according to what I fancy. In summer, it could be sliced green beans, peas, green onions, and shredded spinach or chard; in autumn, perhaps beet, carrot, and kohlrabi matchsticks, plus some shredded savoy cabbage; in winter, diced potato, parsnip, carrot, and celery root or rutabaga.

Serves 4 to 6

For the chicken stock:
1 cooked chicken carcass
Giblets from the chicken, if available (not the liver)
2 onions, coarsely chopped
2 large carrots, coarsely chopped
3 to 4 celery stalks, coarsely chopped
A few leek tops, coarsely chopped (optional)
A few black peppercorns
2 bay leaves
A sprig of thyme
A few parsley stems (optional)
A glass of white wine (optional)

For the broth:
About 1/3 cup pearl barley or pearled spelt (optional)
4 to 6 cups chicken stock
About 1 cup baby carrots, scrubbed and halved
About 1 cup fresh (or frozen) peas
About 1 cup shelled fava beans
Leftover cold chicken (optional)
Sea salt and freshly ground black pepper

To make the stock, after you've picked every last scrap of meat off the carcass, break it up into fairly small pieces (or use kitchen scissors) and pack into a medium saucepan or stockpot, along with the giblets if you have them, plus any bits of skin or gristle or jellied juices left from your roast – anything that's not actually meat. Add all the chopped vegetables, peppercorns, and herbs, plus the wine, if using. Cram everything down with a wooden spoon so you won't need too much water to cover it all – the stock will be that much tastier as a result.

Now pour on enough cold water just to cover the whole lot – you should need no more than 6 cups. Bring to a very gentle simmer, then cover and cook, just barely simmering, for at least 3 hours or up to 5 hours. Strain the stock through a colander and then through a cheesecloth-lined sieve. Let cool completely, then store in the fridge. If there's a significant layer of fat on top, you can scrape it off once it's chilled.

If you're including the pearl barley or spelt in the broth, put them in a saucepan, cover with cold water, and bring to a boil, then reduce the heat and simmer until tender – about 45 minutes for barley, 20 to 25 for spelt. Drain and set aside.

Bring the stock to a gentle simmer in a large saucepan. Add the barley or spelt, if using, and return to a simmer. Add the baby carrots and cook for 3 to 5 minutes, then add the peas and fava beans, as well as any cold chicken you have. Return to a simmer and cook for just 2 to 3 minutes more. Season the soup to taste, then ladle into warm soup plates and serve right away.

Scotch broth salad

This substantial dish combines many of the lovely, earthy elements of a traditional Scotch broth – barley, lamb, greens, and onions – but serves them up in a less wet and soupy format, somewhere between a warm salad and a risotto. Despite being an easy leftovers supper, it's a rather elegant dish, and I wouldn't hesitate to serve it as a starter at a dinner party. There's something about the nutty texture of the barley, robed in a rich dressing, that takes it to a different level.

Serves 3 to 4

$^2/_3$ cup pearl barley or pearled spelt

3 ounces curly kale (2 good handfuls), washed, coarse stems removed, and coarsely chopped

For the dressing:

3 tablespoons canola or olive oil

2 tablespoons cider vinegar or white wine vinegar

1 tablespoon crème fraîche

1 teaspoon light brown sugar

A few fresh mint leaves, finely shredded (optional)

Sea salt and freshly ground black pepper

1 tablespoon canola or olive oil

1 red onion, chopped

About 8 ounces cooked lamb, shredded

A large handful of flat-leaf parsley, coarsely chopped

Put the pearl barley or spelt in a large saucepan, cover with cold water, and bring to a boil. Cover and simmer gently until tender – about 45 minutes for barley, 20 to 25 minutes for spelt. Drain in a colander and set aside.

Blanch the kale in lightly salted boiling water for 2 minutes. Drain, refresh under cold running water, and drain again.

Whisk together all the ingredients for the dressing and set aside.

Heat the oil in a small frying pan, add the onion, and cook gently for about 10 minutes, until softened. Increase the heat slightly, add the lamb, and cook for a few minutes until lightly browned. Add half the dressing and heat through.

Put the barley or spelt into a large bowl, add the kale and parsley, then add the lamb and onion mixture and stir to coat everything well. Check the seasoning, then serve, dotting and dabbing a little more dressing on each plateful.

Split pea and ham soup

This is a wonderfully thrifty sort of dish, using inexpensive ingredients to create a rich, filling, protein-packed soup. You can make it either with a ham bone, which is already cooked (most of the meat having been eaten), or a ham hock, which is cured but uncooked. Either will be available from a good butcher, but this is also a nice way to use the bone and leftover meat from a ham that you've cooked yourself.

Serves 6

1 cooked ham bone or uncooked ham hock

1 tablespoon unsalted butter

1 large onion, finely chopped

1 large carrot, finely chopped

1 celery stalk, finely chopped

2 bay leaves

$1^1/2$ cups yellow or green split peas, soaked in cold water overnight if possible

Sea salt and freshly ground black pepper

If you're using a ham bone, trim all the bits of meat off it, cover, and set aside.

Melt the butter in a large saucepan. Add the onion, carrot, and celery, cover, and cook gently, stirring regularly, for about 10 minutes, until soft. Add the ham bone or ham hock to the pan with the bay leaves, split peas, and 6 cups of water. Bring to a boil and skim off any scum that comes to the surface.

Reduce the heat to low and simmer gently, covering the pan loosely to allow for some evaporation. If you're using a cooked ham bone, you just need to simmer until the peas are completely soft – 45 minutes to an hour, perhaps less if they were presoaked. If you're using a ham hock, the soup will need longer in order to render the bacon good and tender – aim for about $1^1/2$ hours.

Remove the ham hock and set aside, if using; discard the ham bone and bay leaves. You can either use a blender to purée the soup or, for a coarser texture, just mush up the peas and vegetables using a potato masher. Trim all the meat and skin off the ham hock, if using, then cut into small pieces (skin and all, if you like), or cut up the ham from the bone that you set aside earlier.

Return about half of the meat to the soup, taste, and season (the ham may have contributed all the salt you need). Heat through again and serve, topped with the rest of the meat and a grinding of pepper.

Bloody Mary burgers with horseradish dressing

These are exceptionally good burgers; I've never known them fail to please anyone. They are essentially a kind of seared steak tartare – with the spicy seasonings leaning more toward a Bloody Mary.

You can't use any old ground beef for them. Ideally, ask your butcher to grind some top round for you, on a medium rather than a fine setting. If you're shopping in the supermarket, go for ground sirloin – preferably organic. The better the meat, the more you can be inclined to serve these burgers pretty rare.

As an alternative to the horseradish dressing, you could serve the burgers simply with hot mustard and mayonnaise.

Makes 4

1 tablespoon tomato paste

$1^{1}/_{2}$ teaspoons prepared horseradish

$^{1}/_{2}$ teaspoon celery seeds

4 to 8 dashes of Tabasco or other hot sauce, to taste

$^{1}/_{2}$ teaspoon Worcestershire sauce

$^{1}/_{2}$ teaspoon fine sea salt

Freshly ground black pepper

3 pounds ground round

A little canola or olive oil

For the dressing:

$^{3}/_{4}$- to $1^{1}/_{4}$-inch piece horseradish root, freshly grated

1 teaspoon cider vinegar

2 tablespoons crème fraîche

Sea salt and freshly ground black pepper

To serve:

4 good bread buns, ciabatta rolls, or thick slices of baguette

A few romaine lettuce leaves

A few tomatoes, sliced

Ketchup (optional)

In a medium bowl, mix together the tomato paste, horseradish, celery seeds, Tabasco, Worcestershire sauce, salt, and a generous grinding of black pepper. Add the beef and mix thoroughly with your hands, making sure the seasonings are spread throughout the meat. Let stand for at least an hour for the flavors to develop.

Meanwhile, make the horseradish dressing: Mix all the ingredients together in a bowl, seasoning with salt and pepper to taste.

Break off a small piece of the beef mixture, the size of a walnut, and fry in a little oil until well cooked. Taste and adjust the seasonings if necessary.

Shape the meat into 4 patties about $^{3}/_{4}$ inch thick. Lightly brush each one with oil, then place on a grill over high heat. It's hard to give exact cooking instructions due to variables such as the thickness of the burger, the heat of the grill, and personal preference. For a medium-rare burger, you will probably need to grill for 3 to 4 minutes, then flip over and cook the other side for a couple of minutes. If you're cooking the burgers indoors, use a lightly oiled grill pan set over medium-high heat. Let the burgers rest for a minute or two while you prepare the buns.

To serve, toast the buns or other bread lightly on the cut side, then top with the lettuce leaves and tomato slices. Add the burgers and smear with horseradish sauce, and a dollop of ketchup if you like. Top with the other half of the bread.

Good with French fries, obviously, but if they're too much effort, really good potato chips will do.

Venison and pork burgers with sautéed pears

Ground venison shoulder, combined with some pork to keep it succulent, makes a mean burger. If you have a meat grinder, choose the meat yourself and put it through the medium plate. If you don't have one, you can ask your butcher to do the grinding for you. Good-quality ground venison is available by mail order from some online butchers and game dealers.

The fried pears sound unusual but they work really well. So do fried apples, if you go for dessert apples that hold their shape, such as Golden Delicious or Rome. Alternatively, dress your burger with a mild, fruity chutney (nothing too wildly spicy or it'll smother the very lovely seasoning in the burger).

Makes 8

1/2 teaspoon juniper berries

3 bay leaves

4 fresh sage leaves, chopped

1 teaspoon white peppercorns

1 teaspoon sea salt

1 1/2 pounds venison shoulder, coarsely ground

8 ounces fatty pork, such as pork belly, ground

1 tablespoon white wine

A little canola or olive oil

To serve:

1 tablespoon butter

2 to 3 pears, cored and thickly sliced

8 slices of good white bread or rolls, such as sourdough or ciabatta

Put the juniper berries, bay leaves, sage, peppercorns, and salt into a coffee or spice grinder and grind to a fine powder (or chop the bay leaves very finely, then pound to a powder with the other ingredients using a mortar and pestle). Place the seasoning mixture in a bowl with the meat, add the wine, and mix with your hands until well combined. Let stand for an hour for the flavors to develop.

Heat a little oil in a frying pan, break off a small piece of the mixture, and fry it until cooked through. Taste and adjust the seasoning if necessary. Don't be tempted to add too much more in the way of spices, as the flavor will develop as the burgers cook – what you're really checking for is saltiness.

Shape the meat into 8 patties about 3/4 inch thick and fry in a lightly oiled grill pan, or grill them for 4 to 5 minutes on each side, until well browned and cooked through. Remove the burgers to a warm plate and let rest while you fry the pears.

In the same pan, melt the butter over medium heat. Once it is foaming, add the pears and cook, turning occasionally, until they start to take on a little color but still hold their shape.

Serve the burgers on thickly sliced bread or in rolls, topped with the sautéed pears. I like to rub the cut sides of the bread in the pan juices before adding the burger.

Spiced lamb burgers

I do love spicy lamb burgers. Made with good meat, they can be incredibly tender, juicy, and flavorsome. Over the years I've enjoyed seasoning lamb patties with various combinations of herbs and spices. This North African–inspired recipe is my current favorite and an absolute winner when the grill's out.

Makes 8

1 teaspoon cumin seeds
1 teaspoon coriander seeds
1 teaspoon fennel seeds
1 teaspoon black peppercorns
$^1/_2$ cinnamon stick, broken up
A pinch of cayenne pepper or chile powder
3 teaspoons paprika
1 garlic clove, finely crushed
2 teaspoons fine sea salt
2 pounds ground lamb shoulder

For the spiced yogurt:
$^1/_2$ teaspoon cumin seeds
$^1/_2$ teaspoon coriander seeds
1 cup Greek yogurt
A tiny scrap of garlic, crushed with a little sea salt
A dozen fresh mint leaves, finely shredded
A pinch of sea salt
1 tablespoon sesame seeds

To serve:
Canola or olive oil
Flatbreads (page 78) or burger buns
A few romaine lettuce leaves
Some cucumber slices
1 small red onion, very finely sliced

In a dry frying pan, toast the cumin, coriander, and fennel seeds, peppercorns, and cinnamon until fragrant, about a minute or so. (You don't have to toast the spices, but it does get the flavors going.) Grind to a fine powder using a mortar and pestle or spice grinder, then combine with the cayenne or chile powder, paprika, garlic, and salt. Add the ground lamb and mix thoroughly with your hands. Let stand for at least an hour for the flavors to develop.

Meanwhile, for the spiced yogurt, toast the cumin and coriander seeds in the pan you used for the burger spices. Grind to a fine powder using a mortar and pestle, then stir into the Greek yogurt with the garlic, mint, and salt. Toast the sesame seeds in the same pan over medium heat until golden, shaking the pan as you go, for a minute or two. Leave to cool down a bit, then sprinkle over the yogurt.

Break off a small piece of the spiced lamb, about the size of a walnut, and fry it until well cooked. Taste and adjust the seasonings if necessary.

Shape the rest of the meat into 8 patties about $^3/_4$ inch thick. Lightly brush with oil, then place on a grill over high heat. Or, if you're cooking indoors, use a lightly oiled heavy frying pan set over medium-high heat. The cooking time will be determined by the thickness of the burger, the heat of the grill, and your preference. For a medium-rare burger, you will probably need to grill for 3 to 4 minutes, then flip it over and cook the other side for a couple of minutes. Let the burgers rest for a few minutes while you cook or warm up your flatbreads.

Serve the lamb burgers wrapped in the soft flatbreads with some torn lettuce, cucumber, and onion and a dollop of the spiced yogurt. You probably won't need all of the yogurt – what's left over makes a great dip.

My herby grilled chicken

This is a very appealing way to cook chicken, whether you serve it up hot or leave it to cool and make it part of a picnic. There are no hard and fast rules about the herbs – just use what you've got and what you like. Having said that, I think combining one or two "lighter" herbs, such as parsley and chervil, with a smaller quantity of a stronger leaf, such as thyme, marjoram, oregano, or tarragon, is a good way to go.

You can cook the chicken in the oven, but I like it best on a hot grill or in a grill pan.

Serves 6

3 to 4 tablespoons canola or olive oil

1/2 teaspoon English mustard

3 tablespoons chopped mixed fresh herbs, such as parsley and chives, plus a little tarragon or thyme

A little grated lemon zest

A squeeze of lemon juice

1 small garlic clove, very finely chopped

Freshly ground black pepper

1 chicken, cut up, or about 3 pounds chicken pieces on the bone

Sea salt

Combine the oil, mustard, herbs, lemon zest and juice, garlic, and plenty of pepper (but no salt) in a large bowl. Slash the chicken in a few places so the flavors can penetrate, then toss the pieces in the marinade; they should be coated, but not swimming in oil. Let marinate in the fridge for at least an hour or up to 4 hours.

Before cooking, pat off the excess oil, then season the chicken with a little salt. You can either roast it in an oven preheated to 375°F for 40 to 45 minutes, turning once, or grill on a medium-hot grill or in a grill pan, turning regularly until the skin is golden brown and a little charred in places. Check that the juices run clear when the thickest part of the meat is pierced with a knife or skewer. If you are barbecuing, give the breast pieces about 15 minutes on the hotter part; cook the legs and wings on a cooler part for at least 25 minutes.

Transfer the chicken to a warm dish, sprinkle with a little more seasoning, and let rest for 5 to 10 minutes before serving.

VARIATION

Spicy yogurt marinade for chicken

Mix together 4 tablespoons plain yogurt, 1 crushed garlic clove, 1 teaspoon lemon juice, 2 heaping teaspoons medium-hot curry powder, and 1 heaping teaspoon garam masala. Coat on-the-bone chicken portions in the marinade (as above) and marinate in the fridge for at least 3 hours. Season with a little salt before cooking.

Tupperware Mexican chorizo (meatballs)

I find the mild heat and smoky flavor of chorizo goes with so many things, from eggs to vegetables, fish, and shellfish. Making and maturing your own "real" chorizo (as described in *The River Cottage Cookbook*) is fun but undeniably a commitment, so here's the easy version – very popular in Mexico and also here in East Devon.

It's a highly seasoned mix of coarsely ground pork, which you keep in a tub or plastic container in the fridge and use in a variety of ways. You can shape some into mini meatballs or little patties and fry until browned, then chuck into tomato sauces, bean casseroles, vegetable soups, and the like.

Or you can fry a couple of handfuls of the mixture, breaking it up with the edge of a wooden spatula as you go, until you have a pan of coarse, crisp chorizo crumbs to scatter over salads, soups, and egg dishes – especially scrambled eggs – or toss with pasta (page 208) or vegetables, such as broccoli (page 302).

Makes about 1¹/₂ pounds

1¹/₂ pounds pork shoulder, coarsely ground

1 tablespoon sweet smoked paprika

2 teaspoons hot smoked paprika

2 garlic cloves, finely chopped

2 teaspoons fine sea salt

1¹/₂ teaspoons fennel seeds

¹/₄ teaspoon cayenne pepper

¹/₄ cup red wine

Freshly ground black pepper

A little canola or olive oil for frying

Put all the ingredients except the oil into a bowl and mix thoroughly with your hands, squishing the mix through your fingers to distribute the seasonings evenly.

Heat a little oil in a frying pan, break off a small piece of the mixture, shape into a tiny patty, and fry for a few minutes on each side, until cooked through. Taste to check the seasoning, remembering that the flavors will develop further as the mixture matures. If you're a heat fiend, you can add more cayenne and black pepper.

Cover the mixture and store in the fridge for at least 2 hours before using; this will allow the flavors time to develop. It will keep for about 1 week.

Chorizo carbonara

A bit of a cross-cultural recipe this one, using a classic Mexican sausage in a classic Italian pasta sauce. I'm sure no one will mind. The result is a remarkably delicious – and quick – dish that illustrates why my Mexican Tupperware chorizo has become such a family staple. Combined with a few other everyday ingredients – in this case, pasta, eggs, and cream – it is the key to all sorts of satisfying meals.

Serves 2

5 ounces spaghetti, linguine, or other long pasta

1 tablespoon canola or olive oil

1 cup Tupperware Mexican chorizo (page 206), crumbled (or Spanish chorizo, diced quite small)

2 large egg yolks

1/2 cup heavy cream

Sea salt and freshly ground black pepper

Add the pasta to a large saucepan of well-salted boiling water and cook until al dente.

Meanwhile, heat the oil in a frying pan. Add the chorizo and fry briskly for about 10 minutes, until crisp and cooked through. If you're using the soft Tupperware chorizo, you can start with a bit of a lump and break it up with a spatula as it fries, so it forms lots of succulent little nuggets and crumbs, thereby maximizing the surface area available for crisping.

Beat the egg yolks and cream together and season lightly (since the chorizo is already highly seasoned).

When the pasta is done, drain thoroughly and immediately return it to the hot pan. Tip in the crisp chorizo, followed by the egg mixture. Use 2 forks to mix the eggy cream into the hot pasta. It will cook in the heat of pasta, coating each strand in a light, creamy sauce. Serve right away, with a final grinding of black pepper on top.

Sticky glazed spareribs

These sweet, sticky, spicy ribs make an excellent dish to share with friends – no one can stand on ceremony while tucking into them. They're also brilliant children's party food. Make sure you keep a few back for a solitary treat, nibbled cold, once everyone has gone home.

You can roast the ribs as whole racks, which looks great, or, to make serving easier, ask the butcher to chop them into one- or two-rib pieces.

Serves 4 to 6

For the marinade:

6 tablespoons red currant, plum, crabapple, or other fruit jelly

2 tablespoons honey

2 garlic cloves, crushed to a paste

1 tablespoon finely grated fresh ginger

$1/2$ to 1 medium-hot red chile, finely chopped, or $1/2$ teaspoon red pepper flakes

2 tablespoons soy sauce

3 pounds pork ribs (about 2 whole racks)

Combine all the marinade ingredients, whisking them together well. Put the ribs in a large ovenproof dish, pour the marinade over them, and use your hands or a brush to get them well coated. Cover and marinate in a cool place for at least an hour, or several hours in the refrigerator if possible, turning them from time to time.

Preheat the oven to 350°F.

Turn the ribs in their marinade, cover the dish with foil, and bake for 45 minutes. Raise the temperature to 375°F.

Remove the foil and turn the ribs again, basting them with the sauce. Return the dish to the oven, uncovered, and cook for 35 to 45 minutes, turning and basting the ribs 2 or 3 more times, until they are glossy and dark and coated in the caramelized sauce.

Spoon any remaining sauce from the dish over the ribs. Let stand until they are cool enough to pick up with your fingers, then dive in. Serve with steamed rice and wilted greens.

Leftover pork with fennel and new potatoes

Pork has a great affinity with fennel – the aniseedy note in the vegetable cuts the porky richness beautifully. This is one of those recipes that developed in an impromptu kind of way when I had various leftovers to deal with. It is now a firm favorite. Feel free to make the dish your own by playing fast and loose with the quantities, or adding some different ingredients. It also works well with chicken.

Serves 4

2 large fennel bulbs

3 tablespoons canola or olive oil

About 12 ounces cold cooked new potatoes, cut into chunky pieces

10 to 12 ounces cold roast pork loin, shoulder, or belly, thickly sliced, then cut or torn into strips

Juice of 1/2 lemon

Sea salt and freshly ground black pepper

A few coarsely torn fresh mint leaves (optional)

Trim the top and bottom from the fennel bulbs. Remove the tough outer layers and cut each bulb in half lengthwise. Then place each half, cut side down, on the board and cut into thick wedges, keeping a bit of the root base on each wedge if possible, as it will hold the layers together.

Heat the oil in a large frying pan, add the fennel with a pinch of salt, and sauté over medium heat for 6 to 7 minutes, until tender and golden, or even a little tinged with brown. Add the potatoes to the pan and fry for a few more minutes until they start to turn golden, then add the pork and fry, stirring a few times, until heated through.

Squeeze over the lemon juice, season with salt and pepper to taste, and scatter over the mint, if using. Serve right away.

Chicken and mushroom casserole with cider

Somewhere between a stew and a braise, this rich and warming dish is perfect to serve in autumn, perhaps with mushrooms you've gathered yourself. If you're feeling wild and gamey, you could do this with a cut-up wild rabbit instead of the chicken.

Serves 4

1 chicken, cut into 8 pieces, or 8 skin-on, bone-in chicken pieces (about 3 pounds total)

2 to 3 tablespoons all-purpose flour, seasoned with salt and pepper

3 to 4 tablespoons canola or olive oil

1 to 1¹/₂ cups dry or medium cider

1 tablespoon unsalted butter

12 ounces mushrooms (any kind you like, really), cut into large chunks or slices

1 bay leaf

1 large sprig of thyme

5 tablespoons heavy cream

2 teaspoons English mustard

Sea salt and freshly ground black pepper

1 tablespoon chopped fresh flat-leaf parsley

Dust the chicken pieces with the seasoned flour, shaking off the excess. Heat 2 tablespoons of the oil in a large frying pan over medium-high heat. Brown the chicken pieces well in the hot frying pan (in two batches if necessary, adding a little more oil for the second batch). Transfer the chicken to a large casserole dish or pot.

Add 1 cup cider to the frying pan to deglaze, letting it bubble for a minute or two as you scrape up the bits from the bottom. Pour over the chicken and top up with more cider as necessary, so the liquid comes about halfway up the chicken.

Heat the butter in another pan, add the mushrooms, and cook gently until their juices run. Add them with their juices to the chicken. Tuck the bay leaf and the thyme among the chicken and bring to a simmer. Cook uncovered, or partially covered, very gently over a low heat (or with the lid on in the oven preheated to 300°F) for about 1¹/₂ hours, until the chicken is cooked through and tender, turning the pieces halfway through cooking.

Remove the bay leaf and thyme. Pour the juices off into a pan, leaving the chicken and mushrooms in the casserole. Whisk the cream and mustard into the juices and bring to a simmer. Taste and adjust the seasoning, then pour back over the chicken. Bring the whole lot back to a simmer, and it's ready to serve.

Top with a sprinkling of chopped parsley and serve with creamy mashed or plain boiled potatoes and some steamed greens.

Sausage and root vegetable stew

A hearty dish to put on the table when it's cold and gray outside. It's very good with sausages but also works well with pork chops – or even both together. While pretty much a meal in itself, you could serve it with shredded cabbage or leeks with greens (page 300).

Serves 4

2 to 3 tablespoons canola or olive oil

6 good sausages, cut into large chunks, or 4 pork chops

1 glass of dry cider or white wine

2 onions, chopped

1 leek, white part only, sliced

2 celery stalks, chopped

1/4 to 1/2 celery root, cut into chunky cubes

2 boiling potatoes, peeled and cut into chunky cubes

1 large parsnip, cut into chunky cubes

1 bouquet garni (a bay leaf, 2 sprigs of thyme, and some parsley stems, tied together with string)

Sea salt and freshly ground black pepper

1 tablespoon chopped fresh flat-leaf parsley (optional)

Heat 1 tablespoon of the oil in a flameproof casserole or large saucepan. Add the sausages (and/or chops) and brown them well over medium heat – if you're using chops, you might need to do this in 2 batches. Transfer them to a dish.

Pour the cider or wine into the casserole and stir to deglaze, scraping to release any bits of caramelized meat from the bottom of the pan. Pour the pan juices into the dish with the sausages (and/or chops).

Heat another 1 to 2 tablespoons of oil in the casserole, add the onions, leek, and celery, and cook gently for 10 minutes or so, until softened. Then return the sausages (and/or chops) to the casserole with their juices and add the celery root, potatoes, and parsnip. Add in the bouquet garni, season with salt and pepper, and add enough water to almost cover everything. Bring to a very gentle simmer.

Cook uncovered, or partially covered, very gently over a low heat (or with the lid on in the oven preheated to 300°F) for about 1 hour, until everything is tender.

Take out the bouquet garni and check the seasoning. The potatoes should have started to break down and thicken the liquid a little. If not, just mash some of the vegetables against the side of the dish with a fork. Scatter over some chopped parsley, if you like, and serve.

Rabbit stew with tomato

This is a lovely way to cook rabbit. I've never met anyone who didn't like it, and as a bonus, it also works brilliantly with pheasants, partridges, and gray squirrels. You'll need to use two squirrels for this recipe.

You can adapt the recipe slightly to make a flavorsome rabbit ragù, to serve with pasta or soft polenta (see below).

Serves 3 as a main course, 6 as a starter

1 rabbit, cut up

Sea salt and freshly ground black pepper

2 tablespoons canola or olive oil

4 bacon slices, chopped, or about 3 ounces home-cured bacon belly (see page 186)

2 carrots, sliced

2 celery stalks, sliced

1 onion, sliced

2 bay leaves

A few sprigs of thyme

A few black peppercorns

2 garlic cloves, chopped

2 pounds tomatoes, peeled, seeded, and coarsely chopped, or 2 (14-ounce) cans chopped tomatoes

1/2 glass of white wine

Water or chicken or game stock, to cover

Season the rabbit pieces well with salt and pepper. Heat 1 tablespoon of oil in a large saucepan or flameproof casserole, add the bacon, and brown over medium-high heat. Then add the rabbit and cook, turning frequently, until browned all over.

Stir in the carrots, celery, and onion and let them take a little color too. Add the bay leaves, thyme, peppercorns, garlic, tomatoes, wine, and just enough water or stock to cover everything. Bring to a very low simmer and cook uncovered, or partially covered, very gently (or with the lid on in the oven preheated to 300°F) for about 1 1/2 hours, until the rabbit is very tender.

Take out the thyme and bay leaves. Taste the liquid and adjust the seasoning, then serve with plenty of fluffy mashed potatoes and some steamed greens, or with leeks with greens (page 300).

VARIATION

Rabbit ragù for pasta

After the long, slow simmer, take the rabbit pieces out of the sauce. Strain the sauce into a clean pan, pushing hard through a sieve so that plenty of the tender vegetables go through with the tomatoey liquid. It should be rich and flavorsome as it is, but if you want, you can simmer to reduce it further, until really thick. Adjust the seasoning. Pull all the rabbit meat off the bones, in chunks and shreds, wasting nothing. Return the picked meat to the sauce in the pan. Bring back to a simmer and finish by stirring in a tablespoon of butter.

Serve spooned on top of pappardelle or tagliatelle, or soft polenta if you like, in deep dishes. You can offer Parmesan to grate, but there are already plenty of great flavors here, and I like it better without.

Neck of lamb with lemon and barley

This beautifully simple recipe from my Russian friend Ivan Samarine is one I've revisited and reworked over the years. This latest incarnation makes an easy one-pot supper of it with the addition of pearl barley or pearled spelt and a few handfuls of shredded greens.

Neck is one of the cheapest cuts of lamb you can buy. It rewards thrifty, patient cooks for their trouble with loads of flavor and melting tenderness.

Serves 5 to 6

2 pounds neck of lamb on the bone, cut into chunks about $3/4$ inch thick

Sea salt and freshly ground black pepper

$1/4$ cup canola or olive oil

Juice of $1^1/2$ lemons

4 to 8 sprigs of thyme

Water or stock to cover

$1^1/2$ cups pearl barley or pearled spelt

About 8 ounces kale, mustard greens, or braising greens, coarsely chopped, tough stems removed

Preheat the oven to 300°F.

Season the lamb with salt and pepper. Heat the oil in a large, heavy flameproof casserole, add the lamb, and allow it to sizzle and spit for a few minutes, turning until it is lightly browned all over. Add the lemon juice, thyme, and some salt and pepper, then enough water or stock barely to cover the ingredients.

Bring to a gentle simmer, cover, and put in the oven. Cook for about 2 hours, then add the pearl barley or spelt and cook for a further 30 minutes. Remove the casserole from the oven and place on the stove top over medium heat.

Add the greens and simmer for a couple of minutes, until they are just cooked through. Serve with plenty of good bread to soak up the juices.

Baked chicken curry

This may not be quite as quick as opening a jar of curry sauce, but it tastes far better. If you want to put a little curry "banquet" together, you could serve this dish with flatbreads (page 78), lamb and squash curry (page 224), and green onion bhajis with radish raita (page 256).

Serves 6

2 heaping teaspoons cumin seeds

2 heaping teaspoons coriander seeds

1 heaping teaspoon fennel seeds

2 teaspoons ground turmeric

2 teaspoons ground fenugreek

1 large onion, coarsely chopped

3 large garlic cloves, coarsely chopped

1 large green chile, coarsely chopped

1 thumb-sized piece of fresh ginger, coarsely chopped

3 to 4 tablespoons sunflower or peanut oil

1 chicken, cut into 6 pieces, or 6 skin-on, bone-in chicken pieces (about 3 pounds total)

Sea salt and freshly ground black pepper

1 (14-ounce) can tomatoes

1 (14-ounce) can coconut milk

If you've got the time, toast the cumin, coriander, and fennel seeds in a dry frying pan for a minute or two, until fragrant. Grind the whole spices (toasted or otherwise) to a coarse powder in a spice grinder or with a mortar and pestle, then mix with the turmeric and fenugreek.

Put the onion, garlic, chile, and ginger in a food processor or blender. Blend to a coarse paste, stopping to scrape down the sides a few times.

Preheat the oven to 350°F.

Heat 2 tablespoons of the oil in a large frying pan over medium-high heat. Add half the chicken pieces, season well, and brown them all over, making sure you get the skin a good color. Transfer them to a large roasting dish, skin side up. Repeat with the remaining chicken pieces.

Reduce the heat under the frying pan, add the spice mix, and fry for a minute or two, then add the onion paste. Fry, stirring frequently, for about 5 minutes, until the paste is soft, fragrant, and reduced in volume. Add a little more oil if it seems to be sticking.

Add the tomatoes and coconut milk to the food processor (no need to wash it out first) and blend to combine. Pour into the frying pan and bring to a simmer, stirring constantly. Add 1 teaspoon of salt and a grinding of pepper, then pour the sauce over the chicken pieces. Make sure they are all coated in the sauce, then push most of the sauce off the top of the chicken – if there's too much sauce sitting on them, the skin won't brown in the oven.

Bake, uncovered, for 1 hour or until the chicken is cooked through and nicely browned on top, turning and basting it a couple of times. Serve with lots of basmati rice to soak up the sauce.

Lamb and squash curry

Slow simmering renders the lamb meltingly tender, while adding
a jar of chutney is a great shortcut to creating real depth of flavor.
Use a good, spicy, fruity chutney – if it's homemade, all the better.

I have no qualms about using a good-quality ready-made curry
powder or masala in a recipe like this, but including some freshly
ground cumin and coriander certainly enhances the flavor.

Serves 6 to 8

1 teaspoon cumin seeds

1 teaspoon coriander
seeds

3 pounds shoulder (or
neck) of lamb, trimmed
of excess fat and cut into
1¹/₂-inch cubes

Sea salt and freshly
ground black pepper

3 tablespoons canola or
sunflower oil

1 onion, sliced

2 garlic cloves, chopped

2¹/₂-inch piece of fresh
ginger, grated

3 to 6 teaspoons
medium-hot curry
powder, to taste

1 (16-ounce) jar of
chutney

1 bay leaf

Water or stock to cover

About 3 pounds butternut
squash, peeled and cut
into 1¹/₄-inch cubes

Cayenne pepper
(optional)

A handful of cilantro
sprigs (optional)

If you have time, lightly toast the cumin and coriander seeds
together in a dry frying pan for a minute or so, until fragrant. Then
grind them finely using a mortar and pestle or spice grinder. Season
the meat with the ground spice mix, a little salt, and black pepper.

Heat 2 tablespoons of the oil in a large, heavy frying pan, add the
seasoned meat, and cook over medium-high heat until browned all
over. Don't overcrowd the pan – you will probably need to do this
in batches. Transfer the browned meat to a large, heavy saucepan
using a slotted spoon.

Heat the remaining oil in the frying pan and add the onion, garlic,
ginger, and curry powder. Sauté for 4 to 5 minutes, until softened.
Add the spiced onion mixture into the pan with the meat, then add
the chutney, bay leaf, and enough water or stock just to cover. Bring
to a boil, reduce the heat, and simmer very gently, uncovered, for
1 hour.

Add the squash and cook 1 hour longer, until the lamb is very tender.
Adjust the seasoning, if required – if you want a hotter curry, you
could add a good pinch of cayenne. Serve with flatbreads (page 78)
and/or rice, and a scattering of cilantro sprigs if you like.

Stewed venison with juniper and bay

Juniper's pungent, bracing, and rather piney flavor makes it a natural companion to game and other richly flavored meats, and I particularly like it with venison.

A lot of recipes for venison stew require you to marinate the meat in advance, often in a vast amount of wine, in order to "tenderize" it. This is senseless, as it only pickles the meat and makes it drier. It is long, slow cooking that will tenderize it, and the fat oozing slowly from the bacon that will help to keep it moist.

Serves 6

2 tablespoons canola or sunflower oil, or drippings

8 ounces home-cured pork belly (see page 186) or commercial pancetta, cut into chunky cubes

3 pounds venison neck and shoulder meat, cut into large chunks

2 onions, finely sliced

2 to 3 large carrots, cut into big chunks

2 celery stalks, sliced

6 to 10 juniper berries, crushed slightly

2 bay leaves

A large sprig of thyme

At least 2 cups beef, venison, chicken, or game stock

$^2/_3$ cup red wine

Sea salt and freshly ground black pepper

Heat 1 tablespoon of the oil or drippings in a large, heavy frying pan, add the bacon, and fry until it is lightly browned and the fat runs. Transfer to a flameproof casserole dish. Now brown the venison in the same pan, in batches, transferring it to the casserole as soon as it's well colored.

Add the remaining oil or drippings to the frying pan, then add the onions and cook until soft but not colored. Add the carrots and celery and cook, stirring often, for 5 minutes. Transfer to the casserole and add the juniper berries, bay leaves, and thyme.

Pour a little of the stock into the frying pan and stir well for a few minutes to deglaze the pan, then add this to the casserole too. Pour over the remaining stock and the wine, adding a little water too, if you need it – the liquid should cover the meat by a good inch. Season with pepper, but no salt, as the bacon will be quite salty.

Bring to a simmer and cook, uncovered, at a very low simmer for 2 to 3 hours, until the meat is completely tender, skimming any scum off the top as you go along. You can also cook it in a low oven, about 250°F, with a lid on.

When the meat is cooked, taste the stew and season. The juice will be thin but well flavored; if you prefer a thicker sauce, you can strain the liquid off the meat and boil to reduce and thicken it, then return it to the pan. Serve the stew with a dollop of good buttery mashed potatoes and some steamed cabbage, kale, or other greens.

Oxtail stew with cinnamon and star anise

Succulent and tender oxtail, slowly braised with lots of onions and red wine, is always a treat. Cinnamon and star anise give it an extra flavor dimension that cuts the richness a little. This recipe works well with lamb shanks, and shanks or shoulder of veal and venison too, though with these you'll probably want to leave out the chocolate. The stew improves with keeping, so if you can, make it a day or two in advance.

Serves 6 to 8

4 pounds oxtail (about 2 tails), cut into slices 1½ to 2 inches thick

Sea salt and freshly ground black pepper

2 tablespoons sunflower or peanut oil

3 onions, sliced

1 bottle of red wine

2 to 3 cinnamon sticks

2 star anise pods

2 bay leaves

¼ teaspoon black peppercorns

Thinly pared zest of 1 orange

3 to 4 cups beef stock

1 ounce dark chocolate (about 70 percent cocoa solids; optional)

1 to 2 tablespoons chopped fresh flat-leaf parsley (optional)

Season the oxtail with salt and pepper. Heat the oil in a large, heavy flameproof casserole and fry the meat over medium-high heat in batches, so as not to overcrowd the pan, until browned on all sides. Remove with a slotted spoon and set aside.

Reduce the heat to low and gently cook the onions in the casserole for 15 to 20 minutes, until soft and translucent. Return the meat, raise the heat, then pour in the wine and let it bubble until slightly reduced. Add the cinnamon, star anise, bay leaves, peppercorns, orange zest, and enough stock just to cover the meat.

Bring to a slow simmer and cook very gently, partially covered, for about 3 hours, stirring occasionally and adding more stock as necessary to keep the oxtail moist. When it is ready, the meat should be falling off the bone. (You can also cook it in a low oven at 250°F with a lid on, if it's more convenient.)

Drain the meat in a colander set over a bowl to catch the liquid, then pass the liquid through a fine sieve into a clean pan. Boil until slightly thickened and glossy, then skim off most of the fat. If you'd like to take the meat off the bones, do so once it's cooled a bit. Discard the cinnamon, star anise, and bay leaves, return the meat to the pan, then stir in the chocolate, if using.

If serving right away, warm through; otherwise, let cool and keep in the fridge for a day or two, then reheat slowly and simmer for a minute or two. Check the seasoning before serving with creamy mashed potatoes or noodles and a scattering of chopped parsley, if you like.

Beef shanks with ginger and soy

This is based on one of my recipes for spareribs or pork belly, which turns out to work brilliantly with beef shanks too. Don't be tempted to trim any of the sinewy parts from the meat – they are vital for the final, full-bodied, gelatinous texture.

Serves 4

2 tablespoons sunflower or peanut oil, or beef fat

About 3 pounds beef shanks, cut into $^3/_4$-inch-thick slices, either on or off the bone

Sea salt and freshly ground black pepper

6 large garlic cloves, thinly sliced

2 thumb-sized nuggets of fresh ginger, thinly sliced

3 tablespoons tart fruit jam or jelly, such as red currant, plum, or crabapple

$^2/_3$ cup soy sauce

$1^1/_2$ to 2 cups apple juice

2 tablespoons cider vinegar

2 medium-hot fresh or dried chiles

Preheat the oven to 250°F.

Heat the oil or fat in a wide, heavy flameproof casserole. Season the pieces of meat with salt and pepper and brown them in batches, so you don't overcrowd the pan, turning them to color all over. Remove each batch and set aside while you brown the rest. The meat may curl up a bit as the membranes contract with the heat, especially if the slices are on the bone; snipping the membranes will help release the tension and flatten the meat out again. Once the beef is browned, remove it from the casserole and set aside on a plate.

Reduce the heat to low, add the garlic and ginger to the casserole, and cook gently until softened but not colored. Add the jam or jelly and soy sauce, mix well, then return the meat to the casserole, in a single layer if possible. Pour in enough apple juice barely to cover the meat. Add the vinegar, whole chiles, and a few grinds of black pepper, then cover and place in the oven. Cook for $2^1/2$ to 3 hours, until the meat is completely tender.

The garlic and ginger should just about hold their shape and should be eaten with the meat. The chiles will have done their job and can be discarded – or nibbled by anyone brave enough. Serve with noodles and steamed greens.

Roast chicken with pearl barley or spelt

I don't often stuff a chicken, but when I do I like the stuffing to provide a full accompaniment to the meat. And that's why I love this recipe. The pearl barley (or pearled spelt) makes a kind of risotto inside the chicken and takes on a mildly gamey flavor.

It's important to make sure the chicken is at room temperature before it is stuffed, and to put the stuffing inside while it's still hot. This gets the cooking off to a good start and helps to ensure the bird cooks evenly.

Serves 6

1 teaspoon cumin seeds

$^1/_2$ teaspoon caraway seeds

1 tablespoon canola or olive oil

1 onion, finely chopped

1 garlic clove, finely chopped

$^2/_3$ cup pearl barley or pearled spelt

2 cups chicken stock

6 to 8 dates or dried apricots, chopped

Grated zest and juice of 1 lemon

3 tablespoons finely chopped fresh flat-leaf parsley

A handful of walnuts, toasted and coarsely chopped (optional)

Sea salt and freshly ground black pepper

1 large chicken (4 to 5 pounds), at room temperature

3 tablespoons unsalted butter, softened

Toast the seeds in a small frying pan over medium heat for a minute or so, until fragrant (this isn't essential, but it does boost the flavor). Grind to a coarse powder using a mortar and pestle.

Heat the oil in a large saucepan, add the onion, and sauté for about 10 minutes, until soft and translucent. Add the garlic and sauté for a couple of minutes, then add the ground spices, along with the barley or spelt, and stir until well combined. Pour in the stock and bring to a boil. Reduce the heat and simmer, uncovered, stirring occasionally, until the grain is tender and most of the liquid has been absorbed – this will take 20 to 25 minutes for spelt, a little longer for barley. If the mixture begins to look dry, top it up with boiling water. Remove from the heat and stir in the dates or apricots, lemon zest and juice, parsley, and walnuts, if using, plus salt and pepper to taste.

Preheat the oven to 400°F. Undo any trussing on the chicken, take out the giblets if they're inside (save them to make stock) and pull the legs away from the body a little to help hot air circulate. Stuff the chicken with about half of the hot barley or spelt mixture – the cavity should be no more than two-thirds full, as the stuffing will expand in the oven. Put the chicken into a roasting dish, smear the butter over the breast and legs, and season with salt and pepper.

Pour a glass of hot water into the dish, cover loosely with foil, and place in the oven. Roast for 30 minutes, then uncover, baste the chicken with the buttery juices, and return to the oven. Turn down to 350°F and cook for a further 45 minutes to 1 hour, raising the heat for the last 10 minutes if you want the skin a little browner and crisper. Check the bird is cooked by piercing the thigh close to the bone with a sharp knife – the juices should run clear. Let rest in a warm place for 20 minutes before carving. The rest of the barley or spelt can be reheated gently (or left at room temperature) and served alongside the chicken.

Serve each portion of chicken with a generous spoonful of the stuffing, plus juices from the dish and perhaps some wilted greens or a salad.

Pot-roast pheasant with chorizo, butter beans, and parsley

Pheasant has a slight tendency to dryness, but pot-roasting it like this, with plenty of rich chorizo to provide a little fat and extra flavor, ensures a very satisfying result. The butter beans are a fine addition: they soak up all the flavors of the meat, wine, and herbs, and then you can mash them deliciously into the juices on your plate.

If you prefer, you can cut up the pheasants and brown the individual pieces rather than the whole birds. This recipe works brilliantly for a couple of cut-up rabbits, too.

Serves 4

1 tablespoon unsalted butter

3 tablespoons canola or olive oil

2 onions, finely sliced

4 garlic cloves, finely sliced

A few sprigs of thyme

2 bay leaves

2 oven-ready pheasants

Sea salt and freshly ground black pepper

10 ounces Spanish chorizo, skin removed and cut into ³/₄-inch chunks, or use Tupperware Mexican chorizo (page 206), crumbled into small nuggets

1²/₃ cups white wine

2 cups vegetable, chicken, or light pheasant stock

1 (14-ounce) can butter beans, drained and rinsed

A good handful of flat-leaf parsley, chopped

Preheat the oven to 300°F.

Place a large flameproof casserole (one that will accommodate both birds) over medium heat and heat the butter with 1 tablespoon of the oil until foaming. Add the onions, garlic, thyme, and bay leaves and cook for 10 minutes, until the onions are soft and slightly golden.

Heat the remaining oil in a large frying pan. Season the pheasants all over with salt and pepper, add to the pan, and brown on all sides over high heat for 3 to 4 minutes. Transfer to the casserole. Add the chorizo to the frying pan and fry for 3 to 4 minutes, until browned, then add to the casserole too.

Deglaze the frying pan by pouring in a little of the wine and stirring to scrape up any bits from the bottom of the pan. Add to the pheasants with the rest of the wine, the stock, and the butter beans. The liquid doesn't need to cover the birds, but it should come at least halfway up. Bring to a simmer, cover, and place in the oven. Cook for 2 hours, until the birds are tender.

Remove the pheasants from the casserole and let rest in a warm place for 15 to 20 minutes. If the chorizo has released a lot of fat, skim some off the juices in the pan. Add the parsley to the casserole and season to taste. Cut the birds into halves or quarters and divide among 4 warm plates. Spoon over the chorizo, beans, and sauce, and serve with mashed potatoes or lots of bread.

Slow-roast beef brisket with potatoes and onions

Brisket's open-grained texture and depth of flavor make it perfect for slow cooking. Don't let the butcher trim off too much fat – a certain amount is needed in order to achieve the final full-bodied result. It makes an easy Sunday lunch – you'll need to put the meat into the oven first thing in the morning, but then you can more or less leave it alone until lunchtime. Use any leftovers for sandwiches during the week.

Serves 6 to 8

4- to 5-pound piece of boned, rolled beef brisket, tied with string

4 to 5 garlic cloves, coarsely chopped

A good handful of thyme sprigs

2 to 3 tablespoons canola or olive oil

Sea salt and freshly ground black pepper

2 to 2¹/₂ pounds potatoes, peeled and cut into 1¹/₂-inch chunks

1 pound small onions or shallots, peeled

Preheat the oven to 400°F.

Put the tied brisket in a large roasting pan and tuck the garlic and thyme inside and under it. Massage the oil into the meat, then season well with salt and pepper. Place in the oven and roast for 30 minutes, then take it out of the oven. Turn the temperature down to 300°F, cover the meat with foil, and return it to the oven for 4 hours, by which time it should be very tender.

Baste the meat with its fatty juices, add the potatoes and onions to the roasting pan, and toss them in the juices too. Turn the oven up to 325°F and cook, uncovered, for a further hour, until the roast has crisped up and the spuds and onions are cooked through.

Serve the beef in thick slices, with the potatoes and onions. There won't be much in the way of juices, as they will have been absorbed by the vegetables, but any that remain should be spooned over the meat.

Roast breast of lamb with lemon and apricots

Breast of lamb is inexpensive yet full of flavor. It is one of those cuts that look a little unpromising, being an odd shape and quite fatty, but get the cooking right and it delivers a great result (as you'll see in the photographs on the following pages). Here, the lamb is rolled around a sweet-sharp stuffing that balances its richness. It is then given a long, slow cook to tenderize the meat.

Serves 6

For the stuffing:

1 tablespoon unsalted butter

3 or 4 small shallots, chopped

3 garlic cloves, crushed

2 cups fresh bread crumbs

²/₃ cup dried apricots, chopped

Grated zest of 3 lemons

1 tablespoon thyme leaves

Sea salt and freshly ground black pepper

1 egg, lightly beaten

2 breasts of lamb, boned, any skin and surplus fat removed

2 to 3 fennel bulbs, cut into 6 wedges each

2 large onions, cut into 4 wedges each, or 4 small ones, cut in half

2 lemons (the ones you've zested for the stuffing), cut into quarters

Sea salt and freshly ground black pepper

A little white wine or water (optional)

Preheat the oven to 400°F.

First, make the stuffing. Melt the butter in a small pan, add the shallots and garlic, and cook gently until soft but not colored. Mix the bread crumbs with the apricots, lemon zest, thyme, shallot mixture, and plenty of salt and pepper. Stir in enough egg to bind the mixture lightly.

Lay the breasts of lamb flat on a board and season well. Divide the stuffing between them and spread it evenly, leaving a little space at the edges and at each end. Roll the breasts up tightly, starting at a pointed end, and tie each one in 3 or 4 places with string.

Place the two lamb rolls side by side in a roasting pan. Put into the oven and cook for 30 minutes. Remove from the oven and turn the temperature down to 300°F. Lift the lamb rolls out onto a board. Scatter the fennel, onions, and lemon wedges in the roasting pan, turn in the oily pan juices, and season with salt and pepper.

Place the lamb rolls on top and return to the oven. Cook for about 1¹/₂ hours, turning the fennel, onions, and lemons occasionally, until both meat and vegetables are tender. Check from time to time and sprinkle the vegetables with a little white wine or water if they appear a little dry. If everything seems to be browning too quickly, cover the whole dish with foil.

Transfer the lamb to a warm serving plate and let rest in a warm place for about 15 minutes. Cut the lamb into thick slices and arrange on warm plates with the roasted vegetables and lemons. Spoon over any juices from the roasting pan (they'll be fatty, but tasty). Serve with rice or couscous.

Slow-roast shoulder of lamb with merguez spices

Lamb shoulder is an underrated cut. Treated to a very long, slow roast with pungent spices, it offers meltingly soft, flavorful meat that you can pull off the bone easily – as well as a pool of rich juices. This recipe works best with larger, more mature lambs. You can also rub the spice paste on the inside of a boned lamb shoulder, then roll and tie it. Give it an initial 30 minutes at a high temperature (as below), then roast at 325°F for 2^1/$_2$ hours.

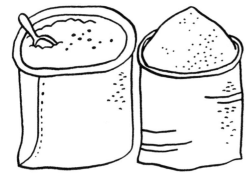

Serves 6 to 10, depending on the size of the roast

For the spice paste:
1 teaspoon cumin seeds
1 teaspoon coriander seeds
1 teaspoon fennel seeds
^{1}/$_2$ cinnamon stick, broken up
1 teaspoon black peppercorns
A pinch of cayenne pepper or chile powder
2 teaspoons sweet smoked paprika
2 garlic cloves, finely chopped
Leaves from 2 large rosemary sprigs, finely chopped
2 teaspoons sea salt
2 tablespoons olive oil

1 shoulder of mature lamb, on the bone

Preheat the oven to 425°F.

If you have time, toast the cumin, coriander, fennel seeds, cinnamon, and peppercorns in a dry frying pan over medium heat for a minute or so, until fragrant (this boosts the flavor but isn't essential). Crush to a coarse powder using a mortar and pestle, then combine with the cayenne or chile powder, paprika, garlic, rosemary, salt, and olive oil.

Lightly score the skin of the meat with a sharp knife, making shallow slashes about ^{1}/$_8$ inch deep and ^{3}/$_4$ inch apart. Rub half the spice paste all over the lamb shoulder, underneath as well as on top, and especially into the cuts. Put into a large roasting pan and place in the oven. Roast for 30 minutes.

Remove from the oven and rub the remaining spice paste over the meat using the back of a wooden spoon. Pour a glass of water into the pan (not over the meat), cover with foil, and return to the oven. Reduce the heat to 250°F and cook for 6 hours, or until the meat is very tender and falling off the bone. You can add another glass of water halfway through, to keep the pan juices from scorching.

Transfer the lamb to a warm serving plate. Skim the excess fat off the juices in the pan. Tear the meat into thick shreds and serve with the juices spooned over. Simple accompaniments are all you need: boiled new potatoes (in summer) or some roasted squash (in winter) and a dish of shredded cabbage, greens, or kale would be ideal.

Roast thick end of pork belly with coriander and fennel crackling

This cut of pork is fantastically forgiving. It's quite fatty, which means you can keep cooking it until the crackling reaches a point of exquisite crunchiness without fear of the meat drying out. The wonderfully aromatic flavor of the coriander and fennel seeds really enhances the flavor of the pork. If you've got one or other of the spices but not both, that's fine.

Serves 6

1 tablespoon coriander seeds

2 teaspoons fennel seeds

1 piece of thick-end pork belly (the last 6 ribs), skin scored by your butcher if possible

Sea salt and freshly ground black pepper

Preheat the oven to 425°F.

Put the coriander and fennel seeds in a mortar and bash lightly with the pestle a few times. You don't need to grind them to a powder, just crack them a bit to release the aromas.

If the butcher hasn't already scored the skin of the meat, do it yourself with a sharp knife. Rub the skin with salt, pepper, and a little more than half the cracked seeds, getting the seasonings right into the cracks.

Scatter the remaining seeds in a roasting pan, put the meat on top, and place in the oven. Roast for 30 minutes, then turn the temperature down to 350°F and cook for about $1^1/2$ hours, until the juices run clear when the meat is pierced with a skewer and the skin has crackled to an irresistible golden brown. If the crackling is reluctant, crank up the heat again, as high as you like, and check every few minutes till it's done. Leave to rest, uncovered, in a warm place for 20 minutes.

Remove the crackling from the pork before carving, then cut the roast into thick slices and break up the crackling into portions. Serve with applesauce (page 339), mashed potatoes, and steamed greens or cabbage. Leftovers are equally delicious cold, with plenty of homemade fruity chutney.

Slow-roast boned shoulder of pork with chestnut stuffing

Shoulder of pork, sometimes confusingly also called pork butt or Boston butt, is economical and very tasty. It stands up well to long, slow cooking and is ideal for stuffing. You'll need a sizable roast for this – anything under 4 pounds really isn't worth stuffing.

Serves 8 to 10

For the chestnut stuffing:

1 tablespoon unsalted butter

1 onion, finely chopped

2 to 3 celery stalks, finely chopped

2 Golden Delicious apples, peeled, cored, and finely chopped

1 pound peeled cooked chestnuts, coarsely mashed with a fork

1 tablespoon finely chopped fresh sage, thyme, or rosemary

Finely grated zest of 1 lemon

1 cup fresh white bread crumbs

1 egg, beaten

Sea salt and freshly ground black pepper

1 boned shoulder of pork, 4 to 6 pounds (ask your butcher to score the skin for you, if possible)

A few sprigs of thyme

3 tablespoons canola or olive oil

Sea salt and freshly ground black pepper

A glass of dry cider

1 teaspoon all-purpose flour

1 to $1^{1}/_{3}$ cups chicken or pork stock

To make the stuffing, melt the butter in a large saucepan, add the onion and celery, and cook gently for 10 to 15 minutes, until softened. Remove from the heat, add the apples, chestnuts, herbs, lemon zest, bread crumbs, and egg, season well, and mix thoroughly. Let cool.

Preheat the oven to 425°F.

Lay out the boned pork shoulder, skin side up, on a work surface. If the butcher hasn't already done so, score the skin at $^{1}/_{2}$-inch intervals with a sharp knife. Turn the meat over and spread the stuffing evenly over the flesh, leaving a margin around the edge. You will have some stuffing left over – this can be packed into a buttered ovenproof dish and put in the oven for the last 30 minutes of the pork's cooking time.

Roll up the meat and tie securely in several places with string. Put it into a smallish roasting pan (this ensures the juices don't reduce and blacken too much) and tuck the thyme underneath it. Drizzle the oil over the skin, season well with salt and pepper, then massage the oil and seasoning into the skin with your fingers. Put in the oven for a 30-minute "sizzle."

Remove from the oven, pour the cider and a glass of water into the dish, and turn the temperature down to 300°F. Cook for another 4 to 5 hours until the meat is very tender, then raise the heat to 375°F and roast for another 20 to 30 minutes to crisp up the crackling. Transfer the pork to a warm dish and let rest, uncovered, in a warm place for 20 minutes.

Pour off most of the fat from the roasting juices in the pan. Place the pan over low heat, sprinkle in the flour, and stir it into the juices to form a smooth paste. Add as much stock as you need to form a thin but tasty gravy, bring to a simmer, and cook for a few minutes. Taste and adjust the seasoning, then pour into a warm gravy bowl.

Cut the crackling from the pork and break it into large pieces. The pork should be tender enough to spoon or tear into thick shreds. Serve with the crackling, gravy, creamy mashed potatoes, and sautéed leeks or shredded savoy cabbage (or both – see page 300).

vegetables galore

The fact that there are way more recipes here than in any other

chapter is no coincidence. Vegetables also play a key role in the Weekday Lunch (Box) chapter, and almost every meat or fish recipe in the book contains at least a suggestion of the kind of vegetables it might be nice to serve it up with. So you'd be right to conclude that I'm serious about vegetables. In fact, I'd go as far as to say that vegetables are, quite simply, the most important food there is. I couldn't even contemplate giving them up. Ever. But let's not get too serious. The last thing I want to do is come over all hair-shirted, virtuous, and ascetic about vegetables. Frankly, there's no need. Because not only should they give us great goodness but they should – must – give us untold pleasure as well.

As I have long been pointing out, vegetables provide the essential variety that is the spice of life in any well-tended kitchen. The range of tastes, textures, and aromas that can be conjured from the roots, shoots, fruits, stems, leaves, seeds, and flowers that we call vegetables is almost beyond limit, and certainly beyond the scope of a single lifetime to explore and experience fully. This becomes more obviously the case when you include all the herbs and spices, fresh and dried, whole and ground, that derive from edible plants. But even if you put that lot on one side, as a special case, your ordinary, nonexotic, common or garden, locally grown, seasonally available vegetables will still do you proud.

There are so many types of vegetables being grown by professionals and amateurs these days, and the subtly differentiating varieties within each type run into the thousands. So if you think you don't like peas, for example, then perhaps you just haven't found the particular pea you like.

The truth is, if ever you are tempted to put the words *vegetables* and *boring* into the same sentence, then something must be not quite right, either in your head or in your kitchen (unless, of course, your sentence is "Vegetables are never boring," to which I would add, "but sometimes cooks are").

I wouldn't presume to judge you guilty of not doing justice to your vegetables on the odd occasion, because that would make me a hypocrite. We are all guilty of it once in a while. The aim of this chapter is to unburden you of that guilt by making it a very rare occurrence indeed. In its place, I want you to feel pride and pleasure, and a sense of possibility oozing from every vegetable-laden corner of your kitchen.

To help make that happen, the guiding principle in the recipes that follow is quite simple: to bring out the very best in each vegetable and make it so irresistibly delicious that you would happily eat it on its own (and perhaps even more happily with something else). Sometimes this means applying to a familiar vegetable a cooking method you may not have tried before: have you ever roasted skin-on wedges of squash as though they were spuds? Or made a well-buttered purée of parsnips? Or grilled a lettuce? Often it means choosing one or two simple additional flavorings: some garlic with your runner beans, a few capers and a little handful of chopped mint with your lovely sliced ripe tomatoes, a yogurty dressing on sliced radishes . . .

Once this process of mild but purposeful elaboration is underway, you'll soon appreciate the extraordinary versatility of vegetables. It struck me only recently that another way of expressing this commitment to making a bit more of, and going a little bit further with, the many vegetables we're in danger of taking for granted is to embrace the notion that there is no vegetable that can't be made the star of a simple dish. It might take a cunning combination of clever cooking methods plus complementary co-stars, but when you put together a dish of kale with chestnuts and bacon, or broccoli with chorizo and soft-boiled egg, or beets with goat cheese and red currants, you'll soon see that the vegetable is in every case the *sine qua non* of the dish in question, and thoroughly deserves its top billing.

This is the thinking that has been applied to all the recipes that follow. Although a fair few of them are principally intended as accompaniments (the three-root mash on page 308 is a killer with roast lamb or game), I'm nevertheless vouching for all of them as stand-alone pleasures (I've served the same mash as a first course, drizzled with canola oil and scattered with shavings of hard goat cheese). Many can be served up as delightful starters or offered, with one or two other dishes, as substantial main courses. One pleasure I hope you'll explore is putting together a simple spread of seasonal vegetable dishes as a kind of meze, or vegetable banquet. You may want it to be strictly vegetarian, or you may not. But it will certainly be the abundance of the season's crop you are celebrating rather than the acquisition of some special piece of meat.

So, before we dive into the recipes and immerse ourselves in the sheer fecundity of what we can take from our soil and use in our kitchens, a few thoughts on where and how you might acquire your vegetables. There are many options open to the modern cook, some quite modern in themselves (ordering vegetables on the Internet is a method on the march), but underlying all the best options is one time-honored principle that can never be cast aside: try to minimize the time and distance between the reaping and the eating, the harvest and the supper.

It could hardly be simpler. Freshly picked seasonal vegetables that haven't traveled far will be sweeter, more flavorsome, and better for you. Time isn't always of the essence. Some vegetables – potatoes, carrots, and onions, for example – store well, mainly because, if kept in the right environment (cool and dark), they remain alive, capable of reproducing when released from their dormant state. But even for these vegetables, long-distance travel will never be conducive to fine quality. It will at best be neutral (though, of course, it will never be neutral to the environment).

Obviously, for all the above reasons, vegetables that you grow yourself are the best you can ever hope to cook with. Add the inescapable psychological factor – the immeasurable pleasure of raising your own food from seed to plate – and it's clear that the home harvest is a kind of miracle food for both body and soul. And while I appreciate that not everyone can grow enough to make a significant contribution to the family diet, I do believe that almost everyone can grow something they can eat – even if it's just a few herbs in a window box, a one-crop wonder such as a tomato plant in a pot, or a trash can full of potatoes. Never underestimate the power of such a project, however small, to bring you joy. It will also do something else very useful: it will serve as a benchmark, both real and in principle, for the vegetables you buy.

So where will they come from? With luck, from the nearest purveyor of top-quality, locally grown seasonal fruit and vegetables. That might be a grocery store on the main street of your nearest town or a nearby farmers' market. Or it may very well be the supermarket. If it is, then you are by no means doomed to second-rate vegetables. The road and air miles supermarkets eat up in transporting fresh produce around the world and around the country are a source of concern, but it is still possible to find good, fresh local vegetables in many of our supermarkets. Such is the speed of their operations that the produce is often in pretty good shape.

The best strategy in a supermarket is to favor what is in season and has not traveled very far. The more shoppers choose this kind of fresh produce over imported out-of-season exotics (especially ones that have traveled by air), the more supermarkets will commit to supporting the farmers who are ready and willing to supply the vast majority of the vegetables we need.

Having said that, there is another way to get a regular supply of top-quality vegetables. If you're not a customer already, I would heartily recommend giving a farm-box scheme a go (called a Community Supported Agriculture, or CSA, plan in the States). Here, you sign up for a weekly delivery from an organic farm, taking whatever fruits and vegetables are in season at the time. We sign up for a farm-box delivery at home during the colder months (my bid for self-sufficiency in winter vegetables is improving every year, but I still haven't got it licked). Ours also brings us local organic milk, and organic and fair trade "exotic essentials" – the bananas, oranges, lemons, and avocados that, like most families, we would find it hard to do without.

As a box-scheme veteran, let me offer you a few tips: always tackle the leafy greens and salads within the first few days of your box's (or bushel basket's) arrival. Try to use up everything in the box before the next one arrives. And never despair at the mounting frequency of roots, cabbages, and kales as the winter wears on. With the recipes that are coming up, you won't be short of exciting and surprising ways to make them sing for your supper.

Asparagus soldiers with soft-boiled egg hollandaise

This is a quick and rather nifty way to enjoy the combination of tender, fresh asparagus and a buttery, eggy sauce without any of the work that a proper hollandaise requires. And it's an awful lot of fun to eat. As with all asparagus recipes, get the very freshest spears you can.

Serves 2

About 20 asparagus spears

2 large eggs, at room temperature

1 tablespoon unsalted butter

A little cider vinegar

Sea salt and freshly ground black pepper

Prepare the asparagus by snapping off any woody ends (the spears will break naturally where they are tender). You could steam the asparagus spears above the boiling eggs – if very freshly cut, they will take about the same amount of time. Otherwise, simmer or steam the asparagus separately until tender but not too floppy – 8 minutes at the most for the thickest stems. Time them so they are ready just ahead of the eggs.

Meanwhile, bring another pan of water to a boil. Carefully lower in the eggs and simmer for about 4 minutes (the yolks must be quite runny or the hollandaise effect will be hard to achieve).

Drain the asparagus well as soon as it is cooked and divide the spears between 2 warm plates. Transfer the eggs to egg cups and put them on the plates with the asparagus.

To eat, crack the egg and take off enough of the top to expose the runny yolk. Drop a little butter, a few drops of cider vinegar, and some salt and pepper into the yolk, stir with a bit of asparagus, dip, and eat. You can add a little more butter, vinegar, and seasoning as you go. Some brown bread and butter won't go amiss.

Green onion bhajis with radish raita

Crisp, light, and delicate, these are homemade versions of bhajis, spicy Indian snacks popular in the UK. Served with the minted radish raita, they make a truly summery snack or smart starter.

Obviously this is a dish for those who are not afraid of the deep-fat fryer. But once you've sliced the green onions and assembled the ingredients for the batter, it comes together pretty easily.

Serves 4 to 6

For the radish raita:
1 bunch firm radishes, trimmed
$2/3$ cup fresh, soft goat cheese
$1^1/4$ cups plain yogurt
2 to 3 teaspoons chopped fresh mint
Sea salt and freshly ground black pepper

5 green onions, trimmed
$2/3$ cup chickpea flour (gram or besan flour)
$1/4$ cup all-purpose flour
$1/2$ teaspoon ground coriander
$1/2$ teaspoon fine sea salt
A good pinch of cayenne pepper
A good pinch of black onion (nigella or kalonji) seeds
3 tablespoons finely chopped fresh cilantro, plus extra to serve if you like
$1/3$ to $1/2$ cup beer or water
Sunflower or peanut oil for deep-frying

Make the raita first. Slice the radishes into $1/16$-inch-thick disks. Place the goat cheese in a small bowl and mash well with a fork, then mix in the yogurt a little at a time. The cheese doesn't have to be blended smoothly with the yogurt – in fact, it's nice if there are a few little lumps. Fold in the radishes and mint and season to taste. Set aside.

Finely slice the green onions on the diagonal and set aside. Sift the flours, ground coriander, salt, and cayenne into a bowl. Mix in the black onion seeds and chopped cilantro, then gradually pour in the beer or water, stirring as you go, until you have a smooth, thick batter. You may not need all the liquid. Add the sliced green onions and stir until well coated.

Pour the oil into a deep, heavy saucepan (or a deep-fat fryer) to a depth of 3 to 4 inches and place over medium heat. The oil should be hot but not too hot, to allow the green onions and flour to cook through without the outside of the bhajis burning. Test the temperature by dropping in a cube of white bread: it should turn crisp and golden in about a minute – no faster.

Drop heaped teaspoonfuls of the batter into the oil and cook for 3 to 4 minutes, until deep golden brown. Don't overcrowd the pan; cook them in batches of 3 or 4, tops. Drain briefly on paper towels and then serve with the radish raita, sprinkling with a little chopped cilantro if you like.

Crudités with garlic and anchovy dressing

This punchy anchovy-based dressing – similar to the Italian classic *bagna cauda* – is a year-round favorite of mine and easy to whip up from the sort of ingredients you're likely to have in your pantry and fridge. It's a superb accompaniment to all kinds of vegetables – raw or cooked. I love it as a dip for crunchy summer crudités, but I also serve it as a dressing for steamed broccoli, cauliflower, and kale. It will keep happily in a jar in the fridge for at least a couple of weeks. It will probably separate, but can be reemulsified by shaking or whisking.

Serves 4

For the dressing:
2 anchovy fillets, drained
²/₃ cup olive oil
2 garlic cloves, peeled
Leaves from a sprig of thyme
A few fresh basil leaves (optional)
¹/₂ small red chile, or a pinch of red pepper flakes
1 teaspoon Dijon or English mustard
2 teaspoons cider vinegar or wine vinegar
A few grindings of black pepper

For the crudités:
A selection of raw baby vegetables, such as carrots, zucchini, beets, lettuce hearts, radishes, fresh young peas in pods, and tender celery stalks

For the dressing, simply blend all the ingredients together in a blender until completely smooth. Or, if you are using fresh chile, you might prefer to chop it very finely by hand, then stir it into the blended dressing to give it a little texture.

Let the dressing stand for half an hour or so, to allow the flavors to mingle and develop, then transfer to a bowl.

Prepare the crudités: Halve or quarter lengthwise the lettuce hearts and larger baby vegetables, such as zucchini and carrots. Leave the smaller ones, such as pea pods and radishes, whole. Arrange them on a platter and serve with the dressing.

Fava beans on toast

This is full of bittersweet and salty flavors, with the lovely, nubbly texture of the beans and bacon lubricated by a little oil and lemon juice . . . quite the nicest kind of the English classic, beans on toast.

Serves 2

1^1/$_2$ to 2 pounds young fava beans in the pod

1 tablespoon canola or olive oil

4 ounces pancetta or bacon, cut into ^{1}/$_4$-inch-thick strips

A small bunch of green onions, finely sliced

Juice of ^{1}/$_2$ lemon, or to taste

Sea salt and freshly ground black pepper

2 thick slices of bread (ideally sourdough)

Extra-virgin olive or more canola oil, to finish

Pod the fava beans, putting the large ones in one bowl and the smaller ones in another. Bring a large pan of water to a boil. Add the large beans, let the water return to a simmer and cook for 1 minute. Add the small beans and simmer for a further minute, 90 seconds tops. Drain the beans. Pop the large, thick-skinned ones out of their skins. Very small beans don't need to be skinned.

Place a frying pan over medium-high heat, add 1 tablespoon of oil, then the pancetta or bacon. Cook until just starting to crisp, then add the green onions and cook for a minute longer. Add the beans and toss to combine with the bacon and onions. Add lemon juice, salt, and pepper to taste.

Toast the bread and spoon the fava beans and bacon on top, along with any pan juices. Drizzle with a little oil, add a final squeeze of lemon, and serve.

VARIATION

Beans with sausage on toast

Replace the bacon with a similar quantity of good pork sausage – or try the Tupperware Mexican chorizo on page 206. Remove the skin from the sausage, tear the meat into lumps, then fry it until crisp, breaking it down into nuggets and crumbs as you do so. Add the green onions and beans and finish as above.

Lemony zucchini on toast

Zucchini are very prodigious – one minute you're wondering if you're ever going to see any peeking out from under the leaves in your garden, and the next minute you've got armfuls of them and your friends and neighbors are politely refusing to take any more off your hands. This is one of the ways in which I like to use up mine. Even if you don't grow your own, you should find an abundance of zucchini in farmers' markets and CSA baskets in midsummer.

As a quick, straight-from-the-garden lunch, this is hard to beat. The zucchini are wonderful served hot on toast, but they're just as good cold – as an addition to a couscous or bulgur wheat salad (page 117), or in pita bread with some soft goat cheese.

Serves 2

3 to 4 zucchini, about 1 pound in total

2 tablespoons canola or olive oil

Sea salt and freshly ground black pepper

1 small garlic clove, crushed

$^1/_4$ teaspoon fresh thyme leaves

Grated zest of $^1/_2$ lemon and $1^1/_2$ tablespoons juice

2 thick slices of bread

10 fresh basil leaves, cut into thin strips

Extra-virgin olive or more canola oil, to finish

Slice the zucchini into thin disks. Heat the oil in a large frying pan, add the zucchini with a large pinch of salt, and sauté over medium-high heat for about 5 minutes, until their moisture evaporates and they are just beginning to brown a little.

Stir in the garlic and thyme and cook for another minute or so, until the zucchini are a little softer and a little more colored. Stir in the lemon zest and juice. Season with a few grinds of pepper and some more salt.

Toast the bread. Remove the zucchini from the heat and add the basil. Tip the zucchini mixture with all its juices over the toast, drizzle on a little olive or canola oil, and dive in.

Grilled Little Gems and green onions with goat cheese

I love cooked lettuce – braised in stock, wilted into a risotto, puréed in soups, or, as here, subjected to the fierce heat of the grill. The lettuce softens deliciously, but forms a crisp, charred, pleasantly bitter outer surface. Combined with green onions and some salty cheese, this makes a wonderful summer starter.

If you don't want to use a grill, you can achieve very similar results with a grill pan indoors – just be sure to get it good and hot.

Serves 4

4 Little Gem (baby romaine) lettuces, halved

3 to 4 tablespoons olive or canola oil

12 green onions, trimmed

Sea salt and freshly ground black pepper

2 to 3 ounces fairly mature, crumbly goat cheese

Extra-virgin olive or more canola oil, to finish

When your grill is ready for cooking, brush the cut side of the lettuces with a little of the oil and place on the hot grill. After a minute or so, turn them over. Put the green onions, also brushed with oil, onto the grill alongside the lettuce. When both are nicely charred and slightly softened, divide them among 4 plates and sprinkle with some salt and pepper.

Use a vegetable peeler to shave the goat cheese over the lettuces – or, if it's a very crumbly type, crumble it. Drizzle over a little oil and serve.

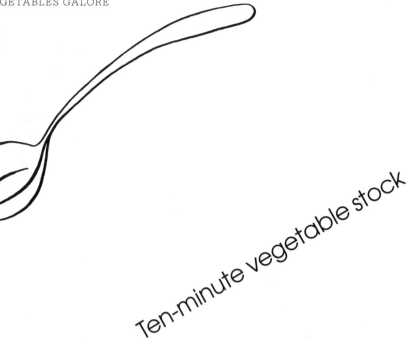

Ten-minute vegetable stock

Few things are more useful
in the kitchen than a pot of
good stock, and this simple,
light vegetable broth is
much quicker to make than
a meat, chicken, or fish stock.

Makes about 4 cups

1 large onion
1 large carrot
2 celery stalks
1 fat garlic clove
1 tablespoon sunflower
or canola oil
1 bay leaf, finely
shredded

Coarsely grate the vegetables and garlic or chop them coarsely in
a food processor.

Heat the oil in a saucepan and add the vegetables, garlic, and bay
leaf. Cover and cook gently for 5 minutes, until softened, then pour
4 cups of boiling water over the vegetables. Bring back to a boil,
reduce the heat, and simmer, uncovered, for 5 minutes.

Strain the stock and it's ready to use right away, or cool it and
refrigerate for a day or two until needed, or freeze.

Seven soups

Soups may be the epitome of thrifty, simple cooking – undemanding both to make and to eat – but that doesn't mean they ever have to be humble or dull. A good soup is a glorious thing, distilling the flavors of its principal ingredients, and the perfect way to show off whatever's fresh and in season at any given time of year. I hope you'll use this clutch of lovely recipes as a guide and an inspiration, and then experiment to your heart's content with the vegetables, herbs, and spices that get your juices flowing.

Potato and fennel soup

A lovely, soothing, creamy soup, like a faintly aniseedy vichyssoise. Served with one of the suggested toppings below, it's posh enough for a dinner party. If you're serving it on a hot summer's day, it's delicious chilled.

Serves 4

1 tablespoon canola or olive oil

1 tablespoon unsalted butter

1 large onion, chopped

1 celery stalk, chopped

1 garlic clove, chopped

3 large fennel bulbs, trimmed and chopped (feathery fronds saved, if they look good)

Sea salt and freshly ground black pepper

1 pound russet potatoes, peeled and coarsely chopped

About 3 cups chicken, fish, or vegetable stock (pages 192, 162, and 266 respectively)

6 tablespoons heavy cream or crème fraîche (optional)

Heat the oil and butter in a large saucepan and add the onion, celery, garlic, and fennel, plus a good pinch of salt. Stir well, then cover and cook gently for about 15 minutes, stirring occasionally. Add the potatoes and stock, bring to a boil, then reduce the heat and simmer, uncovered, for about 15 minutes, until the potatoes are tender.

Purée the soup in a blender and return to the pan (or use an immersion blender in the pan). Add a little more stock or water if it seems too thick. Stir in the cream, if you're using it, then season to taste. Reheat gently before serving.

This is delicious with any of the following toppings:

- The feathery fronds from the fennel, finely snipped and stirred into a little yogurt.

- Croutons or coarse bread crumbs fried in garlicky oil.

- Crumbled fresh goat cheese.

- Any of the pestos on page 132.

- Flakes of cooked smoked pollock or trout, or snippets of smoked salmon.

Pea soup

This soup is the essence of high summer, and an excellent way to use homegrown peas once they've passed the teeny-tiny, supersweet phase and are getting a bit big and "cannonbally." Store-bought peas, fresh or frozen, will work perfectly well too.

Serves 4

1 tablespoon unsalted butter

1 onion, chopped

1 garlic clove, chopped

1 celery stalk, chopped (optional)

A few fresh thyme leaves (optional)

1 pound fresh or frozen peas or petits pois

3 cups chicken or vegetable stock (pages 192 and 266 respectively)

Sea salt and freshly ground black pepper

Melt the butter in a large saucepan. Add the onion and garlic, and the celery and thyme, if using, then cover and cook gently, stirring often, for about 12 minutes, until soft. Stir in the peas and the stock. Bring to a boil, reduce the heat, then simmer, partially covered, until the peas are soft – this will take 3 to 8 minutes, depending on the size and mealiness of the peas.

Purée the soup in a blender and return it to the pan (or use an immersion blender to blend it in the pan). Add a little more stock or some water if it's too thick for your taste. Season well.

You can either reheat the soup and serve it hot or let it cool and chill it thoroughly to serve cold. Either way, you can, if you like, make it more elegant with one of the following garnishes:

- Fine shreds of fresh mint mixed with a little yogurt or crème fraîche.

- A swirl of cream and a sprinkling of snipped fresh chives.

- Fine slivers of prosciutto, or crisp-fried bacon.

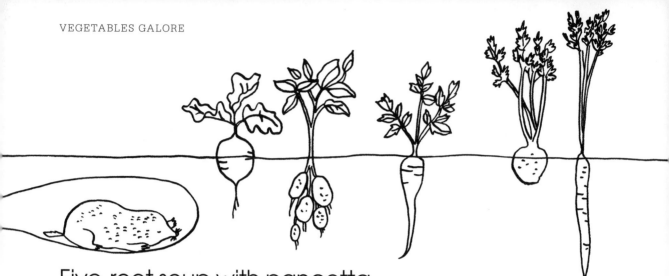

Five-root soup with pancetta

The key to success with this soup is to cut the root vegetables small and keep the pieces all about the same size so they cook evenly. It helps to be in a chopping mood when you make this one.

If you don't have any Cheddar at hand, or you want to go easy on the cheese, you can finish the soup with a drizzle of canola or olive oil instead. You could also leave out the pancetta to make a vegetarian version.

Serves 4 to 6

1 tablespoon canola
or olive oil

3 ounces pancetta, cut
into small dice

1 large onion, finely
chopped

1 cup finely diced carrots

1 cup finely diced
rutabaga

1 cup finely diced boiling
potatoes

1 cup finely diced
parsnip

1 cup finely diced
celery root

4 cups light vegetable or
chicken stock (pages 266
and 192 respectively)

Sea salt and freshly
ground black pepper

To serve:

Fresh chives, snipped

About ¾ cup grated
aged Cheddar cheese

Heat the oil in a large saucepan, add the pancetta, and cook gently until the fat runs and the pancetta starts to turn golden. Add the onion and cook for 10 to 15 minutes, until soft and golden. Add all the diced root vegetables, cover the pan, and let the whole mixture cook and soften for 10 minutes or so, stirring occasionally.

Pour in the stock and bring to a simmer. Cover and cook for about 15 minutes, until all the vegetables are tender.

Taste the soup and season accordingly. Ladle into warm bowls, scatter over some chives, and top with grated cheese. Serve right away, with some thick pieces of toast.

VARIATION

This soup is also very good whizzed in a blender until smooth. Then I like to serve it topped with a dash of pesto, such as the parsley and walnut pesto on page 132.

Beet and cumin soup with spiced yogurt

Sweet beets and earthy cumin are a very seductive combination (see also beet and walnut hummus, page 127).

Served hot or cold, this soup has been known to win over even the most beet-phobic guests. Don't use the spiced yogurt just for the soup, either. It's very good with fried leftover roast chicken or lamb, either with rice or piled into pita bread with shredded lettuce.

Serves 4 to 6

1¹/₂ pounds beets, peeled

1 tablespoon unsalted butter

1 tablespoon canola or olive oil

1 large onion, coarsely chopped

1 fat garlic clove, chopped

1 teaspoon cumin seeds

3 cups vegetable or chicken stock (pages 266 and 192 respectively)

For the spiced yogurt:

1 teaspoon cumin seeds

1 teaspoon coriander seeds

A pinch of caraway seeds

¹/₂ teaspoon sweet paprika

A pinch of cayenne pepper

Sea salt and freshly ground black pepper

¹/₄ cup plain yogurt

1 tablespoon canola or olive oil

Chopped fresh flat-leaf parsley, to serve

Cut the beets into small chunks. Heat the butter and oil in a large saucepan until foaming, then add the onion, garlic, and cumin. Cook gently for 5 to 10 minutes, until soft but not colored. Add the beets, toss well with the onion, then pour in the stock. Bring to a simmer, cover, and cook for 20 to 30 minutes, until the beets are tender.

Meanwhile, for the spiced yogurt, toast the cumin, coriander, and caraway seeds in a dry frying pan over medium heat for a minute or so, until fragrant (this stage isn't essential but it does enhance the flavor). Transfer to a spice grinder, coffee mill, or mortar and grind to a powder. Combine with the paprika, cayenne, and a pinch of salt. Stir a heaped teaspoon of this mixture into the yogurt (keep the remaining spice mix for another batch of the spiced yogurt – it's very good with lamb or chicken). Add the oil and whisk until combined.

Purée the soup in a blender and return it to the pan (or use an immersion blender to purée it in the pan). Season to taste. If it seems excessively thick, you can thin it down with a little more stock or water. Serve hot or chilled, with spiced yogurt swirled or dotted in at the last moment and parsley sprinkled on top.

Celery root soup

Given its humble ingredients, this soup has a surprisingly sophisticated flavor. Celery root's earthy intensity and velvety texture are wonderful combined with the spicy, salty, or sweet finishes I recommend here, and a swirl of parsley and walnut pesto (page 132) works very well too. For a rather splendid starter, you could also top each bowlful with a fat, juicy oyster – steamed open in a little white wine.

Serves 6

3 tablespoons unsalted butter

1 large celery root, about 2 pounds, peeled and coarsely chopped

About 12 ounces leeks, white parts only, sliced

$2/3$ cup peeled and diced potato

1 onion, chopped

2 garlic cloves, chopped

4 cups vegetable or chicken stock (pages 266 and 192 respectively)

$1/2$ cup heavy cream (optional)

Sea salt and freshly ground black pepper

Melt the butter in a large, heavy saucepan. Add the celery root, leeks, potato, onion, and garlic; season generously, then cook for about 10 minutes, until the vegetables are starting to soften.

Add the stock, bring to a boil, then turn down the heat and simmer for 20 to 25 minutes, until the celery root is tender.

Purée the soup in a blender and return it to the pan (or use an immersion blender to purée it in the pan). Reheat gently. If the soup is too thick, thin it with some water or stock, though remember you may be adding cream.

Just before serving, check the soup for seasoning and stir in the cream if you want to enrich it a little.

Garnish with one of the following:

- Diced apple, fried gently in butter until golden, then spooned onto the soup, buttery juices and all.

- A few crisp shreds of fried smoked bacon or ham.

- A little chile confit. To make this, seed and finely slice a few hot red chiles. Put them in a small saucepan with a couple of peeled garlic cloves and cover with olive oil. Cook slowly over an extremely low heat for 45 minutes to 1 hour, until the chiles are really soft. Spoon a teaspoonful of the chile confit and its oil onto each bowl of soup. Alternatively, just use a drizzle of any good chile-infused olive oil.

Lentil soup with caraway and minted yogurt

This soup is a brilliant standby if you need to produce a quick meal from pantry ingredients. The humble lentil is elevated to great heights when enhanced with coriander, caraway, and garlic. Should you happen to have some chile confit at hand (see left), it makes an excellent alternative to the minted yogurt. Any good bread is a suitable accompaniment, but I think this soup goes particularly well with flatbreads (page 78).

Serves 6

2 tablespoons canola or olive oil

2 onions, coarsely chopped

1 carrot, coarsely chopped

2 teaspoons coriander seeds

1 teaspoon caraway seeds

2 garlic cloves, crushed

1^1/$_2$ cups red lentils

6 cups water or vegetable stock (page 266)

Sea salt and freshly ground black pepper

To finish:

5 tablespoons plain yogurt

2 tablespoons finely chopped fresh mint

Heat the oil in a large saucepan, add the onions and carrot, and cook gently for about 10 minutes, until soft.

Meanwhile, if you have time, toast the coriander and caraway seeds in a small frying pan over medium heat for a minute or so, until fragrant (this enhances the flavor, but is not essential). Grind to a fine powder in a spice grinder, coffee grinder, or mortar and pestle. Add half the ground spices to the softened vegetables along with the garlic and stir over medium heat for a minute or two.

Add the lentils and water or stock and bring to a boil, skimming off any scum that comes to the surface. Reduce the heat, then cover and simmer gently for 15 minutes or until the lentils are soft. Purée in a blender or food processor until smooth, adding more water if it is a little thick. Return to the pan and heat through. Adjust the seasoning with salt, pepper, and more of the ground spices, if you like.

In a small bowl, whisk together the yogurt and mint and season well. Serve the soup with a dollop of the minted yogurt swirled on top of each portion.

Butternut and nut butter soup

This might sound like too clever a joke by half, but it's a really good soup. Peanut (or other nut) butter is a very handy way to add richness and nuttiness to a soup. You can use smooth or crunchy peanut butter, depending on whether you want a silky soup or one with a slightly chunkier texture. To make it easier to whisk the peanut butter into the soup, warm it slightly first to soften it. You can do this by standing the jar in a bowl of hot water or leaving it in a warm place (I put it on top of my wood-burning stove) for 10 minutes or so.

You can use other squash varieties too, or indeed a fifty-fifty mixture of sweet and regular potatoes, but then you wouldn't have the joke. And let's be fair, it's a good one, isn't it?

Serves 6 to 8

1 butternut squash, about 2 pounds

1 tablespoon unsalted butter

1 large onion, chopped

1 small medium-hot chile, seeded and chopped, or a pinch of red pepper flakes

A 1-inch piece of fresh ginger, grated

1 small garlic clove, chopped

Sea salt and freshly ground black pepper

About 4 cups chicken or vegetable stock (pages 192 and 266 respectively)

3/4 cup commercial crunchy or smooth peanut butter (or use homemade; see page 52)

Juice of 1 lime

3 tablespoons finely chopped fresh cilantro

To serve:

Plain yogurt

Fresh cilantro leaves

2 tablespoons toasted pumpkin seeds or chopped toasted peanuts (optional)

A little finely chopped chile (optional)

Halve and peel the squash, then scoop out the seeds and cut the flesh into 3/8-inch cubes. Melt the butter in a large saucepan, add the onion, and cook gently until soft and translucent. Add the chile, ginger, and garlic and cook for another couple of minutes. Add the squash, a sprinkling of salt, and a few grinds of pepper. Stir well and cook for 5 minutes.

Pour in the stock. Bring to a boil and simmer gently, partially covered, for about 20 minutes, until the squash is soft – you should be able to mash it easily against the side of the pan with the back of a wooden spoon. Whiz in a blender (or use an immersion blender to purée it in the pan) until very smooth; you may need to do this in batches.

In a bowl, whisk the peanut butter with a ladleful of the hot soup until well blended. Return this mixture to the soup in the pan, stir well, and heat through. Remove from the heat, add the lime juice and cilantro, then taste and adjust the seasoning with salt and pepper.

Serve each portion topped with a dollop of yogurt and a few cilantro leaves. Sprinkle toasted pumpkin seeds or peanuts and/or a little finely chopped chile on top, if you like.

Ten salads

I eat a salad of one kind or another pretty much every day. Often that means just a few lettuce leaves tossed with a light vinaigrette to be eaten with or after something more substantial. But sometimes our salads are big, seasonal family affairs that become the main meal. Fresh vegetables – raw or cooked – tossed with a flavorful dressing, and augmented with nuts, seeds, meat, fish, or cheese, make a meal that's wholesome, delicious, easy to eat, and beautiful to look at. Add to this the fact that salads are easy to prepare (and to adapt or invent) and you'll understand why I see them as a cornerstone of good everyday cooking.

Warm leek and white bean salad with mustard dressing

This simple little dish works very well as a vegetarian starter, but can also function as a side dish to something robust, such as pork chops or sausages. It's all about the sweetness of the leeks and the creaminess of the beans. Put the extra whole-grain mustard into the dressing if you like real bite.

Serves 4

2 tablespoons canola or olive oil

2 large leeks, white part only, finely sliced

Sea salt and freshly ground black pepper

1 (14-ounce) can white beans such as cannellini, drained and rinsed

1 heaping tablespoon chopped fresh flat-leaf parsley

Lettuce leaves, to serve

For the dressing:

1 tablespoon Dijon mustard

1 teaspoon whole-grain mustard (optional)

3 tablespoons canola or extra-virgin olive oil

2 teaspoons cider vinegar

A pinch each of sea salt, freshly ground black pepper, and superfine sugar

Heat the oil in a large frying pan over medium heat, then add the leeks and a good pinch of salt. As soon as the leeks begin to soften, turn the heat down fairly low and continue to cook, stirring from time to time, for 6 to 7 minutes, until they are soft; don't let them color. Add the beans and toss together until heated through. Remove from the heat and stir in the parsley and plenty of black pepper.

For the dressing, whisk all the ingredients together to combine. Add to the pan of warm leeks and beans and stir well.

Divide the salad leaves among 4 plates and spoon the warm bean and leek mixture on top. Serve right away, accompanied by toasted sourdough bread. Alternatively, forget the leaves and just serve the dressed beans on toast.

Celery root Waldorf salad

I've used celery root as well as celery in my take on this classic salad, plus raisins plumped in orange juice. Try it with some brown bread and perhaps some cold chicken or pork. If you don't want to make your own mayonnaise, you could simply add a dab of mustard and a squeeze of lemon to your favorite commercial version. Or, for a lighter dressing, mix mayonnaise with an equal quantity of yogurt.

Serves 4

$1/3$ cup dark or golden raisins

Juice of 2 oranges

$3/4$ cup walnuts

5 ounces celery root, peeled

5 ounces celery stalks

2 crisp eating apples, such as Fuji or Gala

5 to 6 tablespoons mayonnaise (see below)

Sea salt and freshly ground black pepper

Put the raisins in a saucepan with the orange juice and bring to a simmer. Remove from the heat and let stand for an hour or so to plump up.

Preheat the oven to 350°F. Scatter the walnuts in a pie pan and toast in the oven for 5 to 7 minutes, until fragrant – check them regularly, as they can burn easily. Let cool, then chop coarsely.

Cut the celery root into thick matchsticks. Cut the celery, slightly on the diagonal, into slices $1^1/_2$ inches thick. Core the apples, leaving the skin on, and cut into fine slices. Drain the raisins (reserve the orange juice and drink it later) and toss them with the celery root, celery, apples, and walnuts. Add enough mayonnaise to coat everything lightly, toss to mix, then check the seasoning and serve.

Mayonnaise

I'm not a total mayo fascist: like most families, we usually have a jar of commercial mayo in the fridge. However, I make my own if I have time and I hope you will too, as it will be far superior to standard store-bought options. Adding a teaspoonful of ready-made mayo to your raw egg yolk at the start reduces the risk of separating.

Makes about $3/4$ cup

$1/4$ garlic clove

Sea salt, freshly ground black pepper, and a little superfine sugar

$1/4$ teaspoon English mustard

1 egg yolk

1 teaspoon wine vinegar or cider vinegar

1 generous teaspoon commercial mayonnaise (optional)

$1/3$ cup sunflower oil

$1/3$ cup canola oil or a mild olive oil

Lemon juice (optional)

Crush the garlic to a paste with a pinch of salt. Transfer it to a bowl, add the mustard, egg yolk, vinegar, mayo if using, plus a little pepper and a tiny pinch of sugar, then whisk together.

Combine the oils in a pitcher. Pour a few drops into the yolk mixture and whisk to emulsify. Repeat this once or twice, then start pouring in the oil in a very thin, steady stream, whisking all the time.

When all the oil has been whisked in and you have a thick, glossy mayonnaise, taste it and add more salt, pepper, sugar, and some lemon juice if it needs it. If it's too thick, thin it with a little warm water. Refrigerate until needed and use within a week.

Carrot, orange, and chervil salad

This is one of those simple combinations of just a few ingredients that complement each other beautifully. The sharp, juicy tang of the oranges; the sweet crunch of the carrot; the nutty texture of the seeds – it just works. It's also very good if you replace the seeds with around $1/2$ cup crumbled freshly roasted chestnuts.

Serves 2 to 3

2 oranges
1 large carrot
$1/2$ cup mixed pumpkin and sunflower (or other) seeds

For the dressing:
1 tablespoon lemon juice or cider vinegar
1 tablespoon sunflower oil
2 tablespoons canola or extra-virgin olive oil
Sea salt and freshly ground black pepper

A few sprigs of chervil (or tender flat-leaf parsley)

Cut the top and bottom off one of the oranges. Place it cut side down on a chopping board and cut down around it with a sharp knife, cutting off the peel and pith in strips so that the juicy flesh is exposed. Then, holding the orange in the palm of your hand and working over a bowl to catch the juice, slice down either side of each membrane, as close as you can, to release the segments. Drop the segments into the bowl. Repeat with the other orange.

Peel the carrot and cut into matchsticks using a sharp knife or a mandoline. Add these to the orange segments with the seeds and toss to mix.

To make the dressing, whisk all the ingredients together, along with any juice saved from the oranges.

Add the chervil or parsley to the salad along with the dressing, toss everything together, and serve.

Tomato salsa salad with capers and mint

What's the difference between a fresh tomato salsa and a tomato salad? Not much really, but for me, a tomato salsa should always include some kind of raw allium – shallot, onion, green onion – to give it an edge. And if you chopped the tomatoes more finely for this recipe, you'd have a definite salsa, I'd say – perfect for eating with burgers or spicy chicken. But leave the tomatoes in fat chunks and this is a salad, needing only some torn fresh bread to mop up the juices, and perhaps some buffalo mozzarella or tangy fresh goat cheese alongside.

Capers are not everyone's favorite thing, so just leave them out if they don't appeal. And if you don't fancy mint, torn basil leaves and coarsely chopped parsley are good options, too.

Serves 4

1 pound ripe, tasty tomatoes

1 shallot or $1/2$ small red onion, very finely chopped

1 to 2 tablespoons tiny capers, rinsed

A small squeeze of lemon juice

2 to 3 tablespoons canola or extra-virgin olive oil

Sea salt and freshly ground black pepper

A tiny pinch of sugar

A few torn fresh mint leaves

Cut the tomatoes into quarters, then halve each quarter crosswise. Place in a bowl and lightly stir in the shallot or onion and capers.

Put the lemon juice and oil in a small pitcher, season well, and add the sugar. Whisk together, then drizzle over the tomatoes. Scatter over the torn mint leaves and serve.

Salad of baby peas, ricotta, and green onions

A stunning, fresh, and pretty salad to serve as a starter or light lunch in the summer, when young peas can be popped straight from the pod into the pan.

Serves 4 to 6

1 pound very fresh baby peas or frozen petits pois

2 tablespoons canola or olive oil

10 to 12 green onions, trimmed and sliced on the diagonal

For the dressing:

1 tablespoon lemon juice

2 tablespoons extra-virgin olive or canola oil

Sea salt and freshly ground black pepper

1/2 cup ricotta or other soft, fresh cheese

1 teaspoon chopped fresh thyme (optional)

Bring a pan of lightly salted water to a boil, drop in the peas, cook for a maximum of 2 minutes, then drain.

Heat the oil in a frying pan, add the green onions, and cook gently for 4 to 5 minutes, until soft. Transfer to a bowl and mix in the still-warm peas.

To make the dressing, whisk the lemon juice and oil together in a bowl with plenty of salt and pepper, or shake the ingredients in a screw-top jar to combine. Drizzle this dressing over the green onions and peas and stir gently until well coated.

Spoon the salad onto plates or dishes. Crumble the cheese over the top, scatter on the thyme if using, and serve immediately.

Roast Jerusalem artichoke, hazelnut, and goat cheese salad

The earthy flavor of roasted artichokes is delicious with toasted hazelnuts. Jerusalem artichokes have a tendency to collapse into fluffiness when roasted, but keeping the skin on keeps them from breaking up too much when you toss them into the salad.

Serves 4 to 6

$\frac{1}{3}$ cup hazelnuts

1 pound Jerusalem artichokes

4 tablespoons canola or olive oil

2 sprigs of thyme

1 to 2 bay leaves

Sea salt and freshly ground black pepper

1 teaspoon hazelnut oil

$\frac{1}{2}$ lemon

A couple of handfuls of peppery salad greens (optional)

2 ounces hard goat cheese, crumbled or shaved into strips with a vegetable peeler, according to texture

First, toast the hazelnuts. Preheat the oven to 350°F. Spread the nuts out on a baking sheet in a single layer and toast in the oven for about 5 minutes, until they are lightly colored and the skins are blistered and cracked. Wrap them in a clean tea towel for a minute and then rub them vigorously with the towel until the skins fall off. Let cool and chop very coarsely or leave whole.

Turn the oven up to 375°F and put a large roasting pan in to heat up. Scrub the artichokes well and cut into halves or quarters lengthwise, depending on size – you need chunks about $\frac{1}{2}$ inch thick. Put the artichokes in a bowl and turn over in 3 tablespoons of the canola or olive oil with the thyme, bay, and a little salt. Add to the hot roasting pan and roast for about 35 minutes, until tender and lightly golden, taking the pan out after 15 minutes to turn the artichokes over. Allow to cool slightly.

Whisk the remaining tablespoon of oil with the hazelnut oil, drizzle it over the warm artichokes, squeeze on a good spritz of lemon juice, and season with salt and a few grinds of black pepper. Turn the artichokes over gently with your hands so that everything is well combined. Add the hazelnuts and the salad greens if you're using them, toss gently, then divide among serving plates. Scatter over the crumbled or shaved goat cheese and serve right away.

Seedy spinach salad

Obviously this is not seedy in the moral sense – far from it. Indeed it's full of virtues, being packed with lovely, healthy, lightly toasted seeds. I particularly like eating this using the roll-your-own method (see below), which creates a very satisfying leafy, grainy crunch in the mouth.

The fennel or cumin seeds add an intense, aromatic flavor, which some will love and others may wish to avoid. You can, of course, prepare and keep them separate, as an optional sprinkle.

Serves 4

1 to 2 tablespoons pumpkin seeds

1 to 2 tablespoons sesame seeds

1 to 2 tablespoons hempseeds or poppy seeds

1 teaspoon fennel or cumin seeds (optional)

For the dressing:

A good squeeze of lemon juice

A pinch each of sea salt, freshly ground black pepper, and superfine sugar

3 tablespoons canola oil (or half olive and half sunflower oil)

8 ounces young spinach leaves, trimmed

Combine all the seeds in a dry frying pan over medium heat. Toast them for a minute or two, tossing frequently so they don't burn, until they are starting to brown and smell really lovely. Pour into a bowl and set aside to cool.

To make the dressing, stir the lemon juice and seasonings together in a bowl and then whisk in the oil, or shake the ingredients together in a screw-top jar to combine.

Put the spinach leaves in a serving bowl, drizzle over the dressing, and toss together. Scatter over about half the seeds, toss lightly again, then sprinkle the remaining seeds over and serve.

Alternatively, you can turn this into a roll-your-own affair. Put the spinach in a bowl on the table, with the toasted seeds and dressing in separate bowls. Everyone can then help themselves to a leaf, sprinkle a pinch of seeds down the center and roll it up, like a little leafy pancake, then dip it into the dressing and eat. If you choose to serve the salad this way, you'll probably need more seeds, so increase the quantity a touch.

Beet, goat cheese, and red currant salad

Beets are one of my favorite roots, and I particularly like them, post-roasting, in various salad combos with salty cheese. This shamelessly pink-tinged dish has a winning combination of sweet, tart, and salty flavors. I enjoy it most when made with a blue goat cheese, but any crumbly goat cheese will do.

Serves 4 as a starter, 2 as a main course

About 12 ounces small beets

1 garlic clove, finely chopped

A large sprig of thyme (optional)

Sea salt and freshly ground black pepper

2 tablespoons canola or olive oil

For the dressing:

1 tablespoon cider vinegar or lemon juice

3 tablespoons canola or olive oil

A pinch each of sea salt, freshly ground black pepper, and superfine sugar

3 to 4 handfuls of seasonal lettuce leaves

1 cup crumbled goat cheese

1/2 cup red currants

Preheat the oven to 400°F.

Scrub the beets well, but leave them whole, then place on a large piece of foil. Scatter with the garlic, the leaves from the thyme, if you're using it, and some salt and pepper, then drizzle over the oil. Scrunch up the foil to make a baggy but tightly sealed packet, place it on a baking sheet, and put it in the oven. Roast until tender – about an hour, though it could take longer. The beets are cooked when a knife slips easily into the flesh. Let cool, then top and tail them and remove the skin. Cut into wedges and place in a large bowl.

Whisk together all the dressing ingredients. Arrange the lettuce leaves on serving plates and drizzle on a little of the dressing. Sprinkle the cheese over the beets, add the remaining dressing, and toss together loosely with your hands. Arrange on top of the leaves, scatter over the red currants, and serve.

VARIATIONS
Feta, beet, and parsley salad

Prepare the beets as above, then place them in a large bowl with 1 1/4 cups crumbled feta cheese, 1/2 cup fresh flat-leaf parsley leaves, and, if you like, 1/3 cup lightly toasted walnuts. Mix the dressing as above, pour onto the salad, and toss lightly with your hands. Serve right away, with brown bread on the side.

Roast squash salad

You can replace the beets in either of the above recipes with a similar quantity of butternut squash. Seed the squash and cut into chunks with the skin still on. Roast with the garlic, thyme, and oil – in a roasting pan – for about 40 minutes, turning once or twice, until tender and lightly browned. Let cool, then assemble the salad with the roast squash chunks replacing the beets.

Fried halloumi salad

A delicious summer starter or light lunch. I love the Mediterranean tradition of using herbs as a main ingredient. Rather than being relegated to the understudy role of seasoning, big handfuls of mint and parsley are the stars in this salad, adding freshness, flavor, and color. The sweet-sour dressing brings it all together and counterbalances the salty halloumi cheese.

Made from sheep's milk, halloumi is a traditional Cypriot cheese, though you may well be able to find a domestic brand. Along with cucumber, tomatoes, and herbs from the River Cottage garden, this very Mediterranean-feeling dish can actually be surprisingly homegrown.

Serves 4

For the dressing:

1 teaspoon honey

Juice of $^1/_2$ lemon

1 small garlic clove, crushed

A pinch of red pepper flakes

A pinch of sea salt

3 tablespoons canola or olive oil

1 small red onion, very finely sliced

1 small cucumber, cut into chunks

$^2/_3$ cup cherry tomatoes, halved

$^1/_3$ cup kalamata or other black olives, pitted

A large handful of mint leaves, coarsely shredded

A large handful of flat-leaf parsley leaves

$^1/_4$ cup all-purpose flour

A large pinch of smoked paprika

Sea salt and freshly ground black pepper

8 ounces halloumi cheese, cut into 8 slices

2 tablespoons canola or olive oil

First, make the dressing. Stir together the honey, lemon juice, garlic, red pepper flakes, and salt until well combined, then whisk in the oil.

In a large bowl, toss together the onion, cucumber, tomatoes, olives, mint, and parsley.

In a small bowl, whisk together the flour, paprika, and some salt and pepper. Moisten the halloumi slices slightly with water, if necessary, then press them into the seasoned flour and shake off any excess.

Heat the oil in a large frying pan and fry the halloumi slices over medium heat for about 2 minutes on each side, until golden and slightly soft inside.

Toss the salad vegetables with the dressing, turning them over with your hands to make sure everything is lightly coated.

Divide the salad among 4 plates, put 2 pieces of the hot halloumi on each one, and serve immediately.

Hot new potato and sorrel salad

I couldn't resist sneaking this recipe, a firmly established River Cottage favorite, in here. The lemony tang of sorrel is wonderful with the best sweet, creamy, earthy spuds of early summer, and this merits being served as a dish in its own right. But it's also just a lovely way of dressing new potatoes for a side dish – perhaps to serve with fish.

Serves 4

1 pound small new potatoes, mainly whole, the large ones cut in half

2 to 3 handfuls of sorrel, cultivated or wild

3 tablespoons unsalted butter

1 tablespoon extra-virgin olive or canola oil

Fine sea salt and freshly ground black pepper

Scrub the new potatoes. Put them in a pan, cover with cold water, and salt well. Bring to a boil and cook until just tender. Small, freshly dug new potatoes cook much faster than you would think, so be vigilant and taste a small one after just 5 minutes or so.

While the potatoes are cooking, strip the central veins out of the sorrel. Wash the leaves well and shred into ribbons, about $3/8$ inch wide.

As soon as the potatoes are ready, drain and put them into a bowl with the butter and oil. Throw the shredded sorrel into the bowl and toss well. Let stand for a minute, so the heat of the potatoes wilts the sorrel, then toss again. Rest for another minute, then season with salt and pepper and serve at once.

If you do happen to slightly overcook the spuds, don't despair, just stir them vigorously with the sorrel and butter so they break up a little and get a bit "mashy." Pretend it was quite deliberate – your smashed new potatoes will still be delicious.

VARIATION

Parsley potatoes

Garnishing just-boiled new potatoes with a little chopped parsley and some butter is always nice, but here I'm talking about loads of parsley – and quite a lot of butter too. Use a couple of bunches of flat-leaf parsley, stripped of their coarse stalks and washed well. Chop the leaves fairly fine (but not to dust) and proceed as above, using the finely chopped parsley in place of the sorrel. The lightly smashed version of this (see above) is especially scrumptious.

Three greens

I've never had much trouble eating my greens, and I hope these recipes will ensure you don't either. The golden rule with almost any brassica or braising green, whether it's the leaf, stem, or unformed flower (as with broccoli and cauliflower) is to keep the cooking time short. Stick to this, and pair your lightly done greens with a smidgeon of something rich and lubricating, and/or textured and savory – most obviously a knob of butter (garlicky, if you like), but also a little crisp bacon, a just-cooked egg, a few toasted seeds . . . you get the idea.

Leeks with greens

Soft, buttery, wilted leeks bring a lovely sweetness to any kind of lightly cooked cabbage or greens. This simple preparation is one I turn to frequently, both at home and when cooking at River Cottage: it's so easy to throw together, can be made with different seasonal greens throughout most of the year, and works as a side dish to everything from a bit of grilled fish to a full-on Sunday roast.

Serves 4

About 1 pound leeks, white part only

1 tablespoon unsalted butter

1 savoy or other green cabbage, 2 pounds braising greens, or 2 bunches curly kale

Sea salt and freshly ground black pepper

Slice the leeks finely and give them a good rinse to get rid of any grit. Heat the butter in a large frying pan or wide saucepan and add the leeks with a pinch of salt. Let them cook gently for 5 to 6 minutes, stirring or shaking the pan occasionally, until wilted and tender.

Meanwhile, trim and coarsely shred the cabbage, greens, or kale. Cook lightly – in either a steamer or a large saucepan of salted water – for 3 to 4 minutes, until wilted and tender but not too soft. Remove from the heat immediately, drain well, and let the excess moisture steam off for a minute or so. Then add to the pan of buttery leeks, along with some more seasoning, and stir over a low heat for about a minute until thoroughly combined. Serve right away.

PSB with chorizo and soft-hard-boiled eggs

I love purple sprouting broccoli and eat it at least twice a week when it's in season in spring, often just with a little melted butter. It's also excellent in substantial salads like this one, which is equally good as a starter or light meal. If you can't find PSB in the States, use broccoli rabe or broccolini instead.

Serves 4

6 ounces Spanish chorizo or Tupperware Mexican chorizo (page 206)

1 tablespoon canola or olive oil

4 eggs, at room temperature

About 1 pound purple sprouting broccoli, trimmed, or broccoli rabe or broccolini

Sea salt and freshly ground black pepper

If you're using Spanish chorizo, skin and cut into chunks; if using homemade, shape into walnut-sized balls. Heat the oil in a frying pan, add the chorizo, and fry over medium heat, turning regularly, for about 10 minutes, until starting to crisp.

Meanwhile, cook the eggs: Put them in a pan of hand-hot water, cover, and bring quickly to a boil. Boil for exactly 4 minutes – 5 if they are extra-large. Then run them under cold water and peel them as soon as they are cool enough to handle.

At the same time, cook the broccoli in a large saucepan of boiling salted water for 3 to 4 minutes, until just tender. Drain well.

Add the warm broccoli to the chorizo pan and toss it in the hot, spicy fat until well coated. Divide the broccoli and chorizo among 4 warm plates and add a boiled egg, cut in half, to each. Season with salt and pepper and serve right away, with some bread.

Kale with bacon and chestnuts

This is a perfect Christmas-dinner side dish, especially for people who avoid Brussels sprouts. It also makes an excellent accompaniment to roast partridge or pheasant, or can be served with a fried egg for supper.

Serves 6 as a side dish, 2 to 3 as a main course

1½ pounds curly kale (or cavolo nero, or savoy or other winter cabbage)

2 tablespoons canola or olive oil

6 ounces bacon, finely chopped

6 ounces peeled cooked chestnuts, coarsely chopped

1 tablespoon unsalted butter

Sea salt and freshly ground black pepper

Remove the tough stalks from the kale or other greens and coarsely shred the leaves. Cook the kale in a large saucepan of boiling salted water for 3 to 4 minutes, until tender, then drain well and let stand to steam off excess moisture.

Meanwhile, heat a large frying pan, add the oil, then the bacon, and fry over medium heat until it is just starting to become crisp. Toss the chestnuts into the pan, stirring well so they absorb the hot bacon fat. Add the kale, along with the butter and some salt and pepper. Toss well and serve right away.

Three green beans

Green beans grow abundantly in temperate climates during their summer and early autumn season. Since they are also delicious, it pays the prudent cook to have a few nifty bean recipes up their sleeve. Here are three of my absolute favorites.

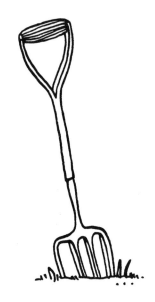

Runner beans stewed with garlic

This recipe is from my friend Sarah Raven. It's a very simple but amazingly good way to cook runner beans. These beans are not so common in the States; if you can't find them, use Italian green beans but cook them for half the time.

Serves 4

1 pound runner beans

2 garlic cloves, finely chopped

1 tablespoon unsalted butter

1 tablespoon canola or olive oil

Sea salt and freshly ground black pepper

Use a potato peeler to remove the strings from the edges of the beans, then chop them into small pieces, on the diagonal. Put them in a large pan with the garlic, butter, oil, and 3 or 4 tablespoons of water, and place over medium-low heat. Heat until steaming, stirring to distribute the melting butter and the garlic over the beans.

Cover the pan, leaving a slight gap, decrease the heat to very low, and stew gently for about 30 minutes, until the beans are completely tender. Stir every now and then and add a splash more water if the beans look as if they are going to catch on the bottom. Remove the lid and let most of the water evaporate for the last 5 to 10 minutes of cooking. Season well and serve hot or warm, with all the buttery, garlicky juices.

Green beans with tomatoes

I always enjoy this combination of tender green beans and garlicky tomatoes during summer and autumn. It can be served as part of an al fresco spread, or with the meats at a barbecue, but even on its own with a good hunk of bread it's a lovely supper dish.

Serves 4

1 tablespoon canola
or olive oil

1 onion, finely chopped

2 garlic cloves, finely
chopped

1 (14-ounce) can of
chopped tomatoes, or
2 pounds fresh tomatoes,
blanched, peeled, seeded,
and coarsely chopped

1 pound green beans,
topped and cut into
2-inch lengths

Sea salt and freshly
ground black pepper

Heat the oil in a large saucepan or frying pan, add the onion, and cook gently for at least 10 minutes, until soft but not colored. Add the garlic and cook gently for another minute or two, then add the tomatoes and stir well. Stir in the beans, bring the mixture to a gentle simmer, and season well. Turn down the heat, partly cover the pan, and cook very gently, stirring frequently, for about 30 minutes, until the beans are fully tender. Season with salt and pepper. If the mixture seems to be in danger of sticking, add a splash of water or stock. Serve warm or cold.

Green beans with seeds and almonds

Dressing green beans with a crunchy, spicy topping is a great way to serve them, and you can customize the recipe to suit your own nut-and-seed preferences.

Serves 4

12 ounces green beans

A handful of blanched
almonds

$1/2$ tablespoon cumin
seeds

1 tablespoon coriander
seeds

2 tablespoons sesame
seeds

1 tablespoon poppy
seeds

2 tablespoons canola
or olive oil

1 small garlic clove,
grated or finely chopped

Sea salt

Cook the beans in a saucepan of boiling salted water for 4 to 5 minutes, until tender but still with a bit of crunch. Drain well.

Meanwhile, coarsely chop the almonds and place in a dry frying pan with all of the seeds. Toast gently over medium heat for a few minutes, until the seeds start to smell fragrant and the almonds are taking on a little color. Remove from the heat, add the oil and garlic to the hot pan, and stir well. Let stand for a minute or so, then stir again, so the residual heat in the pan just takes the edge off the garlic. Season with a little salt.

Put the warm beans on a serving plate and scatter the seedy mixture over the top. Serve right away.

Mixed mashes

Mashed potatoes are hard to beat, but it would be a shame to overlook the mashing potential of other vegetables. Two or three roots combined, seasoned well, and made silky with a little cream, butter, and/or oil can be a revelation served up with stews, grills, and roasts. In all cases, go for floury potatoes; such as russets, and don't be tempted to cut corners at the mashing stage: potatoes need to be mashed by hand or with a potato ricer, as they'll go gluey if put in a food processor. Other roots, however, need processing to achieve a lovely, silky texture. Below are some of my favorite rooty combos.

Three-root mash

Of course, you don't have to stick to three roots: you could use two, four, or as many as suits you. Do always include potatoes, however, to give the mash body and to keep it from getting too sweet.

Serves 6

1 pound carrots, peeled and cut into chunks

1 pound parsnips, peeled and cut into chunks

1 pound russet potatoes, peeled and cut into chunks

3 tablespoons unsalted butter or canola oil

6 tablespoons milk (or half milk and half heavy cream)

Sea salt and freshly ground black pepper

Freshly grated nutmeg (optional)

Cook the carrots and parsnips in a pan of boiling salted water until tender. Cook the potatoes in a separate pan. Drain the vegetables and let them steam dry for a minute or two. Put the carrots and parsnips in a food processor with half the butter or oil and blend to a creamy purée. Heat the milk and the remaining butter or oil in the pan in which the potatoes were cooked, then add the potatoes and mash until smooth. Combine the mashed vegetables, adding plenty of salt and pepper, including nutmeg if you like, to make a creamy, golden mash. Serve steaming hot, with sausages or roast lamb or venison.

VARIATIONS

Celery root and potato mash

Use $1^1/_2$ pounds each celery root and potatoes. Peel both, cut into large chunks, and cook separately in lightly salted boiling water until tender. Drain and let steam dry for a few minutes. Heat the butter or oil and milk in one of the pans, seasoning with salt, pepper, and nutmeg. Add the potatoes and mash until smooth. Rub the celery root through a sieve, or purée it in a food processor, then add to the potatoes and beat well until combined, adding more hot milk and butter or oil if needed. Check the seasoning. Perfect with roast chicken, steak, or baked fish.

Rutabaga and potato mash

Use $1^1/_2$ pounds each rutabagas and potatoes and prepare exactly as for celery root and potato mash. Excellent with roast game.

Mushy squash

I call this buttery purée mushy squash because it's a kind of cold-weather alternative to mushy peas – and I quite often serve this dish with battered or bread-crumbed fish in autumn and winter. It is also excellent with scallops (page 156) or boiled ham or slow-cooked pork belly. A lovely alternative to roasted vegetables or mashed potatoes.

Serves 4

1 tablespoon canola or olive oil

3 tablespoons unsalted butter

About 1 pound butternut squash, peeled, seeded, and cut into small cubes (roughly ¾ inch)

1 garlic clove, finely chopped

3 to 4 fresh sage leaves, finely chopped

Sea salt and freshly ground black pepper

Heat the oil and half the butter in a small frying pan, add the squash, and fry gently for a few minutes, until it begins to take on a hint of color. Add the garlic and sage, season with salt and pepper, and sizzle gently until the garlic just begins to color. Immediately add 2 to 3 tablespoons of water to stop the garlic browning any more. Partly cover the pan with a lid and let the squash finish cooking in the steam from the water; it should be completely tender within about 10 minutes. Add a little more water if the pan becomes dry.

Add the squash and any liquid to a blender or food processor, along with the rest of the butter, and blend until smooth. If it doesn't quite come together, add a dash of hot water to make a thick, creamy purée. Taste and adjust the seasoning, then serve right away.

Thyme and caramelized onion mash

This is delicious – there is nothing better to go with sausages, chops, or roast lamb. It's also great with grilled or roasted fillets of robustly flavored fish, such as mackerel.

Serves 6

2 tablespoons canola or olive oil

1 large onion or 4 to 5 shallots, finely chopped

Sea salt and freshly ground black pepper

2 teaspoons chopped fresh thyme

3 pounds russet potatoes, peeled and cut into chunks

3 tablespoons unsalted butter or canola oil

6 tablespoons milk (or half milk and half heavy cream), warmed

Heat 2 tablespoons oil in a large saucepan over medium heat. Add the onion or shallots and a good sprinkling of salt and pepper, stir well as the onion starts to sizzle, then turn the heat down and cook gently for about 20 minutes, until soft and golden. Add the chopped thyme and cook for another 5 minutes or so. Taste – the onion should be very sweet. If not, cook a little longer. It needs to take on a good golden color, but don't let it start to crisp and brown. Taste for seasoning at this point, too.

Meanwhile, cook the potatoes in a pan of boiling salted water until tender, then drain and let steam dry for a few minutes. Heat the butter or oil and milk in the pan in which the potatoes were cooked, then add the potatoes and plenty of salt and pepper and mash until smooth. Mix in the caramelized onion, check the seasoning, and serve.

Six roasted vegetables

Roasted vegetables – root vegetables and winter squashes in particular – are rarely less than delicious. The roasting process intensifies flavor, brings out sweetness, and adds a rich, caramelized exterior. It's forgiving to the cook (you can be relaxed about timings, and serve your vegetables hot, warm, or cold) and versatile too. The following recipes make fantastic accompaniments but can also be the main focus of a meal, with just a little something else on the side. Leftover roasted roots can be tossed into salads or puréed in soups, or just nibbled cold as an extra something in your lunch box. So you can see why this is a method I return to time and again.

Roast squash with chile, garlic, and rosemary

Butternut squash is delicious roasted in this way, but do try some alternative squashes and pumpkins if you get the chance. Sugar pie pumpkins are outstanding, as are acorn squash.

This makes an excellent side dish for sausages, chops, roast chicken, or robust fish. Since it is creamy and starchy, I tend to serve roast squash instead of, rather than as well as, any kind of spuds. On the other hand, dished up with steamed rice and some sautéed greens or a green salad, this makes a lovely vegetarian main course.

Serves 4

1 large butternut squash, about 2 pounds, or the equivalent weight of acorn or other squash or pumpkin

6 to 8 fat garlic cloves, skin on, lightly squashed

A few sprigs of rosemary

1 fairly hot red chile, seeded and finely chopped

Sea salt and freshly ground black pepper

4 to 5 tablespoons canola or olive oil

$^1/_3$ cup pine nuts or walnuts (optional)

Juice of $^1/_2$ lemon

Preheat the oven to 375°F.

Slice the squash into quarters and seed it, scooping out the seeds with a spoon. I leave the skin on most squashes when I'm roasting them, but you can peel it off if you prefer. Cut the squash into wedges or chunks and put them in a small roasting pan. Add the garlic and rosemary, the chopped chile, and lots of salt and pepper. Drizzle with 2 to 3 tablespoons of oil and toss together. Roast in the oven for 40 to 55 minutes, stirring halfway through, until the squash is completely soft and starting to caramelize.

Meanwhile, if using nuts, toast them in a dry frying pan over medium heat for a few minutes, until golden brown, then scatter over the roasted squash. Add a squeeze of lemon juice and another good drizzle of oil, then serve.

Roasted red onions with port and bay

This is a lovely, simple, and rather beautiful side dish that works very well with most meats – it would make a superb accompaniment to your Christmas roast, whatever that may be. You can serve it hot, warm, or cold, and the rich fragrance that wafts from the oven as it cooks is quite delectable.

Serves 4 to 6

2 tablespoons canola or olive oil

1½ pounds small red onions

About 12 bay leaves

10 to 12 juniper berries, lightly smashed

Sea salt and freshly ground black pepper

¾ cup port

Preheat the oven to 325°F.

Pour the oil into a baking dish and tilt the dish so that the oil more or less covers the bottom. Peel the onions, keeping the root ends intact, and slice into 8 thick wedges from root to tip. The root end should hold the layers of each wedge together.

Put the onions in the baking dish, tuck the bay leaves in among them, scatter over the juniper berries and a good seasoning of salt and pepper, then drizzle the port over everything. Cover with foil and roast in the oven for 45 minutes.

Take off the foil, give the onions a gentle stir, and cook, uncovered, for 30 minutes. At the end of cooking the onions should be very soft and starting to caramelize, and the liquid in the pan should have reduced to a few spoonfuls of intense, aromatic juice. Serve hot, warm, or cold, with roasted meats or as a relish for cheese.

Roasted beets with balsamic, rosemary, and garlic

Sweet, sticky, garlic-scented roasted beets make an ideal side dish for oily fish such as mackerel, or for grilled chicken or pork. But let it cool and you could add some soft goat cheese and salad greens and eat it as a dish in its own right.

Serves 4

About 2 pounds beets

1 large rosemary branch, broken into little sprigs

1 head of garlic, broken into cloves, skin left on, each lightly smashed

3 tablespoons canola or olive oil

Sea salt and freshly ground black pepper

2 tablespoons balsamic vinegar

Preheat the oven to 375°F.

Peel the beets, cut them into thick wedges, and place in a baking dish. Add the sprigs of rosemary and garlic cloves, drizzle on the oil, and season with plenty of salt and pepper. Toss everything together, cover the dish with foil, and roast in the oven for 40 minutes, or until the beets are almost tender.

Remove the foil, drizzle over the vinegar, give everything a good stir, and return to the oven. Cook uncovered, stirring again once, for another 30 to 40 minutes or until the beets are starting to caramelize. Serve right away or let cool.

Roast potatoes with lemon, rosemary, and thyme

It's not just floury potatoes that roast well. An olive oil–roasted new potato, with salty skin and caramelized edges, is a fine thing too. I like to serve this flavor-packed dish alongside a summer roast chicken or barbecued meat or fish. In fact, you can roast a whole fish or two, such as mackerel or small sea bass, right in the middle of the roasting spuds (see page 149 for more on roast fish and potatoes).

The lemons, including the peels, add a bitter note that goes particularly well with fish, but you can leave them out and stick with just the herbs and garlic, if you prefer.

Serves 5 to 6

3 pounds new potatoes

2 lemons, plus an extra lemon half

7 to 8 garlic cloves, skin on, lightly smashed

Several sprigs of rosemary

Several sprigs of thyme

Olive or canola oil

Sea salt and freshly ground black pepper

Preheat the oven to 400°F.

Wash the potatoes to remove the dirt, but try not to remove the skins. Up to, say, golf-ball size, they can be roasted whole, but any larger than that and they should be cut into halves or quarters. Parboil the potatoes in a pan of salted water for 5 minutes, then drain and let dry for a minute or two.

Cut the 2 lemons into thick slices. Put the potatoes in a baking dish and scatter over the lemon slices, garlic, rosemary, and thyme. Drizzle oil generously over everything and toss the whole lot together with your hands, making sure each potato is covered in oil. Season well with salt and pepper. Bake for 35 to 40 minutes, turning everything at least once, until the lemons are starting to caramelize and the potatoes look irresistibly golden brown.

Squeeze on the juice from the extra lemon half, sprinkle with a little more salt, and serve immediately.

Roast carrots with butter, cumin, and orange

This is particularly lovely made with young summer carrots, freshly pulled and no more than thumb thick. Don't peel them unless you really have to – just scrub them before slicing in half down the middle. Or, if they're really slender, leave them whole. If you're using big old winter carrots instead – and there's no reason why not – peel them and slice thickly.

This is very good served with roast lamb, chicken, or pork.

Serves 4 to 6

1 tablespoon canola or olive oil

1 tablespoon unsalted butter

1¹/₂ pounds carrots, small ones scrubbed and halved lengthwise, large ones peeled and cut into thick batons

2 teaspoons cumin seeds

Sea salt and freshly ground black pepper

Finely grated zest of 1 orange, plus some juice

Preheat the oven to 350°F.

Put the oil and butter into a large baking dish and leave in the oven for a couple of minutes, until the butter melts. Remove from the oven and add the carrots, cumin, and plenty of salt and pepper. Toss together, cover with foil, and return to the oven for 30 to 40 minutes, until the carrots are tender.

Remove from the oven, take off the foil, and give everything a good stir. Then return to the oven, uncovered, for about 20 to 30 minutes, so the carrots start to caramelize.

When you take the dish from the oven, stir in the orange zest and a good squeeze or two of the juice. Serve at once.

Roasted roots with mustard, rosemary, and honey

The earthy character of root vegetables is wonderfully enhanced by the addition of hot, sweet, and aromatic flavors. This warming winter side dish goes well with most meats, but I particularly like it with sausages. You could also dish it up with a plate of beans or lentils as a vegetarian main course.

Serves 4 to 6

About 3 pounds mixed root vegetables, such as parsnip, celery root, carrot, salsify, rutabaga, and turnip

3 generous tablespoons whole-grain mustard

2 to 3 tablespoons honey

6 tablespoons canola or olive oil

Sea salt and freshly ground black pepper

2 to 3 large sprigs of rosemary

Preheat the oven to 350°F.

Peel the root vegetables and cut into bite-sized chunks. Combine the mustard, honey and oil in a large bowl. Add plenty of salt and pepper and the rosemary sprigs, then tip in the prepared root vegetables. Mix the whole lot together well with your hands, then transfer to a baking dish that is big enough to hold the vegetables in a single layer, fairly snugly packed.

Cover the dish with foil and place in the oven. Cook for 30 minutes, then uncover, give everything a good stir, and turn the heat up to 400°F. Continue to roast for another 30 to 40 minutes, until the vegetables are tender in the middle, a bit crispy here and nicely caramelized there. Sprinkle with salt and a few grinds of pepper and serve.

Jerusalem artichoke and nettle gratin

This is the lovely creation of our resident River Cottage baker, Dan – hence the stale bread topping. We've made very successful variations using a combination of celery root and potatoes instead of artichokes. It's a big hit as a vegetarian starter or main course.

Serves 4

1 tablespoon sunflower oil

1 tablespoon unsalted butter

2 onions, finely sliced

3 garlic cloves, sliced

1 pound Jerusalem artichokes, peeled and cut into 1-inch-thick rounds

1 teaspoon chopped fresh thyme

Sea salt and freshly ground black pepper

$^3/_4$ cup heavy cream

$^1/_3$ cup vegetable stock (page 266) or water

3 ounces fresh nettle tops or spinach, coarsely chopped

For the topping:
A handful of old-fashioned rolled oats

3 thick slices of stale bread, torn into little pieces or whizzed to coarse crumbs in a food processor

$^1/_2$ handful of hazelnuts or walnuts, toasted, skinned, and coarsely chopped (optional)

2 tablespoons unsalted butter, melted

$^1/_4$ cup grated Cheddar or hard goat cheese

Preheat the oven to 375°F.

Heat the oil and butter in a frying pan, add the onions and garlic, and cook gently until soft and starting to take on a little color. Add the artichokes and thyme, then season well with salt and pepper. Cook, tossing occasionally, for 5 minutes.

Pour over the cream and stock or water and simmer gently until the liquid has reduced by half. Stir in the nettles or spinach, then transfer everything to a greased gratin dish, leveling it out as you go.

Mix all the topping ingredients together. Sprinkle over the artichoke mixture and bake in the oven for 25 to 30 minutes, until golden and bubbling. Serve right away.

Cauliflower cheese

One of the all-time classics. For macaroni and cheese: Make a double quantity of sauce, cook 3 cups macaroni, and combine the two. Put in an oven dish, top with bread crumbs, more grated cheese, and a drizzle of oil and bake until golden.

Serves 3 as a main course, 5 to 6 as a side dish

1¼ cups whole milk

½ onion, cut in two

1 bay leaf, twisted

A few black peppercorns
1 large cauliflower (about 2 pounds), trimmed and cut into large florets

1½ tablespoons unsalted butter

2 tablespoons all-purpose flour

¾ cup grated sharp aged Cheddar cheese

¼ cup grated Parmesan or mature hard goat cheese (optional)

¼ teaspoon English mustard

Sea salt and freshly ground black pepper

Put the milk into a saucepan with the onion, bay, and peppercorns. Bring to just below simmering, then turn off the heat. Let stand for at least 30 minutes, an hour or two if possible.

Preheat the oven to 375°F. Meanwhile, cook the cauliflower in a pan of boiling salted water for 3 to 4 minutes until almost tender but still a bit al dente. Drain well, allowing it to steam for a minute or so, then keep warm.

If the milk has cooled completely, warm it gently before straining it into a pitcher. Melt the butter in a medium saucepan over a fairly low heat, then stir in the flour to form a smooth paste (a roux). Cook gently, stirring frequently, for 1 to 2 minutes. Remove from the heat and add a third of the warm milk. Stir vigorously with a wooden spoon, or a whisk, until you have a thick, smooth paste. Add the rest of the milk in one or two lots. Return the sauce to the heat and bring to a boil, stirring. Let it bubble for 2 minutes, stirring occasionally, to "cook out" any raw taste of flour. Turn the heat down.

Set aside about ¼ cup of the Cheddar and add the rest to the hot sauce, along with the Parmesan, if using, and mustard. Stir gently until the cheese has melted into the sauce; don't let it boil. Add salt and pepper.

Combine the cauliflower with the hot cheese sauce, gently folding the florets into the sauce until well coated. Transfer to a greased ovenproof dish, scatter the remaining cheese over the top, and bake for about 20 minutes, until golden and bubbling. Serve as a main course, with bread, or as a side dish.

VARIATION

Chardy cheese

In place of the cauliflower, use 1½ pounds Swiss, ruby, or rainbow chard. Separate the stalks from the leaves. Blanch the leaves in a pan of boiling salted water for a minute or two until just wilted. Remove with tongs, drain, squeeze out excess water, and chop coarsely. Cut the stalks into ½-inch-thick slices and blanch for 3 to 4 minutes, until just tender. Drain well and toss with a tablespoon of butter and some salt and pepper. Put the stalks in a greased ovenproof dish. Stir the chopped leaves into the hot cheese sauce and pour over. Scatter with coarse bread crumbs and a drizzle of oil and bake as above.

Stuffed butternut squash

This is one of my favorite autumn main courses, another great vegetable idea that I've borrowed from my friend Sarah Raven. It's easy to adapt and alter the stuffing for the squash according to what you have and what you fancy. You can even alter the squash too, for that matter – I've made it very successfully with acorn squashes.

Serves 4

1 large butternut squash (about 3 pounds) or 2 small ones

1 garlic clove, finely chopped

About 3 tablespoons unsalted butter

A little canola or olive oil

Sea salt and freshly ground black pepper

$^1/_2$ cup walnuts, lightly toasted and very coarsely chopped

6 ounces blue cheese, crumbled into small lumps (or use a crumbly goat cheese)

2 teaspoons chopped fresh thyme

1 scant tablespoon honey

Preheat the oven to 375°F.

Make sure the outside of the squash is scrubbed clean. Cut the squash in half lengthwise and scoop out the seeds and soft fibers. Put in a baking dish, add the chopped garlic and butter to each cavity, then brush with a little oil and season well. Place in the oven and bake for 45 minutes to 1 hour, until the flesh feels very tender when pierced with the tip of a knife.

Scoop the soft flesh and all the buttery, garlicky juices out into a bowl, leaving a $^3/_8$-inch-thick layer of flesh still attached to the skin, so the squash holds its shape. Coarsely mash the flesh. Keep back a few pieces of walnut and a little of the cheese, then fold the remaining walnuts and cheese into the soft squash, along with the thyme and some more salt and pepper.

Spoon the filling back into the squash halves and scatter on the reserved cheese and walnuts. Finish with the merest drizzle of honey, then return the squash to the oven and bake for 15 minutes, or until the cheese is bubbling. Serve with a crisp green salad.

VARIATIONS

Crispy bacon-stuffed squash

Chop 4 slices of bacon and fry for a minute or two until crisp and golden. Stir these into the soft squash flesh, along with about $^1/_3$ cup finely grated Gruyère cheese, a tablespoon of chopped fresh chives, and plenty of black pepper. Top with a little more grated Gruyère before returning to the oven.

Crème fraîche- and herb-stuffed squash

Add 1 teaspoon each of finely chopped fresh basil, thyme, and oregano to the mashed squash, stir in 3 to 4 tablespoons of crème fraîche, and season very well before returning to the oven.

Mixed mushroom tart

This is a simple little tart that works well with regular cultivated mushrooms but will be extra special if you include a few wild mushrooms that you've gathered yourself. Serve it as a starter or light lunch.

Lemony zucchini (page 263) are a good summery alternative for topping this tart, so long as you let them cook long enough for most of the juices to evaporate. Tear a little mozzarella over the top before you put it in the oven.

Serves 2

2 tablespoons unsalted butter

About 6 ounces mixed mushrooms, sliced

Sea salt and freshly ground black pepper

1 garlic clove, finely chopped

$^1/_3$ cup fresh white bread crumbs

Finely grated zest of 1 lemon

1 tablespoon finely chopped fresh flat-leaf parsley

6 ounces commercial puff pastry or rough puff pastry (see page 110)

1 egg, lightly beaten

1 heaping tablespoon grated Parmesan or matured hard goat cheese or Cheddar

Preheat the oven to 400°F.

Heat the butter in a large frying pan, add the mushrooms and a pinch of salt, and cook fairly briskly until they start to soften. Stir in the garlic and cook, stirring often, until the mushrooms are tender and all the liquid they release has evaporated. Remove the pan from the heat and stir in the bread crumbs, lemon zest, parsley, and a few grinds of black pepper.

Roll out the pastry on a lightly floured surface to no more than $^1/_4$ inch thick. Using a plate or cake pan as a guide, cut out an 8-inch in diameter circle and place it on a lightly oiled baking sheet. Then, with a small, sharp knife, score a circle $^3/_4$ inch in from the edge of the pastry, without going right through to the bottom. This will create a puffed-up golden rim to the tart.

Brush the pastry border with beaten egg. Spread the mushroom mixture over the pastry, leaving the border clear, and sprinkle the cheese on top. Place in the oven and bake for about 20 minutes, until the pastry is puffed and golden. Serve hot or cold.

Gill's poached leek and blue cheese tart

This recipe of Gill's has become a River Cottage classic, and a particular favorite during the colder months. If you have time, make double the quantity of pastry, partially bake two pastry crusts, and freeze one. This means that next time you want to make a savory tart, you will have already done half the work.

Serves 4 to 6

For the short-crust pastry:
1¹/₂ cups all-purpose flour
¹/₂ cup (1 stick) unsalted butter
A pinch of sea salt
1 egg yolk
2 to 3 tablespoons cold milk

2 large or 3 medium leeks (about 1 pound), white part only, washed and sliced into ³/₈-inch rounds
1 tablespoon unsalted butter
Sea salt and freshly ground black pepper
²/₃ cup crumbled good blue cheese
2 eggs
2 egg yolks
1¹/₃ cups heavy cream

First make the pastry. Put the flour, butter, and salt in a food processor and pulse until the mixture looks like bread crumbs. Add the egg yolk, then pour in the milk in a gradual stream. Watch carefully and stop adding the milk as soon as the dough starts to come together. Turn out and knead lightly a couple of times, then wrap in plastic wrap. Chill for half an hour.

Preheat the oven to 325°F.

On a lightly floured surface, roll the pastry out quite thinly and use to line a 10-inch two-part tart pan, letting the excess pastry hang over the edges. Line the pastry with parchment paper, fill with dried beans, and place in the oven. Bake for 20 minutes, then take the tart out of the oven, remove the paper and beans, lightly prick the bottom all over with a fork, and return to the oven for 5 minutes, until the bottom is dry but not too colored. Carefully trim off the excess pastry with a small, sharp knife. Turn the oven temperature up to 350°F.

To make the filling, put the leeks into a saucepan with ¹/₂ cup water, the butter, and some salt and pepper. Bring to a low simmer, then cover and cook gently, stirring once or twice, for about 10 minutes, until just tender. Drain well, reserving the cooking liquid. Spread the cooked leeks in the tart pan and cover with the crumbled cheese.

Put the eggs and egg yolks, cream, and leek liquid in a bowl and beat until smooth. Season to taste, then pour this custard over the cheese and leeks. Put the tart back into the oven and bake for about 30 minutes – the custard should be just set when you gently shake the pan. Serve warm or cold.

the whole fruit

If we only ever ate one kind of food, it would have to be fruit. Why?

Because fruit is just about the only food we have that was absolutely unambiguously designed to be eaten. Not by us, of course, but by a force whose power to shape things for a purpose is second to none. Evolution has offered us fruit as the perfect food: visually irresistible, cleverly packaged for convenience, full of good things that benefit the eater, and, most importantly, delicious. It's all part of a cunning ploy to keep us coming back for more. And by us, I mean not only humans, but our primate cousins and more distant mammalian relatives – and let's not forget the birds.

It's a symbiotic deal, of course. Fruit eaters do a massive favor for the plants that bear the fruit they eat. They habitually remove the seed some distance from the parent plant and, having devoured the fleshy casing around it, deposit that seed in a new place where it might just have a chance to grow. Sometimes, if they've actually swallowed the seed whole, they'll deposit it with a nice little pile of manure to give it the optimum chance of success.

It's all fiendishly clever, and it looks uncannily as if fruit has the animal kingdom in its thrall. But it hasn't all been one way. We haven't exactly been slouches in our relationship with fruit. A few thousand years ago we learned to nurture and cultivate the fruits we loved best, to make them fatter, riper, juicier, and more delicious than ever before. And a few hundred years ago we worked out how to breed them selectively, effectively "inventing" new varieties with specific characteristics. The sole purpose of such practices was to create fruits that delight us even more.

You could conclude that, having been manipulated by fruit for many millions of years, we have now turned the tables and become the arch manipulators ourselves, "in charge" of the kingdom of fruit. But that would be to underestimate the evolutionary forces at work. One consequence of our incessant dabbling is that certain fruit species are now among the most "successful" living organisms. The apple tree and the grapevine, for example, are the two most prolific fruit-bearing plants on the planet (no coincidence that both lend themselves rather well to conversion into alcohol). We reap a massive harvest of plenty from them. At the same time, you could say they've got us eating out of the palm of their hand . . .

This preamble serves to support a view of mine that might otherwise come across as unsupported hyperbolic prejudice. It is my passionate

332

belief that fruit is the most miraculous of foods, a natural wonder, and that to shun it is an act of the deepest human folly that can lead only to despair. To cultivate a consuming relationship with the best fruits of your region (wherever you are in the world), to understand their seasonality so that you get to enjoy them at their best, is one of the fundamentals of a happy life with food – or even, dare I say, a happy life, full stop.

That's what I've tried to do, over the years, in the way that I have bought fruit, eaten fruit, cooked with fruit, and, for a decade or so now, grown fruit in my own garden. Of course, it's the business of cultivation that really puts you in tune with issues of seasonality and ripeness, and you can become deeply involved, obsessing over varieties, fertilizers, and the limitless possibilities of training and pruning trees and bushes to suit your garden space and maximize productivity. I'm heading that way myself at the moment, having just planted about thirty more fruit trees and ten grapevines at home. I'm about to start training my first espalier of pears. Will they come when I whistle? Roll over when I raise my hand? Only time will tell . . .

However, it's equally possible to grow some fruit in a pretty casual and noninterventionist way. Stick an apple tree or two at the bottom of your garden and let them get on with it. Plant a black currant bush – or a blueberry, a red currant, or a gooseberry – in a good-sized pot on your terrace, and, as long as you water it in a dry spell, it will reward you amply. Often the town gardener with a small plot or even just a backyard can find themselves at a surprising advantage. A sun-trapping corner or wall in a sheltered spot can offer you a chance to grow fruit that will be the envy of those with windswept acres at their disposal. You can ripen figs, apricots, plums, or cherries to the peak of sun-drenched perfection. Don't expect to get many in the kitchen, though. You'll eat most of them right from the tree, the warm juices pouring into you like intravenous sunshine.

Much as I love fruit as a cooking ingredient, I think it's entirely right that you should eat more of it raw and unadulterated than you do cooked or fussed into some kind of dish. Some years I have my fill of strawberries yet barely get round to strawberries and cream, let alone pavlova or jam. But at the same time, it doesn't take much to transform a pile of good fruit into a deeply indulgent dessert. When you look at the recipes that follow, you'll see that the way I like to cook and eat fruit is really by ringing the changes with a few well-chosen companions, thrown together with the fruit of the moment.

Cream appears often enough: whipped into an Eton mess, stirred into a cranachan, served as a topping for a fruit-filled sponge, or added to a panna cotta with a tart compote on the side. A good custard goes hot on a crumble, cold in a trifle, or spooned into a bowl with lightly cooked fruit to make a deconstructed fool. Meringues are just aerated sugar crying out for some fruit and cream to make them a touch less reckless. A sponge is just a sponge, but swamped with raspberries and cream it's almost too good to be true.

If growing fruit in any quantity is wholly impractical for you, then you'll have to take steps to make sure you don't miss out on the seasonal bonanzas. U-picks are the next best thing to grow-your-own – some would say better, since others have done all the hard work. It's a lovely way to spend a few hours with the kids on a sunny afternoon, especially since you come back groaning under a weight of fruity goodies. The real fun starts when you set about transforming your harvest into a summer's worth of ice cream and a winter's worth of jam.

Otherwise, farm stands, farmers' markets, and specialty produce stores that are genuinely plugged into the local supply chain should all be well stocked with the best seasonal fruits. If you're lucky, your nearest farmers' market might have a fruit grower as a vendor. If so, they are likely to be offering exciting varieties that you'll struggle to find in any supermarket. My friends Robin and June Small, for instance, of Charlton Orchards in Somerset, delight the shoppers at Taunton farmers' market from September through to January with baskets of Ashmead's Kernel and Orleans Reinette (apples), and Doyenne du Comice and Beurre Hardy (pears). This is a great way to find a favorite variety – and perhaps you'll be inspired to seek out and plant a tree so you can have your own ready supply.

Having said that, the supermarkets are beginning to sharpen up their act in the way they stock and present seasonal fruits. And the stranglehold of Golden Delicious, Granny Smith, and Red Delicious on the supermarket apple supply is finally being loosened. If ever you see an apple in a supermarket that isn't one of these, then vote for it by sticking a few in your shopping basket. The big retailers are also cottoning on to the fact that increasing numbers of their customers would like their fruit pesticide free, so look out for labels that make this pledge.

You'll have gleaned that my overriding passion is for homegrown and local fruits, and the focus of my recipes is very much on this produce.

But I would never be such a killjoy as to suggest you should boycott fruit from overseas. We get through kilos of citrus fruit and bananas at home, particularly in the winter months, and I always keep an eye out for a box of lovely Italian cherries or Turkish apricots in the market even as I try to grow my own at home. I don't suppose I'll ever grow my own mangoes, but I'll pounce on any I see that seem to have achieved genuine ripeness, though there are a lot of rock-hard disappointments out there. The best mangoes, guavas, papayas, pineapples, etc., are to be found in the ethnic markets of big cities, where discerning shoppers who know what's right will brook no substandard specimens.

In choosing my exotics, I will generally opt for organic, fair trade, or both. That's not a kneejerk approach. I've seen and heard enough, some of it at first hand, about the economic and social conditions for agricultural workers in the third world to believe that these choices make a real difference to real people's lives. The way much fruit is grown for the mass European market is both socially and environmentally unsustainable.

The recipes that follow are hardly elaborate. In most cases a competent cook could read the recipe once, then put the book back on the shelf and get on with it. If you go that route, you'll quickly start adding your own touches, fixing things your way, and that's how it should be. I'd like to think that, after years of tinkering, my crumble recipe is now pretty much perfect. But I'd also be disappointed if you didn't immediately take that as provocation to prove me wrong.

Macerated strawberries

A little touch of vinegar and black pepper can do wonders for the blowsy sweetness of ripe strawberries. The sweet-sour dressing brings out all their delicious juices and rounds out the flavor to something like a complex wine. I like to serve this with a delicate cookie or two on the side, such as caraway shortbread (page 390). It also goes well with a plain sponge cake or the honey whole-wheat cake (page 386) – or, of course, with ice cream. Or, for breakfast, with French toast or pancakes. You don't have to limit yourself to strawberries – raspberries, blueberries, and blackberries can all be given the maceration treatment.

Serves 3 to 4

2 tablespoons superfine sugar

4 cups fresh strawberries, hulled and halved, bigger ones cut into 3 or 4 thick slices (or use a mixture of other summer berries)

1 tablespoon balsamic vinegar or lemon juice

$^1/_2$ teaspoon freshly ground black pepper

Scatter the sugar over the prepared strawberries, toss lightly, and let stand for 5 to 10 minutes to get the juices running. Then add the vinegar or lemon juice and pepper, and toss again. Let macerate for at least an hour – ideally 3 to 4 hours – to draw out the juices from the fruit. Stir again, then serve the strawberries at room temperature with the syrupy juices.

VARIATIONS

Strawberries with mint

Replace the balsamic vinegar with cider vinegar or lemon juice, leave out the black pepper, and add 2 tablespoons of finely chopped fresh mint.

Strawberries with raspberry sauce

In a blender, blend about $^3/_4$ cup raspberries with 2 tablespoons of superfine sugar and 1 tablespoon of balsamic vinegar or lemon juice. Strain to remove the seeds, then pour the purée over your hulled, sliced strawberries. Particularly good with meringues and yogurt or cream.

Apple compote

We have a tradition of dividing our apples into two groups: cookers and eaters (actually, there is a third – cider apples). Cooking apples (McIntosh being one of the most popular) contain lots of malic acid, which gives them a sharp, tangy taste. It also ensures the flesh collapses into a fluffy mush when cooked – perfect for pies and crumbles, and a host of other dishes.

This is the basic way to proceed with cooking apples to gently transform them into a lovely compote, which, sweetened to your taste, can be used in all sorts of ways and not just for dessert. I often have a bowlful for breakfast, with some yogurt and a scattering of muesli (page 34), granola, or wheat flakes.

Makes about 3 cups

4 pounds McIntosh or other cooking apples
2 to 8 tablespoons superfine sugar

Peel, core, and finely slice the apples – be thorough, as any little bits of fiber left from the core or peel will catch in your teeth and spoil the pleasure of the otherwise silky compote.

Put the apples in a large pan and add a good tablespoon of sugar and 2 to 3 tablespoons of water – just to stop them sticking to the bottom of the pan. Cook, covered, over gentle heat, stirring often, until the apple pieces have completely dissolved and you have a thick, slightly translucent purée. It should take about half an hour.

Add more sugar to taste – enough to achieve a purée that is still erring on the tart side but not unpleasantly so. You can always add sugar when you serve it, and in fact the slight graininess of just-sprinkled sugar on the compote is a pleasure in itself.

Leave to cool completely, then store in the fridge in a jar or plastic container. It will keep for a couple of weeks.

VARIATIONS

Apple fool
Keep the compote tart. Whip up $1^1/_2$ cups heavy cream and sweeten with a little sugar. Lightly swirl the cream into the compote, keeping it rippled. Pile into glasses and chill before serving with a sweet, crumbly cookie, such as shortbread (page 390).

Applesauce
The classic accompaniment to roast pork and goose, and rightly so, as the tart fruit cuts the richness of the meat. Keep the compote tart and try adding the finely grated zest of an orange before you heat it for serving.

Two dried-fruit compotes

These sweet, gently spiced concoctions are very easy to make and will keep happily in the fridge for at least a week. They're delicious with yogurt or ice cream, but I often find myself snacking on a spoonful or two throughout the day when hunger strikes.

Spiced fig compote

fig 1.   fig 2.   fig 3.

Serves 6 to 8

1 pound dried figs

2 tablespoons light brown sugar

2 tablespoons honey

2 cardamom pods, lightly crushed

1 star anise pod

1 cinnamon stick

A finely pared strip of orange zest

Separate the dried figs if they are stuck together and give them a quick rinse in cold water to remove any rice flour if necessary. Put them in a heatproof bowl and pour over just enough boiling water to cover. Cover the bowl with a plate and let soak for 4 to 5 hours.

Strain the water from the soaked figs into a saucepan and add the sugar, honey, spices, and orange zest. Stir over low heat to dissolve the sugar, then bring to a gentle simmer.

Add the figs and poach very gently until completely tender. The timing will depend on how moist your figs were to start with – plump, ready-to-eat figs need 10 to 15 minutes, but drier fruit will take longer. If the syrup gets too thick, add a little warm water. Cool, then store the figs in their syrup in an airtight container in the fridge until needed.

Serve as a dessert with yogurt, cream, cold custard, or ice cream, or with a scattering of my independent crumble (see page 358). Alternatively, try it for breakfast with yogurt and muesli or other cereal.

Apricot and prune compote

Serves 4 to 6

1 cup dried apricots

1 cup prunes

$1/2$ cup golden raisins (optional)

$1^1/4$ cups freshly squeezed orange juice (or water)

3 tablespoons lemon juice

A few finely pared strips of orange and lemon zest

$1/2$ vanilla bean (optional)

Put everything in a saucepan and bring to the barest of simmers. Remove from the heat, place a lid on the pan, and allow to cool slowly for an hour or two. The fruit will plump up in the warm juice. Transfer to an airtight container and store in the fridge.

Serve in any of the ways suggested for spiced fig compote, above.

VARIATION

Use $2^1/2$ cups dried apricots and forget the prunes and raisins.

Elderflower panna cotta with gooseberry compote

A delicately wobbly, creamy panna cotta is such a simple but sophisticated dish. Infused with the scent of elderflowers and partnered with a sharp gooseberry compote, it makes a stunning summer dessert. You can use fresh elderflowers during their short season in May, but otherwise elderflower liqueur works fine. Leave out the elderflower altogether and this is a great recipe for a plain panna cotta, with a little tang from the yogurt.

Serves 4

$1/3$ cup whole milk

1 cup heavy cream

1 tablespoon superfine sugar (or $1^1/2$ teaspoons if you're using elderflower liqueur)

3 to 4 large heads of elderflower, or 2 tablespoons elderflower liqueur

$1^1/2$ teaspoons plain gelatin

$2/3$ cup plain yogurt

For the gooseberry compote:

1 pound gooseberries, topped and tailed

$1/4$ cup superfine sugar

A few sprigs of elderflower (optional)

Combine the milk, cream, and sugar in a saucepan. Tie up the elderflower heads in a piece of cheesecloth and add to the pan, or stir in the elderflower cordial. Scald the liquid – bring just to a simmer, but don't let it bubble. If you're using elderflower heads, let stand for half an hour to infuse, then remove the elderflower.

Soak the gelatin in cold water for 5 to 10 minutes, until softened. If you left the cream mixture to infuse for half an hour, reheat it almost to boiling – if you have used liqueur, the cream should still be hot enough. Add the gelatin to the hot cream mixture and stir until dissolved. Let cool to room temperature, stirring from time to time.

Once cooled, stir in the yogurt until thoroughly combined. Pour the mixture into four $1/2$-cup molds, such as ramekins, and chill in the fridge for at least 4 hours, until set.

Meanwhile, make the compote. Put the gooseberries in a pan with the sugar and $1/4$ cup water. Tie up the elderflower sprigs, if using, in a piece of cheesecloth and add to the pan. Bring to a simmer and cook gently for about 10 minutes, until the gooseberries are soft. Let cool completely, then remove the elderflower sprigs and chill the compote.

To turn out the panna cottas, dip each mold very briefly in hot water – literally just a few seconds – then turn upside down onto a serving plate and give it a shake; if necessary, run a knife around the edge. Serve with the gooseberry compote.

Rhubarb and orange yogurt fool

A classic fool combines a fruit compote or purée, cream, and custard to delicious effect. This is a sort of deconstructed version, with the cream replaced by yogurt to give the whole thing a lighter feel. You could mix all three elements together, of course, but I enjoy the look of them unmingled in the dish, and the pleasure of choosing exactly how much of each to put on my spoon.

Serves 6

For the rhubarb compote:
2 pounds rhubarb, cut into 1^1/$_2$- to 2-inch lengths
Juice of 1 large orange
1 cup superfine sugar

Custard (see page 351)
2 cups thick, rich yogurt

To make the compote, put the rhubarb, orange juice, and sugar in a saucepan and bring to a gentle simmer, stirring occasionally. Cook for about 5 minutes, until the rhubarb breaks down into a purée. You can stop cooking when some of the rhubarb is still just holding its shape, but make sure it's quite tender. Use a sieve to drain off a little of the syrupy juice, so you get a slightly denser rhubarb mixture and some good, tart rhubarb syrup. (You could drizzle this syrup on pancakes, or top up with chilled fizzy wine to make a rhubarb bellini.) Cool the rhubarb and then chill.

For each serving, put a couple of tablespoons of the rhubarb into a slightly tilted bowl, turn the tilted bowl slightly, spoon a couple of tablespoons of custard alongside the compote, tilt, and do the same with the thick yogurt. The idea is that the three elements stay more or less separate in the bowl. It's the eater's prerogative to dip and mix, a little, a lot, or not all, sampling different proportions of the three elements, as they wish.

VARIATIONS

This winning threesome of tart fruit purée, sweet custard, and creamy yogurt can be adapted using any fruit that makes a good, tangy compote – the most obvious being plums, apricots, blackberries, and Granny Smith or other cooking apples. Or replace cooked fruit with a pile of fresh raspberries, lightly crushed and sweetened with a few pinches of sugar. In all cases, you can sprinkle over some independent crumble (page 358), if you like.

Two seasonal cranachans

Cranachan is a traditional Scottish dessert, a sublime mixture of toasted oats, honey, cream, fruit, and whisky. Beautifully simple and quick to make, it's ripe for a bit of seasonal variation. I love a classic raspberry version in the summer, laced with some pungent heather honey. But from January to June, when rhubarb is available (first the indoor-grown, "forced" variety, then the sturdier outdoor crop), I find that makes a stunning pink-rippled cranachan, too.

Raspberry and honey cranachan

Serves 4

1/2 cup old-fashioned rolled oats

2 tablespoons whisky

1 cup heavy cream

2 cups fresh raspberries

2 tablespoons heather honey (or other favorite honey)

Warm a small frying pan over medium-low heat. Add the rolled oats and stir until they are golden and toasted – keep a close eye on them, as they can burn easily. Transfer to a plate to cool.

Stir the whisky and cream together in a bowl and then whisk until the cream holds soft peaks. Lightly crush a few of the raspberries, so the juices run. Loosely fold the honey, oats, and raspberries into the cream, spoon into glasses, and serve right away.

Rhubarb and Cointreau cranachan

Serves 4

1 pound rhubarb, cut into 2-inch lengths

Finely grated zest and juice of 1 orange

1 tablespoon superfine sugar

1 vanilla bean, split lengthwise and cut in half

1/2 cup old-fashioned rolled oats

1 tablespoon Cointreau

1 cup heavy cream

3 tablespoons honey

Preheat the oven to 325°F.

Put the rhubarb, orange zest and juice, sugar, and vanilla bean into a roasting pan and stir to combine. Cover with foil and bake for 30 minutes or so, until soft. Let the rhubarb cool completely. Remove the vanilla bean, then transfer the rhubarb and any juices to a bowl.

Warm a small frying pan over medium-low heat. Add the rolled oats and stir until they are golden and toasted – keep a close eye on them, as they can burn easily. Transfer to a plate to cool.

Stir the Cointreau and cream together in a bowl and then whisk until the cream holds soft peaks. Loosely fold in the honey, oats, and rhubarb with its juices, spoon into glasses, and serve right away.

Raspberry and strawberry Eton mess

Though sadly unheard of at Eton in my day, this delicious dessert is now a British classic. It's really just a fool sweetened with broken meringue instead of sugar – but that extra element of texture makes so much difference. I love it with the traditional strawberries alone, but including raspberries adds a whole new dimension to it. Tart fruits such as gooseberries and rhubarb work well, too. Just fold a cooled cooked compote into the cream and meringues.

Serves 6

For the meringue:
2 egg whites
$^1/_2$ cup superfine sugar

2 cups fresh strawberries
2 cups fresh raspberries
$2^1/_2$ tablespoons superfine sugar
$1^1/_2$ cups heavy cream, lightly whipped

Start with the meringue: Preheat the oven to 250°F. Put the egg whites into a spotlessly clean bowl and whisk until they hold soft peaks. Now add half the sugar and whisk to blend well with the egg whites. Add the remaining sugar and whisk again until the mixture is thick and shiny and holds stiff peaks. You should be able to turn the bowl upside down without anything sliding out.

Line a baking sheet with parchment paper. Dollop tablespoonfuls of meringue on the sheet and place in the oven. Leave for 2 hours, until the meringues are completely dry and crisp on the outside (they will still be a bit squidgy in the middle) and can be lifted off the paper easily. Remove and let cool completely.

Meanwhile, halve the strawberries, thickly slicing any whoppers. Put in a large bowl with the raspberries and sugar. Coasely crush and squeeze a few of the berries with your hands so the juices start to run. Cover and let macerate in the fridge for an hour or two.

To assemble the mess, break the meringues into coarse pieces, then fold into the whipped cream. Now lightly fold in the chilled fruit, so everything is rippled together rather than thoroughly blended. Pile into glasses and serve. You can make it an hour or so in advance, but not more, or the meringue will go weepy in the cream.

VARIATIONS

Gooseberry Eton mess
Replace the strawberries and raspberries with gooseberry compote (page 342).

Bramley Eton mess
Replace the berries with apple compote (page 339), and use 1 cup (rather than $1^1/_2$ cups) cream.

Black currant trifle

This simple trifle is faithful to the classic combination of booze-soaked sponge, fruit, custard, and cream. You can make it throughout the year, using all manner of seasonal fruits.

Serves 6

For the black currant purée:
4 cups black currants
$3/4$ cup confectioners' sugar (or possibly more)

For the custard:
1 cup heavy cream
1 cup whole milk
1 vanilla bean, split lengthwise
4 egg yolks
$1/2$ cup superfine sugar
1 heaping teaspoon cornstarch

To assemble:
1 egg white, lightly beaten until frothy
A little superfine sugar
3 ounces plain sponge cake, such as Genoese sponge (page 372), cut into $3/4$-inch cubes
$1/4$ cup crème de cassis
1 cup heavy cream, lightly whipped

Start with the black currant purée: Set aside about 20 fine, plump black currants. Put the rest into a saucepan with $1/3$ cup water, bring to a simmer, and cook gently for about 10 minutes, stirring and crushing the fruit, until soft and pulpy. Rub the black currant pulp through a sieve and discard the skins and seeds. Whisk the confectioners' sugar into the warm purée, then taste and add more sugar if necessary. It needs to remain on the tart side, as the custard will be very sweet. Let cool.

Next, make the custard: Put the cream, milk, and vanilla bean in a saucepan and bring to just below boiling, then set aside to infuse. Put the egg yolks in a bowl, add the sugar and cornstarch, and beat together until smooth. Remove the vanilla bean from the hot cream. Gradually pour the hot cream into the egg yolk mixture, whisking all the time. Pour into a clean pan and heat gently, stirring constantly with a wooden spoon, until the mixture is thick enough to coat the back of the spoon; don't let it boil or it will curdle. Strain the thickened custard through a sieve, let cool, then chill.

Roll the reserved black currants in the egg white, let the excess drain off, then roll them in a little superfine sugar so they take on a "frosty" coating. Set aside in the fridge.

To assemble, divide the sponge cubes between 6 large glasses and drizzle over the crème de cassis. Now layer the black currant purée and custard in the glasses. Finish each with a big spoonful of whipped cream and a few frosted black currants. Serve lightly chilled.

VARIATIONS

Replace the black currant purée with one of the following fruit/booze combinations, keeping the fruit quite tart to counteract the sweet custard. If you don't have the suggested alcohol, use a medium sherry.

• Rhubarb compote (page 344) with Grand Marnier or Cointreau.

• Gooseberry compote (page 342); no alcohol needed for this one.

• Raspberries, coarsely crushed, lightly sugared, and macerated with a drizzle of framboise or crème de cassis.

• Blackberries, cooked, sieved, and sweetened as for black currants above, with a little Calvados or cider brandy.

Roast vanilla plums on toast

This makes a very simple dessert or a rather luxurious breakfast, though for breakfast you might want to forgo the ice cream or crème fraîche and try some yogurt instead. Or you might not.

Serves 4

5 tablespoons unsalted butter, softened

2 large or 4 small thick slices of crusty white bread

About 10 plums, halved and pitted

1 vanilla bean

$1/4$ cup superfine sugar

Preheat the oven to 375°F.

Lightly grease a medium baking dish with a little of the butter, then spread a little more of it on both sides of the bread. Cut the bread in half if large. Lay the pieces in the dish and arrange the plums on top, cut side up.

Split the vanilla bean lengthwise and scrape out the seeds with the tip of a knife. Combine the seeds with the remaining butter and dot it over the plums. Sprinkle the sugar on top, then cut the empty vanilla bean lengthwise into shreds and scatter these over the plums too. Bake for 20 to 30 minutes, until the plums are tender and the bread is caramelized around the edges yet soggy and syrupy under the plums.

Serve right away, with crème fraîche, ice cream, or thick yogurt.

Two seasonal clafoutis

This classic French dessert is traditionally made with cherries. It also works well with plums, pears, and even prunes.

Cherry clafoutis

Serves 6

1 pound sweet cherries
1/3 cup all-purpose flour
A pinch of sea salt
1/2 cup superfine sugar
3 eggs, lightly beaten
1 cup whole milk
Confectioners' sugar for dusting (optional)

Preheat the oven to 350°F.

Lightly butter a 10-inch round baking dish or an 8-by-10-inch rectangular one. Remove the stems from the cherries but do not pit them; you don't want any of the juices – or flavor – to escape until the moment you bite into your first cherry. Spread them out in a single layer in the dish.

Sift the flour and salt into a bowl and stir in the sugar. Make a well in the center and add the beaten eggs. Gradually stir in the flour from the sides, mixing well, then beat in the milk, a little at a time, to form a smooth batter.

Pour the batter over the cherries and bake for 35 to 40 minutes, until golden and puffed up. Clafoutis is best eaten warm, but it's not bad cold either. Dust with confectioners' sugar, if you like, just before serving, on its own or with cream.

Rhubarb clafoutis

Serves 6

1 pound rhubarb
A little ground cinnamon (optional)
Grated zest of 1/2 orange and the juice of the whole fruit
1 cup superfine sugar
1/3 cup all-purpose flour
A pinch of sea salt
3 eggs, lightly beaten
1 cup whole milk
Confectioners' sugar for dusting (optional)

Preheat the oven to 400°F.

Cut the rhubarb into 2-inch lengths and put in a baking pan with a good pinch of cinnamon, if using, the orange juice, and 2 tablespoons of the sugar. Toss well and roast in the oven for 10 to 15 minutes, or until tender and just beginning to caramelize around the edges. Let cool completely and then drain in a sieve.

Turn the oven temperature down to 350°F. Lightly butter a 10-inch round baking dish or an 8-by-10-inch rectangular one. Make the batter as for the cherry clafoutis (above), stirring in the orange zest and a pinch of cinnamon, if you like, with the sugar.

Arrange the drained rhubarb in the buttered dish and assemble and bake as for the cherry clafoutis. When you are just about to serve, mix together about 1/2 teaspoon confectioners" sugar and 1/2 teaspoon ground cinnamon, if you like, then sift a light dusting over the top of the clafoutis. Serve with or without cream.

Baked apples

A perfect baked apple is one of the truly great desserts. It's all about choosing the right variety of apple, and not stinting on the butter and booze that go in the cavity with the dried fruit. Eating apples, such as Golden Delicious and Winesap, work better than cookers such as Granny Smith and Jonagold, which have a tendency to collapse into a fluffy mush. Apple brandy lends a special flavor here.

Serve your baked apples piping hot with a scoop of ice cream on the side. Rum raisin is pretty good, or one flavored with cinnamon or cardamom, but a good-quality vanilla goes well, too.

Serves 6

$^1/_2$ cup dried fruit, such as raisins and chopped prunes

$^1/_4$ cup apple brandy

6 tablespoons unsalted butter, softened

2 tablespoons dark brown sugar

Finely grated zest of 1 lemon

$^1/_2$ teaspoon ground cinnamon (optional)

6 fairly large eating apples

Put the dried fruit in a small bowl and pour over the brandy. Leave to macerate for at least an hour, ideally overnight.

Preheat the oven to 300°F.

Beat the soaked fruit into the softened butter, along with the sugar, lemon zest, and cinnamon, if using. Core the apples and cut a sliver off the base of each one if you think they won't stand up straight in the pan. It's a good idea to score them around their circumference with a sharp knife too, to keep them from bursting. Stuff the cavities with the spiced fruit butter, then arrange the apples in an ovenproof dish, smearing any extra butter over the top.

Cover with foil and bake for 50 to 60 minutes, until soft but not collapsing, removing the foil about two-thirds of the way through cooking and basting with the buttery juices. Serve the apples with the juices spooned over them and a scoop of ice cream on the side.

VARIATION

Christmas baked apples

If you have any leftover mincemeat at Christmas, you can use this instead of the brandy-soaked dried fruit. Punch it up a bit with some lemon zest and a slosh of cider brandy, stuff it into the cavities, and put a tablespoon of butter on top of each one before baking.

Apple and walnut crumble

The nubbly crunch of toasted walnuts adds a new dimension to a classic crumble; pecans are equally good. This basic crumble topping can be used on all sorts of other fruits, from winter rhubarb, through summer gooseberries or plums, to autumnal blackberries, pears, or quince. You can also bake it separately to create my "independent crumble" (see below).

Serves 8

$3/4$ cup walnuts

For the crumble:
$1^1/_2$ cups all-purpose flour
A pinch of sea salt
$3/4$ cup cold unsalted butter, cut into cubes
$2/_3$ cup superfine, granulated, or light brown sugar
$2/_3$ cup quick oats
$2/_3$ cup ground almonds (optional)

$2^1/_2$ pounds cooking apples, peeled, cored, and finely sliced
$1/_4$ to $1/_2$ cup superfine sugar
1 teaspoon ground cinnamon (optional)

Preheat the oven to 350°F. Scatter the walnuts in a pie pan and toast in the oven for 5 to 7 minutes, giving them a shake halfway through, until just beginning to color and develop aroma. Let cool, then chop very coarsely.

To prepare the crumble, sift the flour and salt into a bowl (or food processor). Add the butter and rub in with your fingers (or pulse briefly in the processor) until the mixture resembles coarse crumbs. Stir in the sugar, oatmeal, and ground almonds, if using. Squeeze a few handfuls of crumble in your fist to make lumps – I reckon it's nicer to have a "rocky" crumble rather than a fine, even-textured one.

Put the apples in a large bowl and sprinkle over the sugar (you'll need to estimate the amount according to the tartness of the apples). Add the walnuts and the cinnamon, if using, and mix gently. Spread in a pie dish or other ovenproof dish, getting the fruit as compact as you can.

Scatter the crumble over the apples in a fairly even layer and bake for 40 to 45 minutes, until browned on top. Serve hot, with cream, custard, or ice cream. Eat leftovers cold for breakfast, with thick, rich yogurt.

VARIATION

Independent crumble

Make the crumble as above, squishing a few handfuls of it to make some larger lumps. Spread the mixture out in a baking pan and bake in an oven preheated to 375°F for 20 to 25 minutes, until golden brown and crumbly, taking it out a couple of times to give it a good stir. Let cool completely, then store in an airtight container in the fridge, or in a cool place; it will keep for a couple of weeks.

This ready-to-go topping can be scattered thickly over gooseberry compote (page 342) or rhubarb compote (page 344) in a pie dish and baked at 350°F for 20 minutes to make a quick crumble.

It is also delicious cold, with any tart fruit compote (pages 339–44), or sprinkled over lightly macerated or crushed summer berries. Serve with yogurt or cream, or even ice cream.

Roast plum sorbet
with chocolate brownies

This combination of sweet-tart, icy plums
and warm chocolate brownies is deep
indulgence, producing pleasing contrasts
on so many levels: warm–cold, sweet–sharp,
choc–fruit. Whenever I serve it, my friends
go all gooey, like the brownies.

Serves 6 to 8

**2 pounds plums, halved
and pitted**

2 vanilla beans

**$\frac{1}{2}$ cup superfine sugar
(or more, depending on
the tartness of the
plums)**

**Plain chocolate brownies
(page 397)**

Make the sorbet at least 12 hours before you want to serve it. Preheat
the oven to 400°F. Put the plums in a roasting pan. Split the vanilla
beans lengthwise, chop them into a few pieces, and add to the pan,
along with the sugar and 1 cup water. Roast in the oven for about
30 minutes, until the plums are really soft and slightly blistered
around the edges. Rub the plums and all the juices from the pan
through a sieve into a bowl. Taste the purée and add more sugar
if you think it needs it, then let cool.

Churn the purée in an ice-cream machine until very thick, then
transfer to the freezer to set solid. Alternatively, put the purée in
a shallow container and place in the freezer. Take it out every hour
or so and beat it to distribute the ice crystals throughout the mixture
and make a soft sorbet texture. Three interventions should do the
trick; two will do if you're pushed.

Serve the plum sorbet accompanied by brownies, still a little warm
from the oven.

Apple yogurt ice with blackberry sauce

I love the idea of blackberry and apple ice cream, but it's hard to "fix" the delicate flavor of apple in a rich, custard-based ice. I've now discovered that mixing apple purée with a little yogurt produces a great frozen dessert, full of appley flavor.

Melting some blackberry jelly is a quick way to make a sauce, but at the height of the blackberry season, you could use fresh berries – lightly cook about 2 cups blackberries with about $1/4$ cup sugar and a splash of water, then rub through a sieve to remove the seeds. Adjust the sweetness to taste.

Serves 6

$1^3/_4$ pounds McIntosh apples (or other cooking apples), peeled, cored, and thinly sliced

$1/_2$ cup superfine sugar

Confectioners' sugar, to taste

$1/_2$ cup plain whole-milk yogurt

2 to 3 tablespoons heavy cream (optional)

For the cheaty blackberry sauce:

6 tablespoons blackberry jelly

1 to 2 tablespoons fresh lemon juice

Put the apples in a pan with the superfine sugar and 3 tablespoons of water. Heat gently until the sugar has dissolved, then simmer for about half an hour, stirring frequently, until the apples are completely soft and broken down. Use an immersion blender to purée the apples until really smooth. Let cool completely.

Taste for sweetness, adding a little confectioners' sugar if it is needed – the purée should taste oversweet at this point, as the yogurt is sharp, and things taste less sweet when frozen in any case.

Combine the apple purée with the yogurt, and the heavy cream if you fancy a slightly creamy ice. Taste again for sweetness.

Churn in an ice-cream machine until thick, then freeze until set solid. (Alternatively, freeze in a shallow container, beating several times as it hardens, to distribute the ice crystals.) Remove from the freezer about half an hour before serving so it can soften a little.

To make the sauce, just heat the jelly very gently in a small pan, stirring frequently until it melts, then stir in lemon juice to taste. Let it cool (whisking in a splash of warm water if it resets) or keep it warm – either is good on the yogurt ice.

Scoop the yogurt ice into glasses and drizzle over the sauce.

VARIATION
Apple and blackberry ripple ice
For a stunning-looking dessert, ripple the cooled blackberry sauce directly into the soft-set yogurt ice after churning, or after the final beating if not using an ice-cream machine, then freeze.

Quince and apple sorbet

The fragrant, honey-colored quince is a jewel among fruits, and greatly underexplored. It appears most frequently in hot dishes, such as pies, cobblers, and crumbles, or with roast meats. But it can also be very striking served cold. Combined with tart apples, which soften its powerful, perfumed flavor, it makes a superb sorbet.

Serves 8

1¹/₂ cups superfine sugar

1¹/₄ pounds quince, peeled, cored, and chopped

1 pound Granny Smith apples, peeled, cored, and chopped

Fresh lemon juice, to taste

Put the sugar in a large saucepan with 2 cups water and heat gently, stirring to dissolve the sugar. Add the quince, bring to a simmer, and cook at a gentle bubble for 20 minutes, stirring occasionally.

Add the apples and cook for a further 10 minutes, or until all the fruit is very soft. Blend to a purée using an immersion blender in the pan, then add lemon juice to taste – about 2 tablespoons should do. Pass the purée through a fine sieve and let cool.

Churn the mixture in an ice-cream machine until semifrozen and creamy, then transfer to the freezer. Alternatively, put it in a shallow container in the freezer and beat every hour or so, until you have a soft, fluffy sorbet. Return to the freezer until frozen firm.

Allow the sorbet to soften at room temperature for 20 to 30 minutes before serving, in small dishes, with honey brandy snaps (page 394) or other crisp cookies.

Black currant granita

A granita is one of the easiest of all iced desserts. All you're really doing is freezing a fruit purée/syrup, then flaking it with a fork to create an elegant pile of rough, sparkling, fruity ice crystals. It's not exactly hard work, but the result is very stylish. Once you've got the hang of it, you can easily invent your own, using all manner of summer and autumn fruits. The tart ones, such as raspberries, gooseberries, plums, and rhubarb, are best.

Serves 8

2 pounds black currants
At least 2 cups confectioners' sugar

Put the black currants in a saucepan with 1 cup water, bring to a simmer, and cook gently for 5 to 10 minutes, until the fruit is completely soft. Push it through a sieve to remove the seeds and skins. Sift in the sugar and whisk well. Taste the mixture and add more sugar if you think it's needed (bear in mind that, once frozen, it will taste less sweet).

Pour the mixture into a large, shallow container (if the purée is in a layer no more than 2 inches deep, it will speed up the freezing process). Freeze until rock solid.

Remove the granita from the freezer about 20 minutes before you want to serve it, to allow it to soften slightly. Just before serving, use a fork to scrape the mixture into crystals and shards. Pile into glasses and serve at once.

VARIATIONS

Gooseberry granita
Replace the black currants with gooseberries.

Snow-capped granita
Try drizzling a little heavy cream on the granita in each glass just before you serve it (as illustrated). It will half-freeze in a thin layer on the icy fruit crystals. Both creamy cap and frosty crystals will melt and combine in the warmth of your mouth. Nice.

treats

This chapter is pure indulgence. And why not? Despite my passion

for home-reared meat, fresh local fish, and seasonal garden vegetables, and the unceasing pleasure I get from using such ingredients, I have to admit that the following collection of recipes takes me to a different level of excitement – one in which I rub my hands together, waggle my eyebrows, and break out into a big, broad grin of eager anticipation.

That's not simply because these are my favorite glee-inducing, sweet-treat recipes. It's also because they bring my lifelong culinary adventure full circle, taking me right back to my childhood. There is absolutely no doubt that it was my sweet tooth that led me into the kitchen in the first place. It started with me standing on a chair, age five, mixing confectioners' sugar, egg whites, food coloring, and peppermint essence. This sickly green putty was technically destined to become peppermint creams. And sometimes it actually did. It also proved to be an irresistible "eat me" concoction that got me hooked on cooking and rapidly transported me to the wonderland of baking cakes and cookies, and mixing up indulgent desserts and sticky sweets.

For the first three years or so of my fledgling amateur cooking career, I don't think I made a single thing you would call savory. Instead I built up a repertoire of cakes, sweets, and desserts from the classic cookbooks on my mother's kitchen shelf, mainly the two British domestic goddesses of the 1960s and 1970s respectively, Constance Spry and Katie Stewart. By the age of eight, I was cooking most of the desserts for my mum's dinner parties – a rotating agenda of profiteroles, pavlova, chocolate rum gâteau, and Genoese sponge filled with whipped cream and strawberries or raspberries from the garden. Versions of all these – in my own words, but often not too far from the originals – appear in the pages that follow (or in The Whole Fruit chapter).

I've never lost my sweet tooth, though to my great relief, I managed to find a savory incisor or two as my cooking adventure progressed – and it's still a great thrill for me to discover a new recipe to add to the "sugar lounge" collection. Places on this exclusive list are hard won, but having made the grade they invariably do good service for many years. On reviewing the list, it's interesting to note that at least half the recipes go back a decade or more (and quite soon it will be forty years since I first made fudge and profiteroles). It was Gill Meller, our head chef at River Cottage, who introduced me to the honey whole-wheat cake (page 386) a year or so ago. Now it's become a big favorite at home, as well as with our guests at the cooking school, and I'm sure I'll still be baking it in five years' time. The same goes for the lemon drizzle cake on page 378 (a great way to show kids that chocolate is not the only treat) and the chunky fig, apricot, and prune cake on page 383, which is my latest solution to the challenge of cramming dried fruit into a cake without it becoming austere, sickly, or overtly Christmassy.

So what follows is pretty much my current "sweet-indulgence top twenty" (though a fair few recipes in the fruit chapter could probably also compete for a place in that chart). At home, these recipes get regular outings on all kinds of occasions – and not only "special" ones. Although the easy rich chocolate cake on page 384 is a rock-solid (metaphorically speaking, not literally), dependable birthday cake for chocolate lovers, it's also pressed into service frequently when friends drop by for tea, since it's simple to make and delivers its dose of dense, choccy deliciousness without the need for icing. Personally, I think it's an important principle of treat cooking that it should not be restricted to hallowed celebrations, or even the arrival of guests. The fact that it's raining outside, or that it "seems like ages since we made cookies," is reason enough in our household to get out the kitchen scales, the sugar, the butter, and the big, greedy eyes.

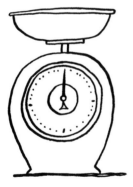

Talking of kitchen scales, it's often said that savory cooking is an art, whereas baking is an exact science – one implication being that you shouldn't meddle with the precise quantities and techniques that have been laid down in print and proven in practice. I concur, but only up to a point. If you meddle with the recipes that follow, they may well not turn out as intended (or as photographed), but stick within the realms of general cakery and all-round dessertness and you won't go too far wrong. Even your worst mishaps are likely to get devoured with gusto (or a good dollop of cream).

I say that not only because I insist on your freedom to adapt my recipes as a matter of principle, but also because in this book many successes have been the result of testing hunches and indulging experimental whims. That includes one of my favorite tweaks in this chapter – the frangipane version of the muffins on page 388. They were the result of a "what if?" conversation of the kind that often occurs when I chat with friends and colleagues: "What if we replaced some of the flour with ground almonds . . . would we get a richer, more gooey muffin that would almost do as a grown-up dessert?" Well, I know what I think, but it's a question you can answer only if you give them a whirl . . .

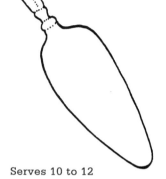

Genoese sponge cake

This is a very useful recipe to have in your repertoire. The light but firm sponge is delicious filled with fresh fruit and cream but is also ideal for a trifle. You do need to whisk the eggs and sugar together for about 10 minutes, but this is easy if you have a handheld electric mixer.

Serves 10 to 12

4 tablespoons unsalted butter
³/₄ cup all-purpose flour
A pinch of sea salt
4 eggs
¹/₂ cup superfine sugar

To serve:
³/₄ cup heavy cream, lightly whipped
2 cups fresh raspberries or strawberries
Vanilla sugar or plain superfine sugar

Preheat the oven to 350°F. Melt the butter gently and let cool slightly. Use a little of it to grease 2 round 7-inch cake pans. Dust the sides generously with flour, knock out any excess, then line the bottoms with parchment paper.

Sift the flour and salt together; set aside. Put the eggs and sugar in a large heatproof bowl that will sit snugly over the top of a saucepan. Pour boiling water into the saucepan and set the bowl on top. The hot water must not actually touch the bowl; it is the steam that is needed to heat it up, which helps the sugar to dissolve and thickens the mixture slightly. Using a handheld electric mixer, beat the eggs and sugar for about 10 minutes, until very pale, thick, moussey, and at least tripled in bulk. The mixture should hold its shape on the surface for a few seconds if you let a little fall from the beaters.

Sift half the flour into the egg and sugar mixture and gently fold it in with a large metal spoon. Repeat with the remaining flour. Carefully pour in the melted butter and fold this in too, until just incorporated.

Pour the mixture into the pans and bake for 25 minutes, until golden brown and firm to the touch. Let cool in the pans for a few minutes and then, running a small, sharp knife around the edge of the cakes if necessary to help release them, turn them out on to a wire rack to cool completely.

Serve topped with, or sandwiched together with, lightly whipped cream and fresh raspberries or strawberries. Finish with a sprinkling of vanilla sugar or plain sugar.

VARIATION

Trifle sponges
Bake the mixture in a large jelly roll pan instead. Once cooled, slice the cake into fingers or cubes to use for a trifle such as my black currant trifle (page 351).

Apple and almond cake

You can serve this warm, with lots of cream, custard, or yogurt. However, it tastes just as good cold, in thick slices, with a cup of tea or coffee. You need fairly sweet, firm dessert apples, such as Rome Beauty, that will hold their shape when cooked (generally speaking, the more acidic the apple, the more it will break down on cooking).

Serves 8

For the apples:

4 Rome Beauty or other dessert apples

2 tablespoons unsalted butter

1 heaping tablespoon granulated sugar

¼ teaspoon ground cinnamon (optional)

⅔ cup (1⅓ sticks) unsalted butter, softened

½ cup superfine sugar

2 eggs

1 teaspoon almond extract (optional – if you like that extra-almondy, frangipane taste)

½ cup white or whole-wheat self-rising flour

½ cup blanched almonds, whizzed in a food processor until finely ground (or use ready-ground almonds)

Preheat the oven to 350°F. Grease an 8-inch springform cake pan and line the bottom with parchment paper.

Peel the apples, quarter them, and cut out the cores, then cut each quarter into about 3 wedges. Melt the butter in a frying pan and let it start to sizzle gently. Add the granulated sugar and stir until the mixture bubbles. Add the apples, sprinkle over the cinnamon, if using, and cook over medium heat for about 5 minutes, turning occasionally, until the apples are just tender and very lightly caramelized. Remove from the heat and let cool.

Put the butter and superfine sugar in a large bowl and beat together with a handheld electric mixer, or using a stand mixer, until light and fluffy. Break in an egg and beat well, then beat in the second egg, along with the almond extract, if using, and a spoonful of flour (this helps to prevent the mixture curdling). Add the ground almonds, sift in the remaining flour, and fold in gently with a large metal spoon.

Scrape the mixture into the prepared pan and gently smooth the surface with a palette knife, then arrange the apples on top. Drizzle over any buttery juices from the pan. Bake for 45 to 50 minutes, until a skewer inserted in the center comes out clean.

Set on a wire rack to cool for a few minutes before releasing the sides. Serve warm, with cream, custard, or Greek yogurt, or cold for tea.

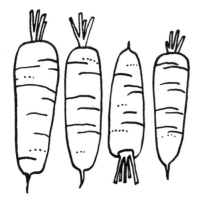

Carrot cake

This wonderful creation, soaked with honey, manages to be both sumptuous and earthy at the same time. It really doesn't need icing – but, if you're a carrot cake traditionalist, you can always whip up a tart cream-cheese-based topping, perhaps laced with a little orange zest.

Serves 12 to 14

4 eggs

$^2/_3$ cup superfine sugar

$1^1/_4$ cups canola oil, or $^1/_2$ cup plus 2 tablespoons each canola and sunflower oil for a slightly lighter flavor

2 cups whole-wheat self-rising flour (see page 386)

$^1/_2$ teaspoon sea salt

$^1/_2$ teaspoon baking soda

3 to 4 large carrots, about 12 ounces in total, peeled and finely grated

About $^1/_2$ cup honey

Preheat the oven to 350°F. Grease a 10-inch springform cake pan and line the bottom with parchment paper.

Put the eggs and sugar in a large bowl and beat together with a handheld electric mixer, or using a stand mixer, for about 10 minutes, until pale, foamy, and slightly thickened. Add the oil and beat for another minute or two.

Sift the flour, salt, and baking soda together into the mixture. Add in any bran left in the sieve, too. Fold in gently. Finally, fold in the grated carrots. Spoon the mixture into the prepared pan and bake for 45 to 50 minutes, or until a skewer inserted in the center comes out clean. Remove from the oven and set the pan on a wire rack.

Put the honey into a small saucepan over low heat and heat gently until it is liquid. Pierce the surface of the hot cake all over with a small knife or a skewer. Slowly pour on the hot honey so it soaks ·into the cake. Let cool slightly in the pan before turning out. Serve warm or cold.

Lemon drizzle cake

This is really a sponge cake flavored with lemon zest and drenched, after baking, in a very lemony liquid icing that soaks through the cake and also forms a glaze. The intense lemony tang saves it from being too sweet.

Serves 10

3/4 cup (1 1/2 sticks) unsalted butter, softened

3/4 cup superfine sugar

Finely grated zest of 3 lemons

3 eggs

1 cup plus 2 tablespoons self-rising flour

A pinch of sea salt

A splash of milk (optional)

1 1/2 cups confectioners' sugar

1/3 cup fresh lemon juice

Preheat the oven to 350°F. Grease a large loaf pan, 4 cups capacity, and line the bottom and sides with parchment paper.

Put the butter and sugar in a large bowl and beat together with a handheld electric mixer, or using a stand mixer, until very pale and fluffy – at least 5 minutes, and up to 10 if you can manage it. This makes all the difference to the lightness of the finished cake. Add the grated lemon zest and then beat in the eggs, one at a time, adding a spoonful of flour with each (to help prevent the mixture curdling).

Sift the remaining flour and salt into the mixture and fold in lightly using a large metal spoon. Add a little milk, if necessary, to achieve a good dropping consistency – i.e., the mixture should drop fairly easily off a spoon when you tap it on the side of the bowl.

Spoon the mixture into the prepared pan, smooth the top gently, and bake for 45 to 50 minutes, until a skewer inserted in the center comes out clean.

Put the confectioners' sugar in a bowl, add the lemon juice, and stir together until smooth. Leaving the hot cake in its pan, use a thin skewer to make lots of holes all over the top of the cake, going quite deep, but not right through to the bottom. Spoon the lemon icing slowly over the cake so that it all soaks in. Let stand in the pan until cool, then turn out and serve in slices.

VARIATION

Victoria sponge cake

This recipe can be adapted to make a classic Victoria sponge. Omit the lemon zest. Increase the butter to 1 cup (2 sticks), the sugar to 1 cup, and the flour to 1 1/2 cups plus 2 tablespoons, and use 4 eggs. Bake the mixture in two greased and parchment paper–lined round 8-inch cake pans at 350°F for 25 minutes. When cool, sandwich the cakes together with raspberry or strawberry jam and dust with superfine sugar. Alternatively, fill with lightly whipped cream and gooseberry compote (page 342).

Sticky Jamaican-style ginger cake

Molasses, rum, and preserved ginger give this cake a deep and sophisticated flavor. It's not for the fainthearted, but it is incredibly addictive – especially if you spread it with butter and serve it for tea.

Serves 14 to 16

5 tablespoons unsalted butter

$^1/_2$ cup dark brown sugar

$^1/_2$ cup dark molasses

$^1/_2$ cup corn syrup

5 tablespoons dark rum

2 eggs, lightly beaten

$1^1/_2$ cups self-rising flour

1 teaspoon ground allspice

1 teaspoon ground ginger

A pinch of sea salt

2 ounces preserved stem ginger, finely chopped, plus a little of its syrup

Preheat the oven to 350°F. Grease a large loaf pan, at least 4 cups in capacity, and line the bottom and sides with parchment paper.

Put the butter, sugar, molasses, and syrup into a saucepan and heat gently until melted and combined. Let cool a little, then mix in the rum, followed by the beaten eggs.

Sift the flour, allspice, ground ginger, and salt into a large bowl and make a well in the center. Add the melted mixture from the pan and stir until smooth. Finally, stir in the chopped ginger.

Pour the mixture into the prepared pan and bake for about 50 minutes, until a skewer inserted in the center comes out clean. If the cake appears to be browning too much, cover it with foil. Let cool in the pan (don't worry if it sinks a bit in the middle).

Once the cake is cold, you can brush some of the syrup from the ginger over the top for extra stickiness. This cake improves after a couple of days and will keep in an airtight container for up to a week.

Chunky fig, apricot, and prune cake

This moist, lightly spiced, fruit-packed cake, devised by my friend Nikki Duffy, is a bit different from your average fruit cake, with its citrusy aromatics and slightly chunkier dried fruit. I absolutely love it. A thick slice is fantastic with morning tea or coffee, and a wedge wrapped in waxed paper is perfect in a lunch box. It will keep well in a tin for a week or more. Should you find, as can happen with fruit cakes, that your fruit sinks, it probably means the cake batter isn't stiff enough. Make sure you stick to the quantities in the recipe, and fold the fruit in as lightly as you can. But don't worry too much – a fruit-on-the-bottom cake is no great tragedy.

Serves 12

1³/₄ cups whole-wheat pastry flour or spelt flour

1 teaspoon baking powder

A pinch of sea salt

1 rounded teaspoon ground allspice

³/₄ cup dried figs

³/₄ cup pitted prunes

³/₄ cup dried apricots

¹/₄ cup orange marmalade

Finely grated zest of 1 lemon

Finely grated zest of 1 orange

³/₄ cup (1¹/₄ sticks) unsalted butter, softened

³/₄ cup dark brown sugar

4 eggs

Preheat the oven to 325°F. Lightly grease an 8-inch springform cake pan and line the bottom with parchment paper. Put the flour, baking powder, salt, and allspice into a bowl and whisk lightly to aerate and combine.

Use kitchen scissors to cut the dried fruit into chunky pieces – cut each fig into about 6, removing the hard stalk, and each prune and apricot into 2 or 3. Combine them in a bowl. Beat the marmalade with a fork to loosen it, then stir in the lemon and orange zest. Combine the marmalade with the dried fruit.

Put the butter and sugar into a large bowl and beat well until very light and fluffy. Beat in the eggs, one at a time, adding a spoonful of the flour/spice mix with each. Fold in the remaining flour with a large metal spoon, then fold in the marmalade and dried fruit as lightly as you can. Try not to overmix it; everything should be just combined.

Spoon into the prepared pan and bake for 1¹/₂ hours, or until a skewer inserted in the center comes out clean. Let cool completely in the pan.

VARIATION

Hot fruit cake with vanilla ice cream

You can make a very lovely dessert with this, or any other fruit-laden cake, by gently frying thick slices of the cake in a little butter for a couple of minutes on each side until thoroughly warmed through. Serve each slice with a scoop of the best vanilla ice cream.

Easy rich chocolate cake

Everyone should have a little black cake in their culinary wardrobe, and this is mine. It is an intensely rich, moist confection. Use the best chocolate you can find and combine it with the other ingredients with the lightest possible touch to ensure a velvety texture.

Serves 10

8 ounces dark chocolate (around 70 percent cocoa solids), broken into chunks

1 cup (2 sticks) unsalted butter, cut into cubes

4 eggs, separated

1 cup superfine sugar (or $1/2$ cup superfine mixed with $1/2$ cup light brown sugar)

$1/4$ cup all-purpose flour

$1/3$ cup ground almonds

Preheat the oven to 325°F. Grease a 10-inch springform cake pan and line the bottom with parchment paper.

Put the chocolate and butter in a heatproof bowl and place it over a pan of barely simmering water, making sure the water doesn't touch the bottom of the bowl. Stir occasionally until the butter and chocolate have melted.

Meanwhile, whisk the egg yolks and sugar together in a large bowl until well combined. (If you use the superfine and brown sugar mix, the cake will have a lovely hint of caramel, but superfine sugar on its own is absolutely fine.) Stir the melted chocolate and butter into the egg and sugar mixture. Combine the flour and almonds and fold these in, too.

In a separate bowl, whisk the egg whites until they hold firm peaks. Stir a large spoonful of egg whites into the chocolate mixture to loosen it, then carefully fold in the rest of the egg whites with a rubber spatula, trying to keep in as much air as possible.

Pour the mixture into the prepared pan. Bake for about 30 minutes, until only just set. It should still wobble slightly in the center – this means the cake will have a divinely sticky, fudgy texture once it's cooled down. Let cool for 10 to 15 minutes before releasing the sides.

Serve warm or cold, on its own or with a dollop of thick cream, crème fraîche, or Greek yogurt. For a more adult version, you could stir a slug of whisky into whipped cream sweetened with a little confectioners' sugar and serve it spooned over each slice of cake.

Honey whole-wheat cake

This soft, moist, dense, almondy cake is always a big hit. It can be served cold for tea, or warm for dessert with cream and some fresh berries or poached fruit, or a big scoop of roast plum sorbet (page 360).

If you can't find whole-wheat self-rising flour, use whole-wheat pastry flour and increase the baking powder to 2 teaspoons.

Serves 10

1¼ cups unsalted butter, softened

1 cup superfine sugar

4 eggs

1 cup whole-wheat self-rising flour

1¼ cups ground almonds

1 teaspoon baking powder

½ cup sliced almonds

¼ cup honey

Preheat the oven to 350°F. Grease a 10-inch springform cake pan and line the bottom with parchment paper. Place the pan on a baking sheet, as some butter may seep out during cooking.

Put the butter and sugar in a large bowl and beat thoroughly until very light and fluffy. Beat in the eggs, one at a time, adding a spoonful of flour with each. Fold in the ground almonds with a large metal spoon, then sift over the remaining flour and baking powder and fold in gently.

Scrape the mixture into the prepared pan, smooth gently, and scatter the sliced almonds over the surface. Bake for about 45 minutes, until a skewer inserted in the center comes out clean.

Remove from the oven and, while the cake is still hot, evenly drizzle over the honey. It will tend to drizzle toward the middle, which will end up more moist and honeyed than the edges, but that's fine. Place the pan on a wire rack and let cool a little before turning out. Serve warm or cold.

Lemon curd marbled muffins

These are indulgent and delicious, but also very quick and easy to make. I sometimes replace ²/₃ cup of the flour with 1 cup ground almonds, and add a few drops of almond extract to the mix, to create lemony frangipane muffins – these are lovely served warm, with cream, as a dessert. If lemon curd isn't your thing, try one of the variations below – the chocolate muffins are always popular with kids.

Makes about 12

1½ cups all-purpose flour

2 teaspoons baking powder

A good pinch of sea salt

½ cup superfine sugar

1 egg

½ cup plain yogurt

½ cup whole milk

5 tablespoons unsalted butter, melted and slightly cooled

²/₃ cup lemon curd

Preheat the oven to 350°F. Line 12 muffin cups with cupcake liners. Put the flour, baking powder, salt, and sugar in a large bowl and whisk lightly to aerate and combine.

Mix the egg, yogurt, milk, and melted butter together in a pitcher. Pour them into the dry ingredients and mix lightly, stopping as soon as everything is combined – it's essential not to overmix or you'll get dense, cakey muffins.

Add the lemon curd in 6 or 7 dollops and quickly "marble" it lightly through the mixture (a couple of light stirs is really all that's needed). If your lemon curd is a bit stiff, just add it in little blobs.

Spoon the mixture into the muffin cups, to three-quarters fill them. Bake for about 30 minutes, until golden brown. Transfer to a wire rack to cool. Eat on the day you bake them, ideally while still slightly warm.

VARIATIONS

Jammy muffins

Replace the lemon curd with your favorite jam, first beating it lightly to soften slightly. Thick, fruity jams work best – strawberry preserves containing whole strawberries are perfect.

Chocolate marble muffins

Replace the lemon curd with ½ cup chocolate-hazelnut spread (warm it gently first, so it's easier to marble).

Fruity muffins

Replace the lemon curd with 1 large or 2 small ripe bananas, thoroughly mashed; or ½ cup blueberries, pitted and halved cherries, raisins, or other dried fruit, such as chopped dried apricots. Stir the fruit into the mixture lightly and quickly, just before spooning into the muffin cups.

Caraway shortbread

These little biscuits are great on their own or as an accompaniment to ice cream or syllabub. Don't work the dough any more than you need in order to combine the ingredients, or your biscuits won't be quite so meltingly delicious. Feel free to leave out the caraway for a classic, very light, and crumbly shortbread.

Makes about 14

$^2/_3$ cup (1$^1/_3$ sticks) unsalted butter, cut into small chunks and softened

$^1/_4$ cup superfine sugar, plus 2 tablespoons for sprinkling

1 teaspoon caraway seeds

1 cup all-purpose flour

$^2/_3$ cup cornstarch

Beat the butter and $^1/_4$ cup sugar together until pale, then stir in the caraway seeds. Sift in the flour and cornstarch and use a fork to stir the mix together into a smooth dough. Place between 2 sheets of parchment paper lightly dusted with flour and roll out to about $^1/_4$ inch thick. Transfer to the fridge and chill for an hour.

Preheat the oven to 325°F.

Use a 2$^1/_2$-inch plain cutter dipped in flour to cut the dough into rounds, then lift them on to a nonstick baking sheet. You can reroll the scraps and chill again to get more cookies, but the resulting cookies will be a little less light.

Bake for about 20 minutes, until very lightly colored and just firm to the touch. Remove from the oven, sprinkle with sugar, and let cool and firm up for a couple of minutes before transferring them to a wire rack to cool completely.

VARIATION

Zesty shortbread

For a lovely citrus-scented cookie that's great with rich fools and ice creams, add the grated zests of $^1/_2$ orange and 1 lemon, omitting the caraway seeds.

Ten-minute chocolate chip cookies

This recipe appears in *The River Cottage Family Cookbook,* but I couldn't resist including it again here because these chewy, vanilla-rich treats are so easy, taking no more than 10 minutes to make and 10 to bake. Ideal when people turn up unexpectedly for tea, they are also a mainstay of rainy-afternoon cooking sessions with the kids. No batch has ever been known to last till the next day.

Makes 14 to 16

$^1/_2$ cup (1 stick) unsalted butter

$^1/_2$ cup superfine sugar

$^1/_3$ cup light brown sugar

1 egg, lightly beaten

2 teaspoons vanilla extract

1 cup all-purpose flour

$^1/_2$ teaspoon baking powder

A pinch of sea salt

3 ounces dark chocolate, chopped into small chunks (or use milk chocolate, if you prefer)

Preheat the oven to 375°F.

Gently melt the butter in a small saucepan. Put both sugars into a mixing bowl, pour in the melted butter, and beat well with a wooden spoon. Beat in the egg and vanilla. Sift the flour, baking powder, and salt into the bowl and stir them in, then add the chocolate. You should have a pretty sloppy sort of mixture.

Dot heaped tablespoonfuls of the mixture onto 2 baking sheets lined with parchment paper, leaving a good 1$^1/_2$ inches in between each one as they really spread out. Bake for 8 to 10 minutes, until the cookies are turning pale golden brown.

Remove from the oven and leave on the baking sheets for a couple of minutes to firm up. Then carefully lift the parchment paper onto a wire rack and let cool completely. Inevitably, they will be eaten as soon as they are cool enough not to burn fingers.

VARIATION

Oat and raisin cookies

Leave out the chocolate and the vanilla extract. Add 2 tablespoons of honey to the butter before melting. Add $^1/_2$ teaspoon of ground cinnamon to the flour, then add $^1/_2$ cup old-fashioned oats, $^1/_2$ cup raisins, and $^1/_2$ cup chopped toasted hazelnuts to the batter before baking as above.

Honey brandy snaps

In the 1970s, my mum often used to make brandy snaps for her dinner parties, and I always admired them hugely. They seemed so grown-up and sophisticated, and learning to make them myself was a kind of coming of age.

They are excellent served with ice cream, panna cotta, mousses, or fools, but don't underestimate the classic seventies approach of filling cigar-shaped tubes of brandy snap with whipped cream. Mum used to serve these treats alongside a simple fruit salad of sliced oranges or a compote of stewed rhubarb. Wonderful.

Makes about 15

3 tablespoons unsalted butter, diced

$^1/_4$ cup superfine sugar

3 tablespoons honey

$^1/_4$ cup all-purpose flour

1 teaspoon brandy (optional)

A good pinch of ground ginger (optional)

Preheat the oven to 350°F.

Gently heat the butter, sugar, and honey in a saucepan, stirring occasionally, until the sugar has dissolved. Remove from the heat. Stir in the flour, mix until smooth, then add the brandy and/or ginger, if using.

Place heaping teaspoonfuls of the mixture on 2 baking sheets lined with parchment paper, spacing them about 4 inches apart. Bake for 7 to 8 minutes, until brown and lacy. Remove from the oven and let cool for a minute or two.

Lift the brandy snaps off the baking sheet with a palette knife while still warm. To make a traditional cigar-tube shape, wrap each one loosely around the handle of a wooden spoon. To create an attractively curled, tuile-shaped biscuit, drape them over a rolling pin. Either way, let cool and set for a minute or so before removing. If they become too brittle to shape, simply put the baking sheet back in the oven for a minute or two to soften them up, then have another go.

Serve plain, with creamy desserts. Or fill with whipped cream, as in the picture, and they *are* your dessert.

Chocolate and beet brownies

The international success of the carrot cake has surely paved the way for experimenting with root vegetables in other cake recipes. Well, this is my contribution to the genre. It's a corker – rich and velvety, and a tad lighter than a traditional fudgy brownie. Warm from the oven, it makes a good dessert brownie to serve with vanilla ice cream.

Makes about 20

1 cup (2 sticks) unsalted butter, cut into cubes

8 ounces dark chocolate (about 70 percent cocoa solids), broken into pieces

3 eggs

1 cup superfine sugar

A pinch of sea salt

1 cup self-rising flour

8 ounces beets, boiled until tender, cooled, peeled, and grated

Grease a shallow baking pan, approximately 8 by 10 inches, and line the bottom with parchment paper.

Put the butter and chocolate in a heatproof bowl. Set the oven at 350°F and put the bowl in it for a few minutes until the chocolate and butter start to melt. Stir, then put back into the oven for a few more minutes to melt completely. Of course, you could melt them together in the traditional way, over a pan of hot water, but it seems a shame not to exploit the warming oven.

Whisk the eggs and sugar together in a large bowl until combined, then beat in the melted chocolate and butter until smooth. Combine the salt with the flour, sift them over the chocolate mixture, then gently fold in with a large metal spoon. Fold in the grated beets – be careful not to overmix or it will make the brownies tough.

Pour the mixture into the prepared pan and smooth the top with a spatula. Bake for 20 to 25 minutes; when the brownies are done, a knife or skewer inserted in the center should come out with a few moist crumbs clinging to it. Don't be tempted to overcook them or they will be dry. Remove the pan from the oven and let cool on a wire rack before cutting into squares.

VARIATION

Plain chocolate brownies

With a little more sugar and a little less flour than the beet version, these are dense and fudgy – a classic brownie. They're very good served warm as a dessert (see roast plum sorbet with chocolate brownies, page 360), but also excellent cold.

Follow the main recipe but increase the sugar to $1^1/_4$ cups, reduce the flour to $^3/_4$ cup, and add 1 teaspoon of vanilla extract to the egg and sugar mixture. Omit the beets.

Foolproof crème brûlée

This is an all-time classic, and deservedly so. My version – baked in ramekins in a hot water bath – is guaranteed to avoid the potential pitfalls of custard that won't set or sugar that somehow scorches before it melts. Using brown sugar for the caramel top may not be authentic, but it has a lower melting point than white sugar and behaves more predictably under the broiler (or kitchen blowtorch). You do need to make the custards well in advance, as chilling them thoroughly in the fridge before the final sugar melting is vital.

In summer and autumn I like to serve crème brûlée with a small bowl of fresh raspberries on the side. These can be eaten as "sharpeners" between mouthfuls of creamy, sugary brûlée – or dropped right into the custard once the burned sugar top has been cracked.

Serves 6

2 cups heavy cream
1 vanilla bean
$1/2$ cup superfine sugar
6 egg yolks
About 3 tablespoons brown sugar

Preheat the oven to 300°F.

Pour the cream into a saucepan. Split the vanilla bean lengthwise and scrape the seeds into the cream with the tip of a sharp knife, then add the pod to the pan too. Scald the cream by bringing to just below boiling, then taking off the heat. Let stand for a few minutes to infuse with the vanilla.

Whisk the sugar and egg yolks together in a bowl, then slowly whisk in the hot vanilla-infused cream. Strain through a fine sieve into a pitcher. Pour the custard into six $1/2$-cup ramekins or custard cups.

Stand the dishes in a roasting pan and add enough hot water to come halfway up their sides. Bake for about 30 minutes until the custards are just set; they should still wobble a bit if you shake the dishes gently. Lift out of the roasting pan and let cool, then chill thoroughly.

Sprinkle a very thin, even layer of soft brown sugar over each custard and put them under a very hot broiler until the sugar melts and bubbles (or use a blowtorch, if you have one). Let cool, return the ramekins to the fridge until the sugar is hard – just 15 minutes or so should do it – then serve.

VARIATION

Apple or rhubarb crème brûlée

I sometimes put a little apple compote (page 339) or rhubarb compote (page 344) in the ramekins before filling them with the custard. The compote should be tart, to cut the richness of the brûlée, and not too runny. Fill the ramekins between a quarter and a third of the way up with the compote, then pour in the custard to within $1/16$ inch of the top. Bake and finish as above.

Lemon sponge pudding

This is a simple, warming pudding for cold days. I love the way the lemon and sugar mixture forms a sweet but tangy goo at the bottom, which then becomes the top of the dessert. Fridge-cold heavy cream is a must – in my house at least.

Serves 4 to 6

Finely grated zest and juice of 2 lemons

2 tablespoons dark brown sugar

6 tablespoons unsalted butter, softened

$^1/_2$ cup superfine sugar

2 eggs

$^2/_3$ cup self-rising flour, sifted

Generously butter a 3$^1/_2$-cup pudding basin, deep ceramic bowl, or charlotte mold. Stir together the juice of 1 lemon and the brown sugar until the sugar dissolves, then pour it into the basin.

Cream together the butter, lemon zest, and sugar until very light and fluffy. Beat in one egg at a time, adding a spoonful of flour with each, then fold in the remaining flour. Finally, stir in the rest of the lemon juice. Spoon the mixture into the basin. The lemon juice and sugar mixture will rise up the side of the basin – don't worry about this, and don't attempt to stir it in with the batter.

Tie a double layer of buttered foil or parchment paper, buttered side down, over the top of the basin. Put a trivet, rack, or upturned small heatproof plate in a large saucepan and stand the pudding on it. Pour in boiling water to come about halfway up the side of the basin, then cover the pan and bring to a very gentle simmer. Steam for 2 hours, topping up the boiling water a couple of times along the way.

Remove the foil and loosen the edges of the pudding with a knife. Place a plate on top, then invert the plate and basin, and unmold the pudding. Enjoy the moment as the sauce drizzles down the sponge like hot lava, and let your guests admire it, too. Then slice or divvy up with a large spoon and serve piping hot, with chilled cream.

Eggy bread pudding

This is really a bread-and-butter pudding made with crumbs instead of slices of bread. It's easier to make – indeed, if you've ever struggled to get neat triangles of buttered bread to stay in serried ranks as you cover them in custard, then this is the recipe for you. What's more, I think it is even better than a traditional bread-and-butter pudding. You can serve it, like rice pudding, with jam (tart fridge jams like the ones on page 50 are ideal) or with stewed/roasted rhubarb or plums.

Serves 4 to 6

3 tablespoons unsalted butter
1 cup whole milk
$^2/_3$ cup heavy cream
2 eggs
2 egg yolks
$^1/_3$ cup superfine sugar
2 cups coarse, slightly stale white bread crumbs

Generously grease a small ovenproof dish with some of the butter. Combine the milk and cream in a saucepan, bring to just below simmering, then remove from the heat.

Whisk the eggs, egg yolks, and all but 1 tablespoon of the sugar together in a bowl, then gradually whisk the hot milk and cream into the egg mixture to form a custard. Stir about 1 cup of the bread crumbs into the custard and let soak for half an hour so the crumbs plump up.

Preheat the oven to 350°F.

Spoon the mixture into the buttered dish. Melt the rest of the butter and combine it with the remaining bread crumbs and sugar. Scatter this mixture over the pudding.

Bake for 30 minutes or until golden and just set, but with a bit of wobble left in the middle. Serve hot with jam or stewed fruit.

VARIATIONS

Boozy fruity eggy bread pudding

For a richer dessert, soak $^1/_3$ cup raisins in $^1/_4$ cup rum or apple brandy for several hours or overnight, then stir them into the bread-crumb custard before transferring to the baking dish.

Lemon curd eggy bread pudding

Lightly marble a few blobs of good lemon curd into the bread-crumb custard once it's in the dish, before you add the bread-crumb topping.

Fudge

Buttery, crumbly homemade fudge, dissolving on the tongue in a rush of creamy sweetness, is a wonderful indulgence. It's also very quick to mix up a batch, so this is a brilliant recipe for a rainy afternoon. You do, however, need a candy thermometer – available from any good kitchenware store and not expensive. A box of fudge is, of course, a lovely homemade present, but I also like to serve tiny squares with coffee after a meal.

Makes 35 to 40 small squares

1¹/₃ cups superfine sugar
1 tablespoon corn syrup
6 tablespoons unsalted butter, cut into chunks
6 tablespoons heavy cream
1 teaspoon vanilla extract

Using a few drops of sunflower oil on a piece of paper towel, lightly oil a 6-by-9-inch baking dish, or small dish with similar dimensions.

Put the sugar, syrup, butter, and cream in a heavy saucepan, making sure it is not more than a third full, as the mixture will bubble up when it boils. Heat gently, stirring all the time, until the sugar has completely dissolved – tip the pan to make sure there are no crystals still visible on the base.

Stop stirring, put a candy thermometer in the pan, and turn up the heat. Let the mixture boil hard until it reaches 240°F (soft-ball stage). This may happen quite fast, or may take 15 minutes or more, depending on the heat of your stove and the conductivity of your pan – so keep a sharp eye on the thermometer. Take the pan off the heat and let stand for 10 minutes.

Add the vanilla and beat vigorously until the mixture thickens, becomes slightly grainy, and starts to come away from the bottom of the pan. This can take up to 10 minutes, so you might want to use an electric mixer. Pour it into the prepared dish, smooth the top with a metal spoon, and let cool.

Mark it into squares with a small, sharp knife while it's still slightly soft, then leave for 3 or 4 hours to firm up completely. Remove from the dish and store in an airtight container.

VARIATIONS

Salted pecan fudge
Omit the vanilla. Add ³/₄ cup lightly toasted, coarsely chopped pecans (or walnuts) and 1 level teaspoon of best-quality coarse sea salt before beating the fudge.

Chocolate fudge
Replace the vanilla with ¹/₂ cup sifted cocoa powder.

Chocolate ginger fudge
Omit the vanilla and add 2 finely chopped pieces of preserved stem ginger along with ¹/₂ cup sifted cocoa powder before beating the fudge.

index

acknowledgments

I've really enjoyed writing this book, not least because of the fantastic support and input of so many talented people.

This is a volume that celebrates the joys of good family food, and I am forever deeply grateful that I have such a lovely family to cook for. Thank you Marie, to whom this book is dedicated, and Chloe, Oscar, and Freddie, not only for your tireless work as tasters-in-chief, but for the inspiration you give me, every day. I love cooking for you, and with you. And I love it when you cook for me!

Very special thanks to my sister, Sophy, and her family, Nick, Max, and Guy. Sophy tested many of the recipes in these pages and her/their careful critiques and excellent suggestions have made this a much better book. My mum and dad have helped no less, if more subliminally, by encouraging me for as long as I can remember to enjoy my cooking, and theirs.

This would simply not be a River Cottage book without Simon Wheeler's stunning photography. He makes it look easy – but I know it's not. I'm absolutely thrilled with the way the book looks, for which I must also thank Lawrence Morton, for his gorgeous, elegant design work, and Mariko Jesse, for her lovely, witty graffiti.

I've worked with my publisher, Richard Atkinson, for a decade now, and I could not wish for a more supportive, collaborative, or conscientious editor. The team at Bloomsbury have worked so hard and given so much to the book: Penny Edwards, in production, and Natalie Hunt, in editorial, have made complicated tasks invisible and seamless.

Jane Middleton has, as ever, provided faultless copyediting, recipe testing, and many inspired suggestions for changes and improvements. And project editor Janet Illsley has calmly and skillfully brought the whole thing together, guiding us through the tricky final stages. Thank you all.

My huge appreciation and thanks also go to Debora Robertson, for her knowledge, enthusiasm, and effort in editing and testing so many of the recipes. And to Nikki Duffy, my right-hand foodie and first-call sounding board, thank you once again. You're brilliant, and it's a total joy working with you.

My team at River Cottage has, of course, played a crucial part in the creation of this book. Immeasurable thanks to Jess Upton, my marvellous PA, who has organized everything with her trademark efficiency, good humor, and élan. Thank you to my chefs Gill Meller, Daniel Stevens, Nonie Dwyer, and Tim Maddams for their incredible hard work, ideas, and inspiration. Thanks to Mark Diacono, Victoria Moorey, and the River Cottage garden team for supplying wonderful produce and ideas too; to Steven Lamb and Ellie Geraghty for looking after River Cottage, body and soul; to Pam "the jam" Corbin for a number of invaluable tips; and to Cat Streatfeild for ensuring our many photo shoots ran smoothly. To Andrew Palmer and Zam Baring, Stephen Leigh and Jacky Sloane, and the team at Keo Films, thank you all for your hard work, support, and patience. And thank you, Rob Love, for your passion and commitment to all things River Cottage.

And finally, thanks to Antony Topping, the best agent I (or anyone else) could possibly have.

Hugh Fearnley-Whittingstall is an award-winning writer, broadcaster, and food campaigner with an uncompromising commitment to seasonal, ethically produced food. He has been presenting programs for Channel Four for more than fifteen years, and this is the sixth River Cottage book he has written. His previous work includes *The River Cottage Cookbook*, for which he won the Glenfiddich Trophy; *The River Cottage Meat Book* and *The River Cottage Fish Book*, both of which won the André Simon Award; and *The River Cottage Family Cookbook*, which was the Guild of Food Writers Cookery Book of the Year. He writes a weekly recipe column for the *Guardian*. Hugh and his family live in Devon, a stone's throw away from River Cottage HQ, where Hugh and his team teach and host events that celebrate their enthusiasm for local, seasonal produce.